FELONY FARMER

Harvesting Meaning from Life

A Memoir

Don McGehe

LUMINARE PRESS

WWW.LUMINAREPRESS.COM

Felony Farmer: Harvesting Meaning from Life
© 2019 Don McGehe

Cover Design: Rick Ferens

Luminare Press
438 Charnelton St., Suite 101
Eugene, OR 97401
www.luminarepress.com

ISBN: 978-1-64388-044-0
LOC: 2018914680

This memoir is dedicated to the former loves of my life.

*My first wife Rosie (nee, Gallo Vin Rose) was part
of my life from 1960 to 1974.*

*Second wife Mary Jane (nee, Cannabis Indica)
succeeded Rosie and was with me 'til June, 1989.*

Table of Contents

Prologue

It Seemed to Make a Lot of Cents...at the Time

Carrie Fisher died on 27 December, 2016. That same day I had lunch at the Kirkland, Washington home of my friend Charlotte Renata Simpson. We talked of dreams and their analysis. I also mentioned to Renata that I had been wanting to write my personal memoir. Renata and I conversed about how that could be best accomplished. We both recalled a book by Steven King titled "On Writing" which I had read several years ago. I had been thinking about writing this memoir for a long time. King's advice in his book was to set aside a specific block of time each day to do nothing but write. Renata strongly urged adopting this approach. That very night I had another dream in which I was the archivist of a photo club. Each of the members of the club had their personal portrait on file in the archives. In the dream, as each member died, their portrait would pop up on my mental screen. My portrait appeared at position number six or seven. At my age 75, this was closer to the start of the photo sequence than I cared to be. It was obviously the time to begin writing. When I awoke, that dream triggered me to act. Thus began the writing.

Memoir writing is a process that takes time. In the art of writing, novelists are often my mentors. Novel writers are constantly confronted by the need to meet deadlines. Author Douglas Adams had this observation: "I love deadlines. I like the whooshing noise they make as they fly by." Unlike novel writers, personal memoir writers need be concerned with only one deadline. That deadline is a very hard one. The grim reaper usually creates this finality. In order to be a successful memoirist, it is critical to finish your writing before this deadline. Many start the writing. Some finish their work.

PART 1

THE BUST

June 1989–September 1998

CHAPTER 1

June 5th, 1989, began as a thing of beauty. A rare Seattle day in the normally cloudy month of June. The sun was out. Dew clung to the morning grass as a transparent raincoat. The heat index read 64 degrees. Warm for June.

I opened the garage door at the English Hill house. The hum of the opening door awoke our house cat, Yankee, from his skybox over the hot water heater in the garage. He stretched languidly. He loved this house. It was his home.

I had scheduled a trip that was to begin this morning. My plan was to be gone for three days. Yankee's food bowl was filled and his water had been checked. The cat door to the garage and outdoor access was unlatched so that Yankee would have the house to himself. I grabbed my gym bag, removed and stowed the Porsche top snugly in the boot of the 914, and proceeded to drive from the English Hill house to downtown Redmond to check on the condo.

The drive was delightful in spite of the ominous KIRO-AM radio reports of the tanks on the streets in Tiananmen Square. That early morning I felt secure as a citizen of "the land of the free." No tanks here. I didn't even look back to see if I was being followed. I was.

I shared this English Hill house with See (a pseudonym for my soulmate in the 1980s). We had met at the dentists. See was a receptionist for Dr. Tom Berthelote, in Bellevue, Washington. I had known her for five years from semi-annual visits to the office. At the time I first visited she was married. Over those next five years she changed.

For several years from 1982 to 1984 she had lost weight by nearly ninety pounds. She had religiously taken up jogging and everyone in the office was proud of her results. With her five- foot-eleven-inch frame she was tall, and high-waisted, with long shapely runner's legs.

At one dental appointment in the spring of 1984 the doctor asked her to come into the exam room, had her do a 360-degree spin, and with a broad smile said "I'd like you to meet our new receptionist."

I was taken by the changes I saw. Knowing her dedication to her fitness program I expressed sincere congratulations. See had cut and curled her hair and looked absolutely stunning.

Towards the end of spring she called to let me know she was leaving her employment at this office. She spoke of a going-away party at a local bar that Friday as a good-bye to some of her favorite dental office clients. I'd been sober since May 1975 and declined the bar invitation but wished her well. See called again on June 14, and suggested meeting that evening at Marina Park in Kirkland. We had our first date of a five-year relationship that night. Thus began a unity of nearly-pure magic. Many details of that relationship are saved for later in this memoir.

See and I had purchased the English Hill house four years earlier in 1985. At the time of purchase, we had moved up from a downtown Redmond condo to the English Hill rambler. I held on to the downtown condo for business purposes.

It was a leisurely and sunny four-mile drive on that June morning, past Theno's Dairy & Ice Cream store down Woodinville-Redmond Road NE to the condo. I parked in the assigned parking spot directly beneath the condo and went in to check on the farm. The automatically-timed lights in both rooms were still on and the gravel was moist from the most recent hydroponic irrigation cycle. Everything appeared normal. My plan was to go to the gym, then to West Seattle to board the Fauntleroy Ferry for Vashon Island to spend several days with See. A month earlier See had moved out of English Hill and had a job, which she enjoyed, working for the owner of an antique Shop on Vashon Island, Washington.

Both of us were friends of a couple who lived south of Cemetery Road on the Island. We had been best man and maid of honor for this couple when they had been married a year or so earlier in Leavenworth, Washington. See and I had even gone to the King County Courthouse in downtown Seattle to get the marriage license application for them (posing as the prospective bride and groom) before the wedding. That was a "grin-a-minute" experience and was as close as I'd ever been to the altar.

The condo inspection was complete. The farm was fine. It would be OK for the several days that I'd planned for the Vashon trip. I walked down the stairs to the lower parking level. There were three City of Redmond Police cars and seven officers awaiting my arrival. Busted!

They asked my name, then frisked and cuffed me. I was then read my rights and presented a copy of the search warrant after I had requested to see one. I thought it ironic that the judge who'd signed the search warrant, James Kaiser, was the same judge who I'd campaigned for in the two previous election cycles. What goes around, comes around—backward?

I surrendered my keys. Two officers went upstairs to open and inspect the grow operation. They soon returned and I was put in the back of one of the squad cars for the ride to Redmond City Hall, two blocks away. In the back of the car I found myself sweating profusely. One female officer mopped my brow and accepted my explanation that being a type one diabetic, the sweating could be from low blood sugar. It was best they know about the diabetes. I had doubts about the blood sugar being low, but since my hands were cuffed behind my back and not available for a finger prick, there was no way to test that hypothesis. My gym bag with my personal belongings was put in the squad car behind me.

At the station I was photographed, finger printed, and booked into a holding cell. This cooling off period in the cell lasted from 8:00 am until 2:40 pm. At noon one of the detectives microwaved me a high carbohydrate, rather lousy lunch. They had a squad of narcotic detectives, who were in the condo during this time stripping all the paraphernalia, grow equipment, records, and anything else they considered evidence for possible conviction like vegetable samples for the testing lab.

Once they confirmed they had what they expected they would need, the 'good cop' - 'bad cop' routine commenced. The 'bad cop' stormed around advocating sending me directly to county jail to be put in with "the rest of the 'perps.'" The 'good cop' had me sit down at his desk and questioned me about my general moral upbringing. He suggested that if I did not have an attorney that I'd best get hold of one. He told me that they would be confiscating the Porsche as evidence. They had previous video tape of me taking CO2 canisters out of the car to carry upstairs for use in the grow rooms. 'Good cop' also indicated that the condo itself would be seized if the drug lab confirmed marijuana.

Since I no longer had a car for transportation 'good cop' offered to have one of the officers give me a ride home if I would allow them to search the English Hill house. They had no evidence for a warrant on English Hill so they needed me to sign off to allow this search. I graciously declined this offer. The 'bad cop' threat to put me in county jail was a ruse. They did not yet have positive identification on the vegetable material samples that had been taken to the lab for testing. These are never confirmed before a one-week period so they must set you free on your own recognizance after any bust where violence or fire-arms are not involved.

When I got out of the holding cell they gave me back my blood test kit and gym bag which had a dozen pre-rolled roaches in it. They did not search the bag (no warrant - thank God). I was planning a two-day trip to the island, after all, with friends. A dozen might not have been enough.

It now appeared that I had just lost twenty years of saving and investing to the 1970s federal government drug crackdown that had started under the Ronald Reagan administration. From the City Hall I walked across the street to the Redmond Transit Center. A blood sugar test at the TC showed 425, which was way too high. Microwaved carbohydrates? I did a booster shot immediately.

Luckily I had a quarter in my gym bag. I called my next-door neighbor at the condo from a pay phone. He drove to the TC to pick me up and delivered me to the English Hill house. Now that I was home my transportation was reduced to an 18-speed bicycle. English Hill is as high as it gets in Redmond (well, not quite). Everything for the next several months was downhill out and uphill back. The work doesn't come until you return home. I became surprised at what I could do with an 18-speed and a city bus.

Home at last. The Redmond Police Department had separated my key chain into two piles, one containing my keys and the other containing theirs. They kept all keys to the Porsche and the condo. I got the keys to the English Hill house. I did not think the Redmond Police would bother me any longer at English Hill but I was not totally sure of that. My first move was to gather all records, papers and any other possibly incriminating evidence I could find and burn it in the fire place.

Next I called a friend, who was free during most days, and asked her to come over, pull into, and park in the garage. I closed the garage door shut after her arrival. I had just over a pound of weed in the house. I asked that she find a home for it, no questions asked. She later said she took it to the dump with some other trash that was at her house. That turned out to be a wise disposal method. Burning it in the fireplace would have created a suspicious odor in the neighborhood. I did mention that it was one of the high spots in Redmond.

That done, I took several deep breaths and attempted to put my life back in order. Yankee was sitting in my lap. His smooth rhythmic breathing and soft purr added some small measure of tranquility to a system in total shock. I saw that my first opportunity to take the bus to the Fauntleroy Ferry would be tomorrow. I needed to let See know of the abrupt change of lifestyle. Tomorrow was the earliest I could do that. I called Vashon, then set up a bus and ferry schedule.

The next morning I arranged food again for Yankee and set the cat door into the garage to allow access for his needs. I then set off on the one-mile walk to catch the bus for the ferry. See did not have a car on the island but was able to meet me at the ferry terminal, and we bussed down-island to the home of our friends. I spent several days on Vashon getting used to the life changes and reviewing those changes with See. It was a new experience to be without wheels; like reverting to a teenage way of life so long forgotten. The rest and reflection offered on Vashon Island were welcome.

I returned to Redmond three days later and called a lawyer friend named Don Desonier to ask for a referral to a criminal defense attorney. He advised me to speak to an excellent counselor and criminal attorney, Mr. Gene Grantham. Gene's office was in Bellevue. I called and set an appointment to meet on June 12, 1989. I wanted to have See with me for this interview. I called and asked her to come over to Redmond. She agreed.

We arrived at Gene Grantham's Bellevue office at 10 am on Monday morning. I explained my situation. I liked him and wanted him to represent me. We agreed to a $1,000.00 retainer which I paid. Gene was interested in seeing how much he could count on support from See as the case progressed. Gene questioned her extensively on our "couple" commitment. See seemed extremely co-operative and confirmed the solidity of our relationship.

So much so that I was silently asking myself "why haven't I asked her to marry me?"

See was not involved in the police altercation. She was on Vashon Island at the time. We had, however, been together for four years. She knew everything there was to know about my activities.

We wrapped up our session with an agreement on how he would represent me and Gene was to get back to me shortly with details after he talked with the Redmond Police. That is what defense attorneys are for.

It was another sunny summer day as we walked the four blocks back to the Bellevue Transit Center from Gene's office.

As we passed under my friend Peter McRae's twelfth floor office window in the Koll Building, next to the Transit Center, the question came back to me. Right there on the street I asked her if she would marry me.

The setting was not nearly as amorous as is often depicted in a Hollywood romantic comedy but she did say "yes," with a surprised grin.

I was relieved and excited. We were both all smiles. I had no idea how I was to explain the need to go to trial to either her folks or to mine. On that particular day the answer to that question didn't really matter.

See and I both loved Kirkland's Marina Park. We had met at this park for our first date on June 14, 1984. Our choice was to be at Marina Park this very day to celebrate our betrothal. That afternoon at the park the St. John's wart yellow blossoms were in profusion everywhere. They bloomed each year before Flag Day. St. John's wort (Hypericum perforatum) had been adopted as "our" flower on that first date in 1984.

Each year we commemorated that anniversary when the St. John's wort blossoms were in bloom. The thought occurred to me in later years, "what is the fate of a relationship with St. John's wort, and not a rose, as it's chosen flower?" The symbolism seems to foretell a somewhat dubious ending. The St. John's wort would likely not have been Shakespeare's nor Umberto Eco's choice.

With a sense of elation, we laughed our way from the bus stop to the park. It all seemed so perfect. I had my camera and asked a nearby photographer to capture our image. We fixed yellow blossoms at both of See's temples at the gathering line of her hair. Then I knelt and offered her a bouquet of the yellow flowers. Click! Click! We were officially engaged with a ring bouquet of flowers. It was all smiles as we frolicked in the flowers and setting sunlight. A peaceful culmination to a memorable day.

Both pairs of parents were familiar with our extended relationship. We'd been living together for four years. During those years we had significant contact with each of the families. We'd had regular dinners with See's folks who were living in Sequim, Washington. My parents had been out to visit from their home in Kansas twice. They knew and liked See already. My mother had been trying to get me married off for 25 years. I was the only one of her three sons who wasn't yet "hitched up." When I called her she was in a state of glee. The phrase "it's about time" never came up in that conversation. That was surprising, what with this type of announcement from a 47-year-old never-married son.

We called See's folks and arranged to meet them in Port Townsend the following weekend for lunch. I was on Vashon Island that Saturday morning and we borrowed a car to drive up to Port Townsend. See and I had earlier conspired to have See ask her mom to go to the ladies room to freshen up after lunch. While they were gone, I asked See's dad for the hand of his daughter in marriage. With a quick smile he agreed and gave his blessing. Everything was going smoothly at that moment. After lunch See's dad and I had our accustomed three hands of gin rummy while See and her mom went shopping in the boutiques of Port Townsend. See had been through a 17-year childless marriage and divorce. This would be my first.

In spite of the upcoming court date I finally felt free. For the first time in the years, alone and together, the specter of the constant, nagging paranoia was finally lifted from my mind and the relationship. I no longer had to hide from the law. The law knew.

Before See, in my single days, I carefully controlled my social contacts. My experience with the Great American Public told me that occupation was always the second question asked. First: "what's your name?" Second: "what do you do?" I believe this question also reflects the feeling of "job snobbery" used in our society to affirm and boost personal status.

When you live in small-town America, no-one has to ask these questions. Everyone knows everyone, and where they all fit within the local society. In million-plus population cities the social sorting is still going on. I had chosen the city, and within it, living the underground life is simpler when you live alone. If you are living with your soulmate as a couple, the number of social contacts expands four to eight fold.

When asked, my usual cover occupation was contract programmer or photographer. I was a photographer. I was a programmer. I had no current contracts. If questions continued I could reply, "I write programs to solve whatever problems a particular business or client is confronted with." These are just convenient cover stories. I detest lying. Untruth has caused problems in my past. I try to be honest. But when your business is growing weed? No.

At a cocktail party it is impossible to be open and honest. The occupation question is asked in order to stratify the society within the group. "Am I better than you are?" This is often the question they are really asking. If you are interesting to the person who asked the "what do you do?" question, they may inquire about your "job" for ten minutes until something else more interesting attracts their attention. It makes easy cocktail party conversation.

After I quit drinking in 1975, I would often have a camera in my hand at a party rather than a drink. Then in the '80s I would use my photography to change the subject and move on. In response to "what do you do?" I might say; "I'm a photographer, may I take your portrait?" This question would often not only change the subject but reroute an entire conversation away from me and toward them. Click, click. Thank you. Move on. As in magic, the hand is still quicker than the eye. The occupation problem is only one part of the personal paranoia spectrum. But it was a big part for me.

Paranoia pervaded my life like a solar eclipse in near totality. Unless you're retired, if folks see you out in the community midday, during a weekday, you can't just always be "out at lunch." People expect you to be at "the office." They want you to be just as miserable at work as they are. Sixty percent of the people who tell me they are happy with their work are lying. Another thirty percent are disillusioned. Ten percent or less may be really enjoying themselves in their profession.

In this underground economy, in the weed patch, I was in constant paranoia. Every time I was seen out in public during a week day my guard was up. Every phone call had the potential to be trouble. Any question from a by-stander or neighbor might lead to other questions I didn't wish to answer. Every contact with law enforcement was a threat. Paying a $365.00 electric bill in mid-summer with cash was highly irregular. I could never call 911. If the Fire Department came to the house I would be busted.

I had to remember exactly which answers I had given to which people to keep all the stories consistent. I also needed constant and excellent communication with my soulmate in order to know what she had told others about my activities. People are basically curious. They want to know what is going on around them at all times. They are not dumb to the realities of their world. It is a very difficult psychological situation to live with paranoia.

Maintaining a cordial loving relationship with your partner is not at all easy with this pressure. I know why people love their dogs. Dogs don't talk. Dogs just love you. It is always verbal communication that gets people in trouble. And that's from a guy who graduated from Kansas State University of Agriculture and Applied Science with a BA in Speech. Who knew I'd wind up in agriculture eventually, as an indoor weed farmer? What goes around…etc. You know the drill.

 DON MCGEHE

CHAPTER 2

After returning to Redmond on Monday some loose ends needed to be tied down. I called Gene to review any information he had received from the City of Redmond. It was now the beginning of July. Gene indicated that he was in negotiations with the City of Redmond on the condo and the Porsche. The City was trying to claim forfeiture on both. Gene thought they would win on the condo but that they didn't have proof that the Porsche was used "to facilitate a sale rather than just to facilitate cultivation" since they had only observed my taking CO_2 canisters from the car into the condo. That was all they had on the Porsche. He said he wanted to get back into these negotiations. He was an intelligent attorney.

Gene used his best judgment and proposed to the City that they take the Porsche. He knew that they could and would use it in their undercover drug surveillance work instead of a marked city vehicle. They went for it. Gene then countered that since we were forfeiting the Porsche that the City forgo a forfeiture hearing and return the condo as well as accepting a $2,000.00 contribution (from me) to the City of Redmond Asset Seizure Fund.

My good friend, and next door neighbor, at the condo, Michael LaGris, (as condo treasurer) was billing the City of Redmond on a monthly basis for the maintenance fees to be paid to the Condo Association. It could be that the City wasn't too eager on keeping up with the real estate details that were involved in their ownership of a condo. They wanted the Porsche. So this negotiated arrangement is what was agreed to on August 14, 1989.

The long term result of these negotiations worked out favorably. My friend Peter McRae called me a year later to say he had seen the Porsche driving around town one day with an undercover officer driving. Three years later another friend Mike Neukirchen said he knew the mechanic who worked for the City and was maintaining the Porsche on a regular basis. Mike also let me know that Redmond was ready to sell the Porsche off and where I could go to bid on the car at auction.

One Saturday I left work for two hours, went down to City Hall and bought the Porsche back at auction for $4,500.00 on a Visa card. Once I had the condo back we tried to sell the English Hill house "by owner" with no success. I soon rehabilitated the condo and was able to move back into that unit and rent out the English Hill house at a positive cash-flow position after the monthly mortgage payment. The English Hill home later sold in a hot market in 2005 and the condo sold three years later in 2008 when I moved to Kirkland.

My attorney and I went to Superior Court on August 8, 1989, for the arraignment. I wore a three-piece Butch Blum suit and tie with spit-shined shoes. Gene wore a sport coat, slacks and a tie. The Judge looked straight at me and asked me how my defendant wished to plea. After pointing out that I *was* the defendant I suddenly realized the importance of showing up at court looking like you were somebody in a previous life. That was a lesson I shall not soon forget.

We pled "not guilty" and were bound over for a hearing of the case on October 20, 1989. We now had over two months to digest the case which the County had to present and still had the option to plead guilty and take the best sentence we could get. In court you quickly learn that everyone pleads "not guilty" in an arraignment. That is the way the system works. By doing that you find out how much the prosecutor knows, how strong their case is, and whether it makes sense to fight it and ask for a jury trial, or to plead guilty, save a lot of money on the trial and lawyer expenses and get a known lesser sentence.

After August 14, I had the keys to the condo and was able to clean it up and move myself back in. Packing the belongings at English Hill amounted to loading up three sets of boxes. One set for the condo. One set to put in the used 1-ton Chevy pick-up truck I had finally purchased—and then to transport those to Vashon Island for See—one other set we were to decide on later.

This took longer than anticipated. You would know if you had ever tried to separate the stuff of the relationship into "yours," "mine," and "ours" piles. The "our" stuff, and See's furniture, went into a storage locker. Even in an amicable divorce situation those yours vs. mine decisions are difficult. I advertised the English Hill house for rent and an agreement was signed within a week.

Before leaving English Hill I got a long, graphically illustrated Dear John booklet/letter from See in the post. The net of this presentation was that she loved me, and all that, but she felt she must back out of the marriage plans. We had seen each other several times in Redmond while trying to sell the house and three times on Vashon Island in the weeks since the bust. I had not been open about my future plans because I had not formulated any yet, and guarded in my emotions during those visits with some good amount of anger still in me about the bust.

My life was in tatters and I was in need of productive work to focus energy on. We had been drifting apart due to the physical separation. The wedding planning had deteriorated into an outdoor Native American ceremony without much support from anyone else in our friendship circle and very little money for ancillary services. See had always been a pleaser. She was able to bring a glimmer of joy into that "kicked in the gut" period in June that was the bust, the threats from authority, and the earthquake of a comfortable, if anxious, way of life completely overturned. For this I was grateful to her.

With wedding planning out of the way I had a much larger piece of dog fish to fry that summer. The dog fish was beginning to smell. It looked more like the killer shark from Jaws. I called both my brothers and my folks to tell them the wedding was off and felt relieved after those conversations were concluded.

I wasn't ready for marriage. Nor was I ready to confront my family. I had to figure out how I was going to reorient my life after getting out of jail. See and I both still cared about each other and continued a strained relationship separated by geography, ferry schedules, and long distance phone service. This was long before the advent of the cell phone.

See was kind enough to come over to help clear out some last minute items from English Hill before the renters moved in. On our last sweep through the house the final thing I picked up was Yankee. As I paused to stroke him and carry him to the truck, tears came to my eyes. Separating from this house was a process of acknowledging the breakup of the dream we had when it was purchased four years earlier; possibly also the breakup of a relationship. It was a sad reflection.

Yankee was a symbol of the dream we'd had. We had found him on the streets of the International District near the King Dome one night in the September after we bought the house. The NY Yankees had defeated the Seattle Mariners 10 to 2 that night. We had left the game early. Here was this lonely kitten in the streets in the International District with a mournful meow. He was hungry. We fed him what snacks we had. I looked at See. We emotionally decided in an instant to keep him and take him home with us.

We had loved Yankee for four years. We had watched him grow. We saw him learn to climb trees. He was part of our family. See did not share my tears of that moment. She was simply patient, quiet, understanding. We got in the truck. I passed Yankee over for See to hold and tried to dry my tears. We drove south into separation.

Communication with Gene increased as September climbed onto the calendar. Gene was of the opinion that the County case was solid and that the safest, least expensive handling of this situation was to plead guilty and accept a sentence of 30–90 days in County Jail. That was the spread that the prosecutor was recommending for the judge to consider. In addition to the jail time I would be responsible for paying court costs and, after release from jail, completing 240 hours of public service work while reporting to the Department of Corrections. The court was also amenable to a "work release" provision with an acceptable employer. Work release was the preferred arrangement for the court in the prosecution of a non-violent first offender. This was the least expensive method of incarceration for the County with the inmate being required to pay the cost of his own board and room (cell).

The only way to get this consideration is for the inmate to have a job. With the inmate getting a regular pay check he simply passes boarding costs along to the County; out of one pocket into another. Government has always worked this way. The defendant would also be responsible for paying for the services of the Community Corrections Officer and for the bi-weekly visits to their offices. Work release was the perfect alternative to County Jail incarceration. Now I had to find a job.

When my parents had come to visit in the past, I had experienced temporary transportation concerns. There were three of us. The Porsche was a two-seater. The solution had been to rent a temporary vehicle from Aero Rent-A-Car in Bellevue, Washington. Aero was owned by Gary Hollenbeck whose son Shaun was a manager at the car rental shop and a long-time friend.

I had lunch with Shaun and asked if it would be possible to get a position at the shop in October to use as a work release location. Shaun said he would talk to his father Gary and let me know. Those arrangements were made and I was relieved that I was accepted into their organization. The job was washing and cleaning the rental cars, pick-up and delivery of customers before and after their rentals, and transportation to and from the airport for Aero customers arriving at and departing from SeaTac Airport.

My preparation schedule for court was still very full. We chose to postpone the start date at Aero until after the trial. I did ask Gene to inform the Court that Aero Rent-A-Car would be the employment source for the work release program.

By August 25, 1989, the decision was made to plead guilty to the charge of "Violation of the Uniform Controlled Substances Act, Possession of a Controlled Substance, To Wit: Marijuana." According to prosecuting attorney Norm Maleng, this was "Contrary to RCW 69.50.401(a), and against the peace and dignity of the state of Washington" (At least until the State of Washington could devise a way to profit from and control the "killer weed." This would not happen until November 6, 2012 on the General Election Ballot with Initiative I-502).

We went to court on October 20, 1989 for the sentencing hearing. See came up that day and met me at the Court House in Seattle. I wore my three-piece court suit to the hearing. As mentioned before: "dress for the best." Because this was a sentencing hearing there were a number of cases on the docket at this proceeding. All the court decisions were already made and the docket was very pro forma. Before sentence was handed down, Judge R. Joseph Wesley asked if I cared to make a statement. I replied in the affirmative. To the court I affirmed:

I have been addicted to drugs for over 25 years. First it was alcohol and nicotine then marijuana. I gave up alcohol in 1975. Cigarettes were next in 1978. I used marijuana as a crutch to wean myself from both the alcohol and the nicotine. In the early eighties the price of marijuana began to rise just as my income began to drop. At that time I had difficulty understanding why alcohol was legal and marijuana not.

In order to sustain my habit I began to grow several plants in my closet. I used what I grew primarily for my own consumption and shared with a few friends. In the ensuing years as my consumption increased the size of the garden did as well. More and more friends also wanted to get a hold of the product. I had a difficult time saying no to my friends. Smoking as much as I did began to lead to para-

Don McGehe

Judge Wesley then read the sentence. Thirty days confinement in the work release unit of the county jail (one day of which was served on June 5th), $85.50 in court costs, twelve months of community supervision by the Department of Corrections, bi-weekly drug urine tests, and 240 hours of community service under DOC supervision. That was it. The most difficult part of the sentence was to be the 240 hours of community service.

None of this was a surprise. Gene kept me in the loop at all times and once out of court mailed me a statement for $2,000.00 for legal fees less the $1,000.00 retainer paid in June. Money extremely well spent. Now all I had to do was complete the sentence, stay clean, and maintain employment. I had a hand shake for Gene Grantham, a hug for See and a thank-you-for-standing-beside-me for them both. I was grateful. I was relieved.

Entry into the work release unit depended on having a bed open up in the facility. That availability occurred on Sunday November 5. I arranged to meet with See in downtown Seattle that Sunday. She was to pick up Yankee and take the truck over to Vashon Island and use it for four weeks while I was in the work release unit. Participants in the program were not allowed to drive their personal vehicles while serving. There was no place to park downtown anyway.

I was to be let out at 6:30 am, Monday through Friday, to catch a bus to work. Work day started at 8:00 am and ended at 5:00 pm. After the return by bus to downtown Seattle the check-in at the facility was 6:30 pm. The work week was five days from Monday through Friday. Saturday and Sunday we were confined to the jail facility. Everyone at Aero knew my schedule and, though it was never mentioned, I assumed many knew I was on work release. It was obvious.

No one else at Aero worked only a 40-hour week. The way the pay scale was structured the first 40 hours each week were at regular time. Everything over 40 was at time and one half. The only way to make living wage money was to work as many overtime hours as possible. The shop was typically open 12 hours a day, six days a week and closed Sunday. The owner, Gary Hollenbeck, himself worked long hours. Everyone did. Once my work release period was over I would typically clock in at over 70 hours a week on a continuing basis. There was always work to be done to maintain a fleet of hundreds of vehicles.

America was not yet in the cell phone era in 1989 so I made arrangements for my land line phone at the condo to be answered by a service which I could call from the Aero office to get messages. I would also call my parents in Kansas once a week on my phone credit card. I had been in the weekly phone call home habit for years and continued it so that no questions would be asked.

  Don McGehe

To check into the Work Release Unit I met with See in down-town Seattle on that Sunday afternoon. I give her the keys to the pick-up truck and the cat carrier with Yankee in it to take over to Vashon Island while I was in stir. Yankee needed supervision and See did not have a car on the island, so this connection would solve both those concerns. Communication with See was difficult while I was incarcerated; she didn't have a land line connection on Vashon.

Her location in any given week was dependent on who she could find to couch-surf with, among her friends on the Island. Many of these friends also had resident pets of their own. Phone calls from the work release unit's only pay phone needed to be made "collect," and depended on the receiving party accepting the call. These were operator intercept calls. Phoning out was virtually impossible. Imagine answering the phone and hearing "I have a collect call from a Mr. McGehe at the County Jail. Will you accept the charges?"

Since she had no permanent address, See later told me that Yankee became confused about where his home was and was not used to competition from other house pets. So he ran away twice while on Vashon. He was, however, a very cute cat. He had a lot of "love me, feed me" skills and after the "lost cat" posters went up, phone calls came into See, and Yankee was recovered both times. He was a con at finding a new home when he thought he was being slighted or ignored. I often wished I had learned those skills at his young age.

The 1989 work release unit was on the 14th floor of the old courthouse building down near Pioneer Square. We would ring a buzzer on the 13th floor, where elevator access ended, and await a "buzz-in" from the guard desk above. Once the door was released we ascended a long ramp to the 14th floor, checked in at the guard desk and walked around the unit to our cell. This was formerly a jail holding unit. Each cell had an iron gate but the gate was never closed or locked. Two inmates shared each cell.

I had a very savvy cellmate and heeded his advice to keep to myself and to be guarded about all contacts. I had several good books to read during the month and even accomplished some art work. The lights in the cell block were always on. There was constant noise in the block no matter what time it was. Some of the inmates worked odd shifts, and nights, and when they returned to the unit they often held poker games that lasted for hours with rotating people entering and leaving the table.

My cellmate offered blinders and ear plugs to aid sleep. Near the guard desk was the food service area and an indoor basketball court. Behind the guard desk was a small personal area which I used for blood sugar testing. When I left for work I'd pick up the test kit. I was not allowed needles and syringes in the cell but went to the guard to access the test kit to check sugar and shoot insulin.

The weekdays went by fast. Saturday and Sunday were far more deliberate. In those long weekends they asked that we reflect on why we were there. I had appealed to the court that since Aero worked on Saturday I should be allowed to work a six-day week. The answer to that was not just "no" but "hell no."

There was fairly good spirit in the Work Release Unit most of the time. People were really happy to be there. Honestly. All one had to do was to consider the alternative of the big county jail and adjust your attitude a bit to appreciate where you were. As the Minnesotans often said on *A Prairie Home Companion,* "it could be worse."

Similar to the military, the Work Release Unit could be a rumor mill. The old expression held. If you don't hear a good rumor by noon, start one. On Monday November 20, the rumor started that we might be given home visitation privileges on Thanksgiving Day. I called See that morning from Aero to let her know of that possibility. She had an invitation from her folks for dinner in Issaquah where she and I had helped them to move in during October when they had sold the Sequim house. My one-ton pickup truck was a very popular choice when someone needed to move. In any case, See's folks had been very kind to me and I would have helped them any way I could.

     DON MCGEHE

By Tuesday the Thanksgiving visitation was confirmed. See could come to pick me up downtown at the let-out time of 11:00 am and I didn't need to be back until 11:00 pm. This was a great break. I was looking forward to seeing her and also enjoying a holiday meal with friends. We were able to stop by the condo to make sure it hadn't burned down, then we drove on to Issaquah. It was a great traditional meal of giving thanks, followed by See and her mom easily defeating me and her father in a thought-provoking game of Trivial Pursuit. See had a great store of knowledge in the popular culture category. She'd been a winning contestant on "The Price Is Right" in LA. We thanked them and left Issaquah about 9:30 pm to get back downtown.

Beginning on Friday, November 24, Christmas activity began in the streets below the 14th floor of the old courthouse building. It seemed odd to look down 14 stories to the holiday merriment in the streets of Seattle and not be able to participate. That is the lesson of being in jail. Regular caroling calls would drift up to the Unit to remind us where we were and where we could return in a very short time. Even though there were bars on the casement windows you could still open them four inches to let the carolers' voices come in.

One of my good friends had an expression that he had shared with me years earlier. He foretold: "if you can't do the time, don't do the crime." The way the system works, you can seldom walk away from the crime before the bust comes. The piper must be paid. It is like gravity. When you get high, you eventually must come down. It is, after all, the law.

The work release sentence was due to end on Monday, December 4, 1989, at 12:01 am. If you served one minute of the release day you were given credit for serving the entire day. Therefore, those of us who were to be let out were assembled at the guard desk at 12:01 am that Monday and given our walking papers. See was parked a block away from the Unit, with Yankee in the pick-up truck, and it was a relief to see them both. Out at last! We drove straight back to the Redmond condo. It was the first time in years we'd been straight on that Seattle-Redmond drive.

CHAPTER 3

THE "I'M OUTTA' HERE" EUPHORIA LASTED LESS THAN 30 HOURS. Monday was my first 12-hour day at Aero. I returned home to the condo just before 8:00 pm on Monday night. I watched some lame TV in the evening and got to bed early in anticipation of a full and early Tuesday morning. I was up at 4:15 am Tuesday to get to the gym at 5:00 am and to work by 7:00 am.

On the way through the bathroom at the condo I spotted a toke pipe on the bathtub ledge. I'd not left it there. See was still asleep and I did not wake her. I felt sabotaged. I imagined that all the cops had to do was find paraphernalia like this on premise and ownership of the condo would be gone again. I was now a convicted felon. Was I being overly cautious? I knew I had no control over See's personal habits. I also knew that a significant piece of real property was on the line with the choices made while living at the condo. That made a difference to me.

I had not made a big deal out of going from the dark side over to the light side and living the straight life. I'd just quietly made the necessary decisions and changed my attitudes and my life. See had not experienced the shock that I had confronted at the bust. Was it possible, for her, that no shock meant no change? Everyone must choose their own time to make life changes. We've all done it.

That decision is a deeply personal and individual choice. When I'd given up drinking in 1975, I'd found it necessary to separate myself from many friends whose only glue was the shared alcoholic content that held the sticky pieces together. At that moment I saw that I might be alone with these new life changes. I tried to

     DON MCGEHE

work that one through my addled brain down at the gym. Many friends at Washington Athletic Club asked me where I'd been for a month. I told them I'd been "…outta' town, thank you very much." Showing up at Aero at 7:00 am, it was a relief to know the reason for being there was simply an honest day's work for an honest day's pay. Back to the basics.

I postponed making the phone call home until after lunch. I felt I was going to have to ask my partner to stop smoking weed in the condo. This sounded a lot like a classic drug intervention. There was just no way to win with this call. I should never have made it. It was all best left unsaid. None the less, I was still hot! I was still stupid!

So I made it. When I finished there was a long pause on the other end of the phone. It was as if the next question was to be…"now, who's telling me this? The guy who grew all this weed?" Don't even remember what else was said now, but I do remember the emotions and the fear that the condo could be taken away. Again! This felt like Monopoly. Serious *MONOPOLY*. "Do not pass GO. Do not collect $ 200.00. Go to jail. Go directly to jail"… once again.

The question that came to mind was "can I abstain from all drugs and yet hang around with friends who are still using?" The DOC would be checking my urine bi-weekly. I had even changed the recipe for my classic poppy-seed salad dressing for the entire next year. I dropped the poppy-seeds knowing that they would show up as opiates in the testing system. I discovered, with patience, that I could abstain while still in the company of users. It was like looking backwards, through a mirror, darkly.

When I started the job at Aero Rent-A-Car, my salary was set at $4.20 per hour. At the time I didn't care. I needed the job. The wash station was right outside the vertical shop door with glass windows. Just inside this door was Gail Leboutillier's desk. She was the company accountant. It was plain to see from her desk what was happening on the wash pad.

I soon found out that Aero management never expected me to do much work while I was on that assignment. I was so eager just to have the job, however, that I had been working my butt off. Gail was surprised. Gary evidently was also surprised. This kept up for a week or so when the salary was suddenly raised to $6.25 an hour. I was now surprised.

Gary had a work ethic that it was tough to stay ahead of. He was there early and stayed late. Saturday was no exception. It seemed that everyone in the organization worked within this same ethic. With everyone working hard, the company worked better. Customers were happier. It was, after all, a service business. Good service was rewarded with customer loyalty.

Gary was also able to price the product so that the customer could get a real bargain. The Seattle Seahawks were customers as were the Seattle Mariners. Fred Hutchinson Cancer Center also referred families from out of town who were supporting cancer patients to Aero. These families were also big fans of Aero Rent-A-Car. By pricing the cars with somewhat limited mileage Gary was able to keep the prices reasonable.

At the time rentals were $19.95/day with 100 free miles, $115/ week with 450 miles free, and $295/month with 450 free miles per month and $.10 per mile for over miles. Nearly all of the long term rentals were in the monthly category. These prices provided basic transportation around town for Seahawk and Mariners players and family transportation for the Fred Hutch families, which worked well as long as you weren't driving to San Francisco every weekend.

Knowing even in early August that there would be a significant community service request in the sentence, I had explored alternatives to accomplish this. The Department of Corrections places and supervises all community service work. The DOC often will accept work with any civic club (Lions, Kiwanis, etc.) or a church-sponsored service job. They especially like church sponsorship, feeling that this is the kind of societal influence that will keep the inmate on the "straight and narrow" path that will lead to productive post release affiliations. The ministers who are involved in these programs are also considered outstanding civic leaders. Awareness of this Department of Corrections' fondness for church-type activities had led me to the Evergreen Church of Religious Sciences.

ECORS rented the Kirkland Women's Club facilities on 1st Street across from City Hall for their weekly services. The organization was founded in 1927 by Ernest Holmes as a religious science/science of mind-based study group. Holmes framed his beliefs to reflect "Religious Science [as] a correlation of laws of science, opinions of philosophy, and revelations of religion applied to human needs and the aspirations of man." To me it sounded like the "Church of the Humanities." Holmes did not originally intend for RS/SOM to be a "church", but rather a teaching institution.

As with many "faith-based" organizations, however, over many years the structure changed slightly to reflect the top-down hierarchical traditions of many other "God-based" church or governmental organizations. Being a church of the 20th Century it was decidedly devoid of dogma. Its strength was a philosophy that focused instead on its emphasis on the humanities.

I'd been attending services at ECORS for several months. One Sunday I approached the pastor with the idea of completing my community service hours working with the church. Pastor Hennie had never worked with the Department of Correction but I assured her that once we developed a plan, designed a program for completion, and presented it to Vandy George at the DOC, it could get rapid approval. The plan called for complete documentation of all computerized programs, updating and regular maintenance of membership name and address listings, documentation and run instructions for each monthly program, and continuing maintenance of all computer systems. The required minimum hours to be completed each month were 30. Vandy George called Pastor Hennie and we got program approval immediately. We began the program in December of 1989. I did not realize, at the time, just how busy the year 1990 was to be for me.

In that next year my schedule at the car rental shop averaged 72 hours per week. Between December 1989 and July 1990 we completed a total of 268.5 hours of community service. On even-numbered weeks I would go to downtown Seattle for an observed urine-drug test. On odd weeks I had appointments with Vandy George at the DOC office in Bellevue to review corrections progress. I was committed to over 82 hours each week in these four projects and the eight hours of community service.

With the exception of the two weeks each year when time changes, there are only 168 available hours in each week. For planning purposes, into whichever available hours each week you have left over, you may carefully place gym time, grocery shopping, preparing and eating food, sleeping, and yes, those interminable hours of social enjoyment that we all crave and allow ourselves to enjoy, with all the emojis that they create in our email texting. Whatever it took, I got just what I needed. I needed to stay busy. I got busy. I stayed busy. Time flew by.

During that next spring my schedule was so full that I would get home at 11:00 pm and leave home at 5:00 am most days. Yankee seldom saw me. He was an outdoor cat, and had been all his life. At the condo I no longer had a cat door. The front door was metal and could not be cut open for a cat door to be added. He no longer had his run of the place. I would let him out at 5:00 am and let him back in at 11:00 pm. But he still loved to be outside at night. He was still a male cat.

The day before Easter, on Holy Saturday night, he was meowing at 1:30 in the morning wanting to be let out. I was trying to get some sleep to get up for early services on Easter morning and I lost my patience with him on his way out the door that night. The next day he did not come back home. He was gone. I felt crushed. I was guilty of lack of love. I posted lost cat fliers and checked humane society shelters all over the East Side for weeks. He never came back. I only hope he found a good home and a new care-giver who had better access to their home and more time to spend with him. I missed him. Another casualty to incarceration.

     Don McGehe

CHAPTER 4

IN JUNE 1990, MY PARENTS SUGGESTED THAT I JOIN THEM IN A one-week visit to relatives in Missouri. For this I needed Court permission to leave the State. Judge Wesley quickly granted the leave. I met my parents, Helen and Jay McGehe, in Kansas City and we drove to Bethany, Missouri to see my aunt Eva Belle Romig. I was carrying a black and white film camera on this trip. Eva was aged 91 that summer.

It was good that we visited. Eva lasted only two more years. I got some good portraits of her on the trip. Eva had always been a favorite Aunt, living on their eastern Missouri farm with Uncle Arthur, horses, dairy cattle, as well as acres and acres of wild blackberries. All the things that an eight-year-old boy loves to horse around with. I had many memories from that farm in the late 1940s. Every morning we would eat cold blackberries we had picked the afternoon before with fresh unpasteurized cream on the patio behind the kitchen.

Eva now lived in town with a house full of memorabilia dedicated to her hero and President Ronald Wilson Reagan. I had my own opinions of Reagan based on his administration's drug policies. Eva, however, must have experienced ecstasy when her movie hero moved into the White House. Of such things are political traditions cemented. Once you are able to hook those dependable votes you have them for a career. And, if it is closer to Chicago, you can vote them in even after you pass. That's what the Great American Heartland is all about.

Leaving Eva's house in Bethany, Missouri, we passed by the

former home of my grandparents, David Benjamin Romig, Jr. and Mary Augusta Buxbaum Romig. Ben and Mary Romig were living in this home in June of 1935 when my parents were married there. I took many photos of the house and listened to both of them as they spoke of their efforts to get out of Bethany the day after the wedding. There was general flooding in the entire area and they nearly did not make it to Kansas City to begin their honeymoon. With all the memories flowing out, this was a special part of the trip on the way up to Cameron, to the home of Helen's older sister Edith Florence Romig Parker.

Florence had lived at 320 Little Brick Street in Cameron, Missouri for years. I recall using that street address for over a decade to get cards and letters to and from Florence. Dad and I had one day's worth of work around the house putting up clothes lines and doing electrical repairs for Florence. I enjoyed working with Dad. Most of the stuff we did could have been done alone by either of us in our thirties. At fifty and seventy-five, respectively, we were holding each other up and making sure neither was getting set up for a fall.

We had more than ample time, and for the most part just enjoyed our time together. With a 35mm lens and an f1.7 aperture, I was able to shoot indoors in the available light and would simply wait until Dad or Florence and Mom were oblivious to my presence, and then I would shoot. I was quiet. Some of the truth of their lives appeared in those images. I'd watch my father work at a crossword puzzle to the point of drowsiness then arise to fetch another cup of coffee.

The trait that Jay knew stronger than any other was patience. He used that very quality to allow Mom and her sister all the time they needed to re-establish their relationship. We were all extremely relaxed through those three days. At this time Florence was the eldest of the group at 86. Many of us would be back in Cameron again in 2003 for her 100 birthday party.

Florence was married to Frank Charles Parker in 1924. Both were aged 21 at that time. Florence and Frank Parker then lived in St. Joseph, Missouri until 1946 when they bought a farm near Winston, Missouri. Florence, in fact, was present at the funeral services for both of my parents and outlived that entire generation of the family to her last year at 105. Florence was far more prepared to survive the widowed years than was her sister, Helen. After the passing of Frank, Florence prospered a further 44 years as a widow and family matriarch; Helen lasted only three after Jay's death.

In 1996, my brothers and I were making plans for my mother's 90th Birthday party in Kansas. I called Florence asking for a photo of them as young girls. She sent me one that was taken in 1907 when she was four years old and Helen only one. I had it published in the local Manhattan Mercury newspaper on Mom's 90th birthday. One of Mom's good friends, Edna Edwards, saw the photo in the paper. Edna called to tell Helen to look for it in Mom's copy of the Mercury about one hour before our birthday dinner celebration. I did not even have to mention it. Who said it's not a small world?

The folks dropped me off in Kansas City at the airport on their way back to Manhattan. It was a wonderful week of quiet sharing with the folks I loved most. A quiet road trip with Mom and Dad; something you seldom get in our modern lives. The question of why I was working such long shifts in a service job never came up. Mom always seemed to be happy with the fact that I had a job—any job. It didn't matter to her what the job was.

Dad could have known more than I ever gave him credit for knowing. I was never quite sure. He said nothing. I had explained my felony situation to my older brother, John David a year earlier when he was kind enough to come through Seattle to see me in a one-on-one visit. I had asked Dave to tell no one else in the family. I wanted to keep from breaking my mother's heart. And it would have. I'm sure she never knew.

Dad may have understood if I had told him. His family was more diverse growing up than Mother's was. I didn't know that Dad could or would keep that kind of news from Mom. I elected to avoid that possibility just in case. It had always been nearly impossible to talk to Dad alone. He listened very well. He never asked questions. Whenever we were together, though, he insisted on sharing every moment with my Mother because he knew her deep and palpable need for that togetherness time with her sons. Besides, after 62 years of marriage he still loved her.

Close to the end of summer of 1990, See called me from Vashon Island. She hoped to come over to Bellevue soon to close out the storage locker in Redmond and also to sign over a Quit-claim Deed on the English Hill rambler. Gail, the accountant at Aero Rent-A-Car, was also a Washington State notary. She volunteered to organize the paperwork for the deed. When See came over to Bellevue, the first thing we did was sign off on the deed to the English Hill house.

Following that I jumped into the van that See and her girlfriend had driven over from the island and we all went up to the Redmond storage locker, emptied out its contents, and loaded it all into the van. At that time, the only thing in the storage locker was the furniture that See had left at the English Hill house. We then closed the arrangements on the rental of the storage locker and went to lunch at a cafe in Redmond. This was the end of the year-long separation in my relationship with See. It was also the end of the relationship. It was an amicable parting.

In the past year when it became a question in my own mind between truth or evasion with my family and friends, I often chose an option that was still evasion. I was dealing with what the Drug Enforcement Administration told us was a major felony. I didn't use that exact wording because I had already been there and done that. The cat was out of that bag for me. I had now been working through the problem for over a year. Little did I know I still had eight more years to go.

While working the problem, I still did not yet know where it would all come out. I still was not ready to be that open with my assessment of the situation with friends and family. As I've said before, everyone wants to know everything. How far towards open

I was yet willing to pry that can of worms was still up to me. People only know what you tell them. I could still dance around that can by avoiding it. That was my preference before playing a fully-fledged game of kick-the-can down the street.

I was still working the problem. I didn't have the answers yet. I still had years to go before I would. As yet, I did not know how to explain a felony conviction to someone whose biggest problem with the law in their life to date was a 10 MPH over ticket for speeding in a school zone. Weed was prevalent in society. There were people who looked on marijuana as "not a crime." Those were the ones who had not yet been prosecuted by their Government. The DEA had a quite different view.

After returning to Bellevue from the Kansas trip, I had begun working with Vandy George at the Department of Corrections to complete the requirements of sentence. Thirty days' confinement in the Work Release Unit at King County were completed in December, 1989. The 240 hours of community service was completed and signed off by July 14, 1990. All urine tests were negative. Court costs of $85.50 were paid in addition to the $2,000.00 contribution to the City of Redmond Assett Seizure Fund on August 18, 1989. This was partly to cover the city's cost of the $1.000.00 reward that was paid out for the information leading to my arrest. I never knew who got it. I suspect it was the wise-ass clerk at the store where I had bought the CO2 every eight days for over three years.

The Certificate and Order of Discharge in Case No. 89-1-04210-6 was signed by Judge R. Joseph Wesley on September 19, 1990. It certified that the defendant had completed the requirements of the sentence imposed. It ordered that the defendant be discharged from the confinement and supervision of the Secretary of the Department of Corrections. It further ordered that the defendant's civil rights lost by operation of the law upon conviction be hereby restored. I could now vote again. The lawyer's fees were paid. It had taken over a year. The legal work was now complete. The Court and the Law were satisfied. I was sober. I was clean. I still felt that I had a hole in my soul.

At Aero Rent-A-Car there were both outside jobs and inside positions. New hires always started outside. Washing and gassing cars, as well as transporting clients before and after rentals was the function of the outside crew. Answering the phones and writing up rental contracts was the inside function. The inside positions were always promotions up from the outside crew. It took a year, but eventually the inside crew had changed and an opening became available.

One bright, sunny day that summer, Gary's younger son, Glenn Hollenbeck, came out to the wash pad with a big smile on his face. He told me there was an opening on the inside desk. He asked me if I would be interested. After that brief two sentence promotion interview, I accepted. It was not possible to burn as many calories inside as I did outside but the weather indoors was far superior and the dress code offered a more stylish appearance. From the inside you also got a greater opportunity to get to know the customer base.

Many of these folks I saw each month when they would come in for their monthly renewal. I made many friends from this group. I sometimes see them on the streets today and have pleasant conversations with them. Though he is no longer in the Seattle area, defensive lineman Joe Nash of the Seahawks was that type of friend, with an open and gregarious personality and a welcomed monthly visitor for three seasons. I had spent a year outside and would spend eight more years inside.

After September of 1990, with the Department of Corrections work completed, I had openings in my schedule to expand my hobby and travel interests. This presented a perfect opportunity for photography. I had purchased a Nikon full frame film camera, utilizing Fuji Velvia slide film, that I could use in this pursuit. Lake Washington Vocational Technical Institute in Kirkland, Washington was offering low-cost, workshop-focused classes with titles like Photography 1, 2, and 3. These were run by an accomplished local photographer named Fern Kennedy. I called the school that fall and spoke to Ms. Kennedy about any availability.

 DON MCGEHE

Her Photography 1 class for the fall semester was full. Photography 1 was also a prerequisite course for the second and third classes. That Photography 1 course would be available again in the spring semester. Fern did, however, offer me a spot in her class called Night Photography for the fall semester. I assumed this was a joke. You can't photograph at night! It's too dark! How wrong I was.

I signed up for the class and was enthralled with the course content. By mounting the camera on a tripod to make it steady, using a remote exposure trigger, and employing longer shutter speeds and wider lens openings you can easily capture night time photographs. One of the favorite venues for this class was Gas Works Park on the north side of Lake Union. We would shoot south toward the lights of downtown Seattle. Another favorite was to shoot toward downtown Seattle from Rizal Park, high above the intersection of I-5 and I-90 on Beacon Hill, and capture the white headlights of southbound I-5 traffic and the red tail lights of northbound I-5 traffic with the lights of the downtown high-rise buildings and the sports stadiums to add contrast. I was hooked. Have Nikon, will travel.

The Night Photography class shoehorned me into, and through, Photography 1, 2, and 3 to complete a two-year course of photography training and develop an enthusiastic new hobby. Fern was also a source of referrals into other shooting opportunities. She recommended that I join the Mountaineers Photo Club, which offers the most extensive schedule of photographic field trips of any club in Seattle. They offer some kind of shooting opportunity every weekend, even in the winter. These are all guided group outings to places were the veterans in the group have been before; they are willing to share with the novices all their experience and knowledge.

The field trips cover a three-state area and include excursions into Canada with emphasis on Vancouver Island and the Canadian Rockies. They do it all. The Club also offers the finest short introductory course to photography each spring starting in March. Due to the fact that I had been through Fern's series of courses, I have never been a student on the Mountaineers basic course but I have assisted in its teaching several times.

My new-found interest in photography also got me back in touch with a fellow high school graduate of the class of 1959 from Manhattan High School who loved to go to the southwest United States to shoot. Larry Blanchard Hofman had spent his working life at NASA Ames Research Center in California and regarded Arizona, New Mexico, Colorado and Utah as his favorite locations in the country for photography. His home was in Grand Junction, Colorado and he, Dr. Mickey Shanabarger and Michael Antonelli introduced me to shooting the national parks of Utah. These guys were serious photographers. Mickey and Michael both had 4" x 5" view cameras in addition to SLRs. I learned a lot and had some fantastic vacation shooting experiences with this crew. Larry died on June 9, 2003, at age 60. I am still in touch with Mickey who now lives with his wife, Lily, in Fruita, Colorado, a suburb of Grand Junction.

One year in the early 1990s I decided to surprise my father by showing up in Manhattan for Father's Day. I called both my brothers to see if either, or both, would be interested in joining me on this trip. Dave had commitments but Bruce was eager to go. I arranged a flight that arrived at Kansas City International Airport, Saturday morning before Father's Day Sunday, at 9:30 am. Bruce left Norwalk, Iowa early that morning and met me at the flight arrival. We drove straight to Manhattan in Bruce's car. We pulled up in the driveway at 420 Oakdale Drive just before 1pm.

The day was sunny but cool, for Kansas in June, at about 60 degrees. We walked around the north side of the garage into the back yard. Looking through the backdoor glass screen I saw Mother sitting in the living room reading. Father was out in the back yard digging in his garden. We said "Happy Father's Day, Dad." He looked around. His jaw dropped, his eyes lit up, he dropped his hoe, stepped over the six-inch-high stone wall and rushed to hug us.

Hugging was something we'd had to teach him to do. With the exception of a hand shake, there had never been much male-to-male touching in his family when growing up. He had accepted it willingly from about the age of 70. We let Dad walk through the back door first to tell Mom she had company. I thought Dad had shown surprise but for Mom it was flabbergast. If you were born again you'd have thought her expression was a recognition of the second coming.

We all sat down and reviewed the recent happenings in our lives. Dinner that night was at the Country Club. The family all went to church on Father's Day Sunday to honor Dad, on his day, in front of his congregation. Dad was touched. I'd made that vow, in 1960, to honor him more. This was a small token deposited into that bank. Bruce had to leave on the Monday morning to get back to work. I stayed until catching a shuttle to Kansas City for a Wednesday afternoon flight to Seattle.

CHAPTER 5

A GROUP THAT I ASSOCIATED WITH AT THE CHURCH OF RELI-gious Sciences organized a trip to the Big Island of Hawaii in 1991. The retreat center that was used by this group was on the south end of the big island near the Black Sand Beach. We did yoga daily and toured the Kilauea Volcano lava flow by helicopter once. A daily trip around the south end of Hawaii Island was dedicated to discovering fumaroles where we could bask in the steam from the underground volcanic springs, then wind up at the Black Sand Beach for a swim and body surfing.

During this trip I stopped to visit Marge and Keith Yokum, old friends from Portland, Oregon, who were living on the Kailua-Kaneohe side of Oahu Island. I spent a day with them and also a day with Bob and Sharon Price, additional Portland friends, who also lived in Kailua at their bed and breakfast home and business, named Sharon's Serenity. I've always loved this place. Sharon's Kailua address is on Kakahiaka Street. Kakahiaka means "good morning" in Hawaiian. The pronunciation is "kah-kah-hee-akah." I could say that all morning and smile 'til noon.

The entire McGehe family coalesced in Des Moines, Iowa during the summer solstice in 1997. The celebration was for the marriage of my nephew Robert Jason McGehe and Miss Piper Christine Sargent, of Indianola, Iowa. This was a picture-perfect wedding. The church was The Basilica of St. John in Des Moines. The western wall of the Basilica is covered with ornate stained glass windows that are nearly floor to ceiling. The evening wedding was bathed with the setting solstice sun, streaming through those stained glass windows. The dappled light, in rainbow shades, spread out to honor the bride and groom and then bathe the congregation.

What made this wedding unique was the presence of a complete, intact, family of in-laws. Both the bride's and groom's parents were in attendance, and both were still married couples. There were four complete sets of grandparents, all still alive and present as married couples. Six sets of witnesses that marriages can and do endure. Jason smiled to express his deep pride as he ushered first the four sets of grandparents in, and next his parents and those of Piper to their seats of honor in the second pew. The vows were said in front of a hushed and reverent congregation. Then Piper and Jason turned, smiled, and immediately sought out both sets of parents to exchange hugs of sincere thanks and appreciation. In joy they then retreated back up the aisle to the jubilation of their family and friends. The reception was held at a local country club with champagne and dancing. I've never seen a more perfect wedding.

Our meeting in Des Moines gave me, without knowing, my last face-to-face communication with our father, Wilbur Jay McGehe. We had three glorious days of meaningful close conversation and meal sharing with Dad. Mother held up well at Des Moines even though she felt ill much of the time. Her incapacity gave us more intimate time with our father though. I had my camera there. Using a tripod and remote release exposure, I captured a final image of we three boys together with our dad, which I will always treasure. This was taken in the front yard of my brother Bruce's Norwalk, Iowa home. This is just my observation, but it seemed that the women of the family were spending so much time "getting ready" for the ceremonies that we men had more time to enjoy a relaxing experience with Dad together. We left Des Moines all the richer for the perfect wedding and a last companionship with our father.

In those first thirty years since college I had quit alcohol and marijuana cold turkey. I could not say the same about nicotine. I had given up smoking while living in Portland, Oregon for six months in 1971 but unfortunately accepted one lousy stinking cigarette from

Per Bjerkman while riding with Per and Nancy Corwin in a car coming back from the Portland Airport that fall, and consequently had smoked again until early 1978. That drug had a real hook in me. I saw my Father Jay give up cigarettes cold turkey when I was in Junior High School. I had always admired him for that. I was not quite so fortunate.

I've always been an addict with an addictive personality. I've always wanted to alter my mind. We used to have an expression that we coined when I lived in Manhattan Beach, California, that went "let's get drunk and be somebody." What the hell was the matter with just being me, anyway? I got clean after 1989 and I've been clean ever since. Working those long hours in car rental certainly assisted that recovery. And I realized just how important staying busy had been a causal factor in my staying clean.

I also knew that the prospect of changing jobs was going to be very difficult with the marijuana felony conviction on my record. After eight years at Aero I was comfortable with the situation that I was in. I did realize that I was putting in a lot more hours than most folks did to earn a living. There was also the apprehension about being able to land a better job elsewhere. I was frankly becoming complacent. I was shocked out of that in April 1998.

I called Kansas that night at 9:30 pm, Central time. I let the phone ring more than seven times. There was no answer. That was very odd. It was Saturday April 18, 1998. My folks had a standing Scrabble game every Saturday night, when I would normally call them at 7:30 pm Pacific Time. They would interrupt their game at their 9:30 Central Time hour and we would talk for half an hour to forty minutes and catch up on all our weekly activities. This weekly phone call had been going on for years. It was habit. Mom and Dad's Scrabble had been going on for years as well. Another habit. At that point Mom was ahead in the all-time score, 530 games to Jay's 430 games. There were 14 ties on the sheet. They kept that continuing tote sheet in the Scrabble game box, which I still have to this day.

I waited until 9:30 pm, after I had eaten dinner, to call back. Mom answered the phone sounding distraught.

"Hello?" Mom said.

"This is Don. What's the matter, Mom?" I asked.

"Oh Don, your Father was sitting here this evening, after getting back from his golf game and something happened where he couldn't move his left arm and left leg. I was so worried about him. We got in the car and Dad drove to the hospital and went to the emergency room. They said he'd had a mild stroke." Mother said.

"Where is he now, Mom?" I asked.

"They checked him into a room in the hospital and I sat with him for a while. Then they called a cab for me so I could get home. I haven't had a driver's license for years, you know. We left the car over at the hospital." Mom responded.

"So Mom, what's Dad's status now?" I asked.

"Well, he called me ten minutes ago from his room and wondered where he had left his glasses. He said he was resting all right when he called."

I talked to Mom for another half hour and ended the call telling her that he was under care now and everything was probably as good as it could be for the moment.

I immediately called my younger brother Bruce and his wife Betty Gail. I talked to Betty Gail, who has a master's degree in nursing. I told her that I had talked to Mom and was concerned. I asked that she keep tabs on Mom tomorrow since they were closest to her home in Manhattan at only four hours' driving time. I next called my older brother David and his wife Lily in Rhinebeck, N.Y. I gave them what information I had and just asked that they remain alert for further word. My message to them both was not dire but cautionary, considering it was a stroke. Strokes can be serious.

Sunday came with a call that Dad had had another more serious stroke overnight in the hospital. On Monday I called Northwest Airlines and booked a ticket for seven days in advance to get to Manhattan. That was just far enough ahead to get a reasonable fare.

Betty Gail was of invaluable assistance to the family that week. In her own words:

"Bruce had a meeting in Dallas so I went to Manhattan by myself. I got there before Jay went into a coma. He wasn't able to talk when I got there. He was not receiving nutrition (because he was unable to eat and hyperalimentation had not been initiated). He was receiving fluids by IV. When it was determined that his brain was so swollen that it was herniating into the brain stem and death was imminent, the decision was made not to insert another IV when the present IV required change. So the decision was not to stop the fluids he was presently receiving but to not put him through a futile procedure."

Jay passed beyond the veil on Friday April 24, 1998. I flew into Kansas City and Bruce met me at Kansas City Airport to go on to Manhattan early Monday 27 April, to join the family, who were already there for services scheduled on April 29. That entire week I had planned to stay in Kansas. In a week of marked sadness there was yet a light moment. We are, after all, still very human and prone to the foibles that can add humor to tragedy.

On Tuesday April 28 we were all to go down to the funeral home for a final viewing before the service the next day. As we were dressing in the afternoon, Bruce could not find his good suit which he had brought from Norwalk. He had hung it in the sewing room closet but it was not there. My younger brother was in utter consternation. Finally we consulted David.

In questioning him we discovered that the funeral director had been at the house late Monday (after Bruce had hung his clothes in that same closet) to pick up one of Jay's suits to dress the body for viewing. Mom directed Dave to the sewing room closet to choose a suit to give to the director. Dave chose the nicest suit he could find and handed it to the director. He had chosen Bruce's mourning suit. We called the funeral home, quickly grabbed another suit from Jay's collection, took it down to the funeral home and swapped the suits out in the parking

        DON McGEHE

lot. All of us, in that exchange, sported a broad grin and had a good laugh. We hustled back to the house and presented Bruce with his suit. The suit caper postponed our viewing until later in the day.

The funeral home was apologetic and accommodating, remaining there late into the evening. Mother now had a good half hour to be alone with the casket after the rest of the family had moved out into the reception area at the funeral home. This patience provided my Mother with the final privacy to say good-by, and to close a 62-year loving relationship. It was good that we did this. Mother had anticipated another viewing with an open casket at the funeral. Jay's will had requested cremation. When we got to the church there was only the urn at the service. Everything seems to work out all right in the end. And if it doesn't work out…that means it's not the end…yet.

After the services we assisted Mother in writing thank-you notes for flowers and gifts, and I got to work on the family home to get it ready for sale. Mother already had arrangements to move into Meadowlark Hills Retirement Community where she and Jay had been on a waiting list for years but had been postponing any openings that came available due to Jay's continuing good health. Change! My dear and trusted friend Karen Williamson was given selling responsibilities for the home and she worked very closely with Mother on coordinating the sale. My work in Kansas was completed and I flew home to Seattle on Monday May 4.

Back in the late 1990s I used to listen to KIRO radio at 710 on the AM band. KIRO had a program on Sunday evening that I would tune into on my day off. It was a call-in show hosted by a Seattle attorney who answered legal questions from callers. One night on this show in June 1998, I learned that by making application to the courts someone who had a felony conviction on their record could get that conviction expunged if they had completed their sentence, paid all restitution, and had been crime-free for five years. *BINGO!* That sure sounded like me.

I called the show and confirmed this using the cover name "John" from Redmond. It was true. On Monday I called my attorney Gene Grantham. Gene was familiar with the statute and asked that I mail him a check for $200.00 and he would pursue the matter. The Redmond Post Office was a block from the condo. I was at that post office in ten minutes flat. Envelope, with check enclosed, in hand.

On July 15, 1998, I received the notification that read:

In the superior court of the State of Washington in and for King County:

State of Washington, Plaintiff, v. Donald McGehe, Defendant

No. 89-1-04210-6 Order Vacating Record of Conviction

The Court having heard the defendant's Motion for Vacation of his conviction and having reviewed the files herein and finding good cause to grant the defendant's motion now HEREBY ORDERS:

The judgment of conviction under the above-captioned cause number is hereby vacated pursuant to RCW 9.94A.230 For all purposes, including responding to questions on employment applications, the defendant may state that he has never been convicted of the offenses charged under this cause number.

DATED this 15th day of July, 1998.

The Hon. Joseph Wesley

Thank you Counselor Grantham. Thank you Judge Wesley.

The death of my father was a shock to my entire outlook on life. It is intuitively obvious, to even the most casual observer, that once my immediate parent dies, my generation is next in line for that self-same, once in a lifetime, experience. I was now free and cleared by the courts for the opportunity to change my work and change my life. I began looking at once.

 DON MCGEHE

In 1997 Safeco Mutual Funds had the number one fund in the small-cap mutual fund market. It was called the Safeco Growth Opportunities Fund. Small investors have always loved to follow a number one fund. The Safeco Growth Opportunities Fund was no different. This is not always the wisest investing choice. If you are investing in last year's leader, you are following the market. If you are lucky enough to pick the next, upcoming fund sector, you are anticipating future growth. If you are correct in your forecast, you can ride the tide upwards.

But now, suddenly the mutual fund consumers were speed-dialing Safeco trying to get into the growth fund. Safeco Mutual Funds offices were located just across the valley from my condo on Willows Road in Redmond. They were advertising in the newspapers in the summer of 1998, trying to find customer service phone representatives to cover the increased call volume they were receiving on a daily basis. I asked Gary Hollenbeck if he would be willing to give me a good recommendation. Gary said he would, so I applied for the position.

Three interviews later I was offered a phone representative job. I accepted. I then expressed sincere appreciation to Gary Hollenbeck and the crew at Aero Rent-A-Car for their steadfast contribution to my recovery efforts. I could not have been successful without that unwavering support and reliable employment for nine years. When I have dreams about being at work, even after a time lag of more than 20 years, the physical setting of those dreams is always at that Aero Rent-A-Car office.

The change to Safeco came with an increase in gross pay, shortening of hours from 70 to 37.5 each week, paid medical, and paid vacation. Once on the Mutual Funds payroll, I took the Series 6 Mutual Fund Sales training including fingerprinting, in the same Redmond Police Department where I had been fingerprinted and "mug" photographed nine years earlier. The complete criminal records check was performed and reviewed, and I was granted the Series 6 Securities License by the U. S. Securities & Exchange Commission.

The court was true to its word. The record was clean. I had done the time. I was moving on. It had been a long nine years.

I was ready to rejoin the human race…at a slightly slower pace.

— PART 2 —

MANHATTAN

November 1941 – June 1963

CHAPTER 6

I WAS BORN IN A PREVIOUS CENTURY: THE 20TH, ANNO DOMINI. This was 46 years before United States citizens were automatically issued social security numbers at birth. Back then professional baseball was played in the afternoon. The date was November 3rd, 1941; the time was 2:15 AM. It was a Monday.

I should have been born on the 2nd, but I wasn't. My older brother John David McGehe celebrated his second birthday party on November 2nd, 1941. I'm sure my Mother, Helen Katherine Romig McGehe, not wanting her first and second children born on the same date, tightened up a bit and held off until after midnight. This was likely all for the best. I wasn't yet ready to eat cake and ice cream at Dave's second birthday party anyway.

As she told the story later, Mom was feeling rapid dilations just after midnight on the 3rd. She was calling on my father to hurry up and tie his bow tie in the bathroom, so they could bolt to the hospital. Dr. R. R. Cave was on his way to the apartment at 1015 Fremont Street by car. St. Mary's Hospital was only half a block away. Word has it that Dr. Cave delivered me at home and carried me to the hospital [not true, my Father did]. It was a fast delivery. I'm sure that Mom just wanted to wait for Dr. Cave's arrival. This is because even though Dad had his bow tie adequately tied by then, he was not properly gowned in acceptable surgical scrubs.

After moving to the Pacific Coast in 1963, whenever I was asked, "Where were you born?" I would often smile and respond: "Manhattan." It sounded so much bigger than just "Kansas."

[Four months after I wrote the opening paragraphs to this section, I was cleaning out a safe-deposit box in preparation for a move to Oregon. In that box clean-out I discovered a letter that my mother wrote the day after I was born to her parents David Benjamin and Mary Augusta Romig in Bethany, Missouri. This letter was an eye-witness account of my birth and I include it here for its historic purpose.]

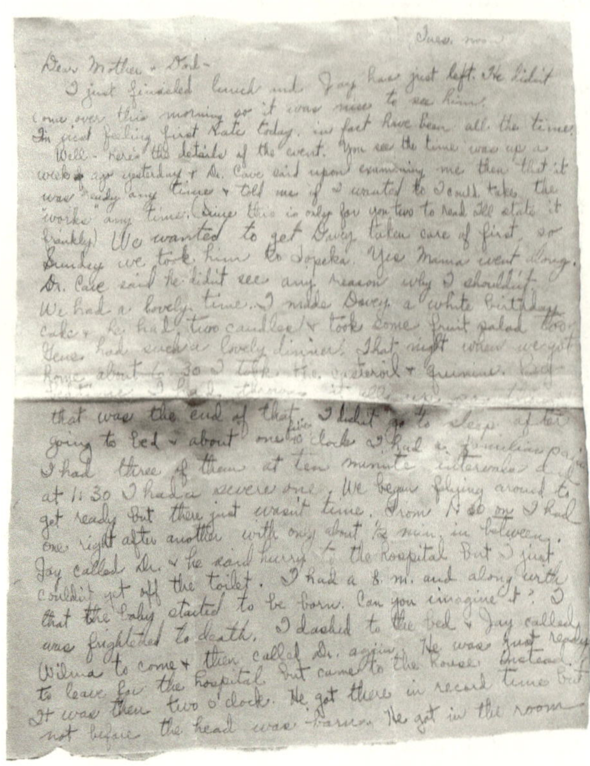

DON MCGEHE

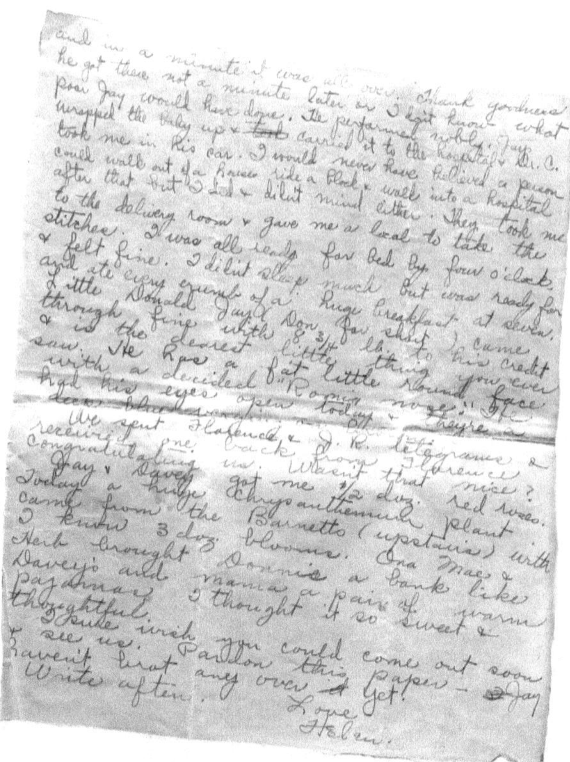

Due to the age of the letter I have taken the contents and transcribed them to a more easily-readable type face for presentation in this manuscript. The letter was written Tuesday, November 4th, 1941 (34 days before Pearl Harbor):

Tues. noon

Dear Mother & Dad -

I just finished lunch and Jay has just left. He didn't come over this morning so it was nice to see him.

I'm just feeling first rate today, in fact have been all the time. Well - here's the details of the event. You see the time was up a week ago yesterday & Dr. Cave said upon examining me then that it was ready any time & told me if I wanted to I could take the "works" any time. (Since this is only for you two to read I'll state it frankly) We wanted to get Davey taken care of first so Sunday we took him to Topeka. Yes Mama went along. Dr. Cave said he didn't see any reason why I shouldn't. We had a lovely time. I made Davey a white birthday cake & he had two candles & took some fruit salad too.

Gene [Dad's sister Imogene Heitman] had such a lovely dinner. That night when we got home about 6:30 I took the castor oil & quinine. By bedtime I had thrown it all up so thought that was the end of that. I didn't go to sleep after going to bed & about one o'clock I had a familiar pain. I had three of them at ten minute intervals and at 1:30 I had a severe one. We began flying around to get ready but there just wasn't time. From 1:30 on I had one right after another with only about 1/2 min. in between. Jay called Dr. & he said hurry to the hospital but I just couldn't get off the toilet. I had a b. m. and along with that the baby started to be born. Can you imagine it? I was frightened to death. I dashed to the bed & Jay called Wilma [a neighbor] to come & then called Dr. again. He was just ready to leave for the hospital but came to the house instead. It was then two o'clock. He got there in record time but not before the head was born. He got in the room and in a minute it was all over. Thank goodness he got there not a minute later or I don't know what poor Jay would have done. He performed nobly. Jay wrapped the baby up & carried it to the hospital & Dr. C. took me in his car. I would never have believed a person could walk out of a house ride a block & walk into a hospital after that but I did & didn't mind either. They took me to the delivery room & gave me a local to take the stitches. I was all ready for bed by four o'clock, & felt fine. I didn't sleep much but was ready for and ate every crumb of a huge breakfast at seven. Little Donald

Jay (Don for short) came through fine with 8 3/4 lb. to his credit & is the dearest little thing you ever saw. He has a fat little round face with a decided "Romig nose." He had his eyes open today & they're a deep blue verging on brown.

We sent Florence, [Helen's sister] & J. R. [Helen's brother] telegrams & received one back from Florence congratulating us. Wasn't that nice? Jay & Davey got me 1/2 doz. red roses. Today a huge chrysanthemum plant came from the Barnetts (upstairs) with I know 3 doz. blooms. Ona Mae & Herb [Bishop] brought Donnie a bank like Davey's and Mama a pair of warm pajamas. I thought it so sweet & thoughtful.

I sure wish you could come out soon & see us. Pardon this paper – Jay hasn't brought any over yet.

Write often.

Love
Helen.

PEARL HARBOR WAS BOMBED 34 DAYS LATER. ON THE FOLLOWing day, December 8th, 1941, the US was in World War II. My Mother would give birth to three sons in this "Silent Generation" between those years of 1925-1945. The total birth figure for this twenty-one year "Lucky Few" generation, which included the 12 years of the Great Depression, is only 30 million. Compare this to the Baby Boom generation which numbered 75 million in only 18 years.

My first cognizant memory was of sitting on an 18" high stool in the kitchen of the 1015 Fremont apartment and learning to tie my shoes for the first time. It was during the winter. The neighborhood was in darkness but it was warm inside the kitchen. I do not remember how old I was on that day. I do remember the overwhelming sense of accomplishment.

Military service was nearly universal in the United States during WW II. My father, then 33, was included in the 1944 draft calls. A total of 16.1 million citizens served in the armed forces out of a population of 134.9 million; nearly 12%. As of 2015 that figure had dropped to 0.4%.

Father served navy basic training in Farragut, Idaho. He was released with medical waivers to return home in August of 1944. I was too young to remember his being gone, but we did preserve filmed footage in his absence. While he was away my brothers John David, Bruce Alan, and I went with Mother to spend several months visiting her parents on their farm near Bethany, Missouri. Mom took along Father's 8mm movie camera.

We have footage of David and me, both running out to the front yard water pump, to pump water on a sunny summer day. The camera, however, was upside down. We appeared to be defying gravity on that run. The water ran uphill into the upside-down ground.

The next significant recollection that is cemented in my young memory is a scene from the first day of preschool at the age of four. I entered half-day kindergarten in September of 1946. The teacher organized the class and then instructed us to choose a play activity. Two of my friends, Sarah Lynn and May Rogers gravitated to the doll house and I followed them. I picked out a male doll and we all played "house" for half an hour.

With only three sons and no daughters in my home, I'd never experienced "playing house." It looked like fun. I do not recall my motivation to join with May and Sarah at the time, rather than building roads out of wooden blocks with the boys. Was I there to play dolls or was I with them because they were the only kids in the kindergarten class that I really knew well, and I simply sought someone familiar to play with? In the 1940s the binary male/female separation was near polarity.

In my mature years I have been more willing to consider myself as falling somewhere within a broad androgyny spectrum between male and female and not on the hard male end of that line. My emotions are never ruled solely by either estrogen or testosterone. They appear somewhere on a bell curve distribution between the two. That flexibility is understood in today's society. The separations were more hard and fast in 1946. On that day I chose, by pure gut impulse, what felt good at the time.

I have often thought back on this day as if I had made a personal choice that reflected the duality of hormones influencing my choices at the time. But that's all adult talk. It comes out of a senior citizen's brain; not a four year-old's. At that moment, I chose what I chose.

The name of that first school was Woodrow Wilson Elementary School on Juliette Avenue. Elementary school was kindergarten through 6th grade in the Manhattan School system. I would attend that school for all elementary years except 4th grade when I was at Bluemont School. Evidently the school board was gerrymandering the districts in that fourth grade year to balance out the youth population. Woodrow Wilson was six blocks away. Bluemont was only one block distant from home.

One cold winter weekend in that kindergarten year, our family moved to a new rental house at 619 N. Juliette Avenue. Father was back from Idaho by now to ramrod that move. We were no longer in an apartment. We now had a whole house. It felt great to have more room to horse around in and play. I shared a bedroom on the second floor with my older brother Dave. My folks and my younger brother Bruce shared the other upstairs bedroom with its walk-in closet. At the head of the stairs, up from the first floor, was our only bathroom, with a tub but no shower.

Kindergarten was only half a day at that time and the first Monday after the move I was walking home for lunch and could not remember the route to the new house at #619. I had walked north on Juliette Avenue as far as Fremont Street, where I used to turn left, and forgot where to go from there. I asked the people who lived on the corner of Fremont and Juliette for help but I did not know the address or the phone number of our new house. I was bewildered, so I just sat on the corner of the street with the soft snowflakes falling around me and teared up.

Within ten minutes (it seemed) my father drove along and I recognized his car and stood up. He stopped, let me in, and we drove the two additional blocks to the new house for a hot navy bean soup lunch with Nabisco saltine crackers and Kraft Velveeta cheese. Next day I had no problem on the six-block walk. I was in school to learn something…if only the way home.

August in Kansas was often listless and sometimes rather dreamy. It was always hot. Hand fans advertising funeral homes were stuck behind the hymnals in all the pew backs of the churches. Homes used oscillating electric fans to circulate the heat. It was best to avoid second story rooms during daytime hours.

One August day I was at home, in my bedroom, with mother downstairs cleaning and cooking. I was bored and wandered out of my room to the folks' bedroom and into their walk-in-closet. There was a wood casement window to the backyard which was open and screened to keep out the mosquitoes. It was so still and so quiet. The only sound I noticed was that of the birds calling from the maple tree behind the house.

There, on a dressing table was a white feminine garment. It was my mother's bra. I picked it up. It felt warm and cotton-soft to the touch. I felt sexual excitement stirring up from the base of my brain. I wanted to put it on. I slid it over my shoulders without fastening the back. I closed my eyes in a fantasy, near-dream state, imagining what it would feel like to be a girl.

Suddenly I heard my mother's footsteps on the stairs. Popping open my eyes, I dropped the bra on the dressing table, and slipped out into the bedroom. I was near the top of the stairway before mother's slow plodding up the stairs was completed. I do not remember the ensuing conversation. I'd not been caught. It was close.

 Don McGehe

Mother went into the bathroom, and closed the door. I retreated to my room and plopped face-down on my bed to stare out of the window onto Juliette Ave. Since that day, I've never spoken of this incident. It was the first time in my life that I had experienced the thrill of that feminine side of my character.

CHAPTER 7

IN THE LATE 1940S THERE WERE STILL TRADITIONS OF SMALL-town daily life occurring in Manhattan that you no longer hear of today. My folks had an electric refrigerator. Not everyone did. Some neighbors around the block on Laramie Street still had ice boxes. These homes had square card signs posted in their front windows with four quadrants and a rotatable arrow in the center. With this sign they could request 25 lb., 50 lb., 75 lb., or 100 lb. ice deliveries.

The ice man would look at that sign, and leave the requested amount of ice off each morning to keep the ice box cold. In those early years he drove a horse-pulled wagon with his ice up and down his route. Summer was his heavy delivery season. The horse-drawn wagon had become widespread during the war. Gasoline was a rationed commodity. Milk delivery was still done in glass bottles by a similar horse-drawn conveyance. The order that triggered the delivery here was the number and size of empty milk bottles left on the porch in the carry container.

U.S. Mail was delivered by a walking carrier to a slot on the side of the porch or the side of the door and dropped directly into your house. Within two weeks of Christmas, mail deliveries doubled to twice each day. Times did change in mail service. That's why they called it mail service. There was still service involved. In addition to being your neighbors, these delivery people were part of the normal heartbeat of the neighborhood.

There was a core of kids who lived within a rock's throw of the Juliette Avenue address. North was one block were William Frank LaShell (known as Bill), his sister Joan Ellen, and next-door to their house Owen "Packy" Sherman. Across Moro street was Mel Bond, and a block east were brothers Duane and Dick Roepke. On the other side of Moro was Sharon Openlander.

Somewhere back then we found a 45 mm brass cannon shell about 30 inches long. It likely came from Ft. Riley Military Reservation, 10 miles west of town on Hwy. 18. In the summer, when school was out, Bill LaShell and I would mount that shell on a stable wooden rack stand, throw a lit cherry bomb or M-80 down its spout, slip a Hersey chocolate can over the snout and fire the can towards Bluemont School in July around the 4th. We thought that was great fun. That was until we broke a window in the main door of the school from 100 yards away one day. Lord did we run, cannon shell in hand, to hide in the alley behind Bill's house. As I look back on that caper, I realize I couldn't have found a more appropriately named co-conspirator for a stunt like that than Bill LaShell. N'est-ce pas?

The business area of Manhattan, Kansas, in the 40s and 50s, was along Poyntz Avenue, down near the Kansas River. The storefronts stretched for just over six blocks and were two more blocks deep on either side. The town, at the time, had a population of 18,000 townies (local citizens), swelling to 24,000 while Kansas State College was in session. It was also a bedroom community for Fort Riley Military Reservation, ten miles west of the city.

At the time of my birth, my father was employed as a shoe clerk at the largest department store in downtown Manhattan. His department even had one of the old shoe store fluoroscopes where you could X-ray the shoe for correct fit. These machines were later discontinued due to possible excess exposure to harmful radiation. The store was named Cole Brothers Department Store after the Cole family who owned the business, or just "Cole's" if you were asked where you were going to shop. Over the years, and through several ownership changes, Jay McGehe worked his way up to become general manager of the store.

The store was open six days a week with late hours on Saturday night. They were dark on Sunday. This was, after all, Kansas in the 40s and 50s. Dad spent a lot of time at the store. But Sunday was family day. Bill and Joan LaShell would regularly walk down Juliette on the way to the movies on Sunday and ask us boys if we wanted to go too. Dad asked that we did not. That was family day. We would all attend services at the First Presbyterian Church, come home for a pot roast Sunday dinner, and often in the evening all five of us would sit around the Philco radio and listen to the Lone Ranger radio broadcast together. This was early cave man TV.

At our house the three meals each day were breakfast, dinner, and supper. Later in my life those names would transition into breakfast, lunch, and dinner. Times change. Terms change. Eating habits also change with age.

Dad spent 42 years at—and retired from—this Cole's store location. When I say retired, he was actually let go at age 64 because a new owner was cutting costs and Dad was the highest salaried employee. The store went downhill after that and closed its doors within three years. I would often put in part-time hours at that store. Some summers I would work three months as substitute elevator operator. Dad's regular operator, Velma, liked to be home with her children in the summers so I would have a solid, if boring, three months' work on the lift.

One day a traveling ladies undergarment salesman came into the elevator. Turns out he wanted to go to the second floor for the Ladies Department, but he said "Foundations please," so I took him to the basement. There was nothing but storage down there. In a boring job, I'd do anything for a laugh.

Often I could find magic in the ancillary benefits of that job. Across Poyntz Avenue from Cole's was a Duckwall's "five & dime" store which had a lunch counter that was open early. Every business person in town would show up at that counter. It would be jammed weekday mornings. They served a home-made, saucer-plate-sized cinnamon roll with real country butter that would melt in your mouth.

     DON MCGEHE

Dad and I would frequent those calories often before Cole's opening. Back then I could get away with it. That was pre-diabetes. It didn't bother Dad either. At six-foot-tall he was always skinny as a split-rail fence. If you wanted something done in business in Manhattan, Duckwall's was the place to be in the early morning.

My mother, Helen, was a slender woman of 5' 7" with a warm smile and brown hair that was as curly as her beautician could make it. She had a provisional elementary school teaching certificate from the State of Kansas. In our youth Mom was required to continue taking classes at Kansas State College toward completion of her Bachelors Degree requirements and therefore maintain her certificate. She would eventually earn that BA when I was in High School. While she was raising three boys her focus was on being a stay-at-home mom.

She would take on substitute teaching assignments to cover for ill instructors, in any of the elementary schools in the Manhattan system. Occasionally that would be in one of her boys' classes. We had to be alert while she was in our room as a substitute and cause no problems whatsoever. All three of her sons did regular homework and thus were prepared if she were to show up as a sub. Mom was, after all, supervising the homework.

In the pre and elementary school years Saturday night was always bath night. Dad was at work so Mom was an integral part of this process. She would line us all up and have us jump in the bathtub one at a time and scrub us silly in serial order. This was done in an oldest-to-youngest sequence. You had to get your body clean in the Saturday night bath to qualify to get your soul clean in the Sunday morning church service. First things first.

There didn't seem to be any showers built into the homes designed in and before the 1940s. If you wanted a shower you had to rig one yourself. We finally did that and built one in between the furnace and the Maytag washing machine in the basement. Big improvement.

If we boys got in trouble at home (no, not if, but when) mother would say, "there'll be consequences for this. Wait 'till your father gets home."

Dad was so level headed with us. Of course he didn't have to put up with our shenanigans, except on Sunday. When he got home he would get the daily crime report from Mom and if it was warranted he would calmly take us to the basement and get the paddle out and give us a swat or two. Not much emotion was involved in these punishments. It was always so far after the commission of the offense, that the sting was usually taken out of the swats. Dad always remained calm though.

There was, over time, a conspiracy among the children to hide these paddles. When we felt we had been overly punished, we would shove the offending paddle under the furnace. This remained a mystery in the family until one winter when the old furnace went out and had to be replaced. When they took out that old furnace, on the floor beneath it magically appeared seven paddles.

Kansas has always had weird-ass weather. You can, however, depend on four distinct seasons. Two of these are somewhat agreeable. The other two should be avoided. Spring and fall were always my choices. Summer was hot, humid and nearly unbearable. Before the advent of air-conditioning in the 1950s you may as well treat the climate like you dealt with the summer New York stock market, leave town in May and return in September.

Each August there was always a piece in the Manhattan Mercury newspaper about some "yahoo" downtown chef trying to fry an egg on the pavement on Poyntz Avenue. This was something everyone could relate to. Winter could be all over the place depending on weather coming across the Rockies or out of the Gulf of Mexico. I've played golf on New Year's Day and also gone sledding down Bluemont Hill a week later. Bluemont was a great hill that leveled out onto Juliette Avenue about six blocks north of home. It was the site of soap-box derby races in the summer and great sledding in the winter.

    DON McGEHE

In some of my more stupid days I've also been involved in B-B-Gun fights between gangs on the east side and the west side of the hill with the street of cars running down through the center. Dumb! You know…it's all fun and games until somebody loses an eye. I didn't know why I ever did that. I am not, and never have been, a gun person. I qualified with a 22 caliber pistol in the Air Force but not with the big gun, the M-1 Rifle. Our father wasn't a gun person. We didn't learn hunting at home.

Time together with my family was a visit to the park with a still and a motion-picture camera in hand to "shoot." We would skate in the winter and attempt hockey games on Wildcat Creek when it was frozen. One of the main reasons that I finally left Kansas at the age of 21 was to move somewhere like California with better, more predictable weather. But in the 1950s I wasn't through with Kansas quite yet.

For my fourth grade year they transferred me to Bluemont School. The teacher in that class organized reading circles. This was public speaking, it was new to me. Each student was asked to read a paragraph aloud, in turn, around the circle. In this oral reading exercise I had a problem. I would come to a word and not be able to say it. I'd stammer. These were not unusually difficult words that would cause these blockages. The words that I would stammer on were "this" or "that" and sometimes "the."

The teacher referred me to a speech coach who would visit the school weekly. We worked on this stammering problem for six or seven weeks. The coach was able to get me past these stammer blocks and the problem was resolved. I do not know what was discussed between the coach and my mother. As I look back on it now, I would suspect that total lack of confidence and stage fright in public speaking was the cause of the stammering. The words were simple. I just could not say them out loud in front of the group. Some significant boost in self-confidence was likely the solution.

I'd go on in high school and college to perform in plays, musicals, and eventually graduate from KSU with a bachelor degree in speech. I do not remember who this coach was but she gave me the opportunity to overcome a major social obstacle and let me emerge, still shy, often quiet, yet more confident. Where theatre was concerned I didn't have to be myself. I'd put on the mask and make-up of another character and play a role.

In 1951 the Kansas River flooded. The highest crest of the flood was at Manhattan on July 13th. Between July 9th and 13th there were 8 to 16 inches of rain which fell on the area around Manhattan. At the crest the river was 15.4 feet above flood stage with between 8 and 9 feet of water over the streets in downtown Manhattan. Dad was in the Cole's store during the flood and was not heard from for four days.

As the water level rose to 2 feet high on Juliette Avenue all I wanted to do was wade and splash in it with an open sore on my shin. Mother and we three boys were evacuated from our home when flood water reached the first floor. We were taken by boat to the College Field House on the KSC campus. While there, we were all shot for possible tetanus infection and then we walked on up to the home of our family friend Grace Derby in the hills above the College. After four days Dad came walking up the alley at the Derby home in a pair of pajamas, a baseball cap, and house slippers which were all they could rescue from the flood water. Those items were all they had left that were clean and dry in the men's department at the store. They had survived on the second story of the building and were rescued by a "duck" type amphibious boat from a second story window.

The flood clean-up was horrendous. Mud was everywhere. Naturally there were calls for flood control measures. Because the flood was on the Kansas River, and it was too flat to dam, they proposed a dam on the Blue River, which did not flood. This was because government entities wanted to use the flood relief money to build a bass fishing and water sport lake up the Blue Valley as a civic improvement project and to sell lake front homes to prospective buyers. Your tax dollars at work.

   DON McGEHE

There were civic campaigns throughout the area to protest against this recreation dam building blunder. The motto was "Let's Stop Big Dam Foolishness." Strong words in Kansas parlance. The protests were not able to halt the march of progress in the Blue Valley. The dam was built.

When the McGehe family went on vacation, I don't know how our parents survived it. Three rowdy boys in the back seat, and all the territorial disputes that causes, would have driven the average person to drink. My parents weren't average. Mother used to drag us to "Dry" rallies at the Methodist Church before Kansas voted to relax drinking laws in the '50s. There was never alcohol around the house when I was young and we didn't know anyone who drank.

Our vacation favorite was to drive west to Estes Park, Colorado. We would rent a cabin and tour the Rockies for two weeks. The first sight of the Rockies from the flat plains of Kansas was the revelation of another world. We were eight hours from the mountains in Manhattan but each time we drove west it was like the pioneers on The Oregon Trail nearly 100 years before. Wow! Purple mountain majesty? That's really something else!

That eight-hour drive will teach you that the world is, in fact, not flat but round. As you drive through flat western Kansas, the Rockies come up a fraction of an inch every ten miles until you get to this special spot on the highway where there is a tower on a hill that you can pay money to climb up and see the full panorama. Geometry talks. Another roadside attraction, as Tom Robbins would later write. Look and listen.

I now drive from Seattle to Yellowstone National Park in one, very long, day. Try that with three kids. It can't be accomplished. Our family could possibly make it across the Colorado State line before having to find a motel for the night. It taught me the travel lesson of a lifetime; "He travels fastest, who travels alone."

We used to count cows and horses along the roadside with subtractions when you had a cemetery on your side. Automobile identification was also a time killer on the road. There were not nearly as many makes and models as there are now and only one in fifty was foreign. It may be that that was what made America Great Again back in the 50s. When we reached our Colorado destination we would buddy up with other campers' kids and get lost in the sage brush and rocky creeks for hours and days.

That's what being a kid is all about. We knew that if we saw a creek with a rocky stream bed, and the water flowed over those rocks for more than 50 yards, the water was safe to drink. The germ term "giardia" was not in common use yet. Still, nobody died.

When I was in sixth grade, the popular shoe style for boys was black engineering boots. I was on my father all summer to get me a pair of them. He argued that they were not the best thing for the health of the feet, and that oxfords were a better choice. And he knew shoes. One week before I was to go for the first time to junior high school at the 7th grade level he relented and I proudly had my engineering boots. I wore them to school that first day and discovered that they were no longer the style everyone wanted. I was the only one with new boots in the school. As I discovered, fashions change, and had changed. I didn't say much when I got home but I did push the heavy new black boots off to the corner of the closet. Style lesson learned.

But it still didn't keep me from buying a Nehru jacket in the 70s. Ouch! Something else occurred that first month of junior high. Several professional Hispanic yo-yo twirlers showed up in front of school one day. These were 18- to 20-year-olds who were real whiz-bangs with the yo-yo. They could do walk-the-dog and any number of other amazing tricks with the yo-yo that amazed all the kids. They had been hired and sent by the Duncan Yo-Yo Company to stimulate sales. Fortunately, Duncan Yo-Yos were available at the corner grocery store across the street from the junior high. Such convenience.

At junior high I was also among a lot more students. I was overwhelmed and scared at first. I learned in later years that there was a term for this. I was an introvert. Susan Cain wrote a book titled

was pert and cute with long brown hair, glinting expressive eyes, and a pixie smile. On the fourth night of camp I had arranged to meet with Shirley. Over behind the mess hall in a secluded area near the lake we kissed. That was a first for me.

I was so excited I didn't even notice that Molly Hoover, guessing what was to be going on, was observing this whole episode with two of her cabin buddies from over in the bushes. That excitement did not ease up, so later that night I helped to organize a raid on the girls' cabin where Shirley and Molly were bunked. We didn't get in the cabin. We had no intention of getting in the cabin, but we did take sticks and knock out all the struts that kept the storm shutters propped up. When propped open, these storm shutters allowed ventilation through the cabin.

We whooped it up and made a lot of noise but caused no damage. That was enough, though, to get our entire cabin assigned to a two-hour clean-up of the chapel the next day. In a magnanimous move, Shirley even came over to help in the chapel clean-up. What a move. Proud? I was ready to pin a medal on her chest.

As a teenager I was observant of the reactions of my mother to the deportment of my older brother Dave. As the first born son, it was his function to test the family behavior rules for all of his siblings. David was quite open in his activities and hid very little from my folks. When they, usually my mother, came down on him for some alleged offense I was able to see which way the wood grain was running in the family paddle. I use this only as a figure of speech. Paddling ceased when that furnace was replaced years ago.

Dave was always able and willing to argue his point of view on his activities, sometimes quite successfully. These discussions sometimes ended in a stalemate without any grounding. That was a win for Dave, to my way of thinking. By watching and listening, this enabled me to avoid parental confrontations. I was far more secretive than Dave was. I couldn't, or more likely didn't, talk to either of my parents. It was my custom to be attentive and avoid any trouble.

I often wished that I had an uncle or cousin whom I could feel comfortable talking to. The closest I came to that relationship was my cousin Richard Lee Cox. Richard had that Arthur Fonzarelli look with rolled-up white t-shirt sleeves. And this was in the late 1940s, 25 years before the first airing of *Happy Days* in 1974. Richard was 10 years my senior and too distant in age to fill the role I sought.

In those teenage years, Mother had fairly strong opinions on who her boys should date. She was also eager to share these opinions. She often chose the daughters of her good friends. These were always wholesome, intelligent, Protestant, young ladies. The kind you *should* want to marry, if you had marrying in mind.

I wasn't looking for marriage. Excitement was more attractive to me. Like most young boys I found an excess of testosterone ruling my choices. Hormones, however, don't automatically overcome introversion. I was still too shy to ask.

Tenth grade of senior high was a simple move to the building adjoining the junior high. Both schools shared a common auditorium, gym, and food service area. The building was familiar. I played varsity football as a sophomore but did not letter. Upper class men got the time on the field.

As a sophomore I earned my first letter in track. I ran the quarter mile (440 yard) dash. That was the major problem with the 1/4 mile. It was a dash. I was asked to run two of these races each meet. I would lose my lunch after each race. When the season was over I was tired of puking. As a junior I went out for the golf team in the spring.

When my class came back for our junior year we moved into a brand new high school, 18 blocks up Poyntz Avenue next to Sunset Cemetery. In 1957, during the spring of that sophomore year, my folks bought their first home at 420 Oakdale Drive. This home was across the cemetery from the new school property. I could now walk across Sunset Cemetery to school. With a new auditorium and a new football field, two of my main areas of interest were significantly enhanced in this new building.

I participated in three stage performances, including "Briga-doon", and lettered in football that junior year. In the third game of that season my good friend John Montgomery (Monty) Williamson got a slight injury. I was sent in to replace him at left defensive end. I did the job the coach was looking for and earned a starting job on defense. Many of my friends, including Monty, were seniors that year and in the class ahead of me. These were kids I had known for years from Westminster Fellowship, a youth group associated with the Presbyterian Church.

That junior year summer, and for the previous three summers, I had worked for Leo Cross at the Manhattan Municipal Swimming Pool in City Park. I would check baskets on the men's side and do all the clean-up and maintenance at the pool. I enjoyed that job. The clean-up was done alone and either before opening or after closing. On breaks I could get sunshine around the pool.

The summer between my junior and senior year I met my first serious girlfriend. I was 16, she was 15. Peggy Sue Hoffman was a year behind me at MHS and a cheerleader. I had known who she was for months. All it took was to get up the guts to ask her out. I had always been afraid to ask questions. Someone could say no. I still have that problem.

As we went back to school in the fall, we became a steady couple. I thought I was in love. It is often like that with the first relationship. It was a relief not to wonder who I would take to the next school dance or function. The 1958 football team won the Central Kansas League championship that year. We enjoyed the best MHS season in years, until my younger brother Bruce's team won the State Championship three years later. They went undefeated. That was a rare accomplishment in anyone's league.

After football season was over, I played around with cigarettes. I didn't get hooked but thought it was "Marlboro Cool." I had fallen for the advertising; the line. At Peggy's folks' house they also had alcohol. I had my first drink there over Christmas break. I was able to postpone that addiction until 1960 or so. In a three-month period I had introduced myself to two habits that would plague me for years. Nice start, McGehe.

I also had a fun role as Jud Fry in "Oklahoma" that year. I was a baritone. It seemed that I was always the villain in the musicals. The hero role was always reserved for the tenor. Was this the foreshadowing of a life persona or just a reflection of my vocal range?

During my senior year I had not done much spade work on getting into college. I knew that I could enroll at Kansas State which would entail staying in town and continuing to live at home. In the spring of that year, a Captain Tom Bakke visited my football coach, Dick Towers, in Manhattan. He was looking for recruits to play football in the USAFA Class of 1963 at the Air Force Academy in Colorado Springs, Colorado. When Towers called me into his office I was floored. I expressed interest and was told there were several hurdles.

First I had to pass the scholastic tests. Second was a flight physical. Third, if those went well, they had to find me an appointment from a U.S. Senator or Representative to the U.S. House. I went to Topeka for the scholastic tests and passed them. I don't know by how much, but they said I passed. Then I bussed up to Offutt AFB in Nebraska for the flight physical. The body was in good shape. That was a pass.

I then communicated with Captain Bakke and he went to work on the appointment. I imagined that the football program at a major academy had appointments in their back pocket that they could call up and use for the favor of putting an Air Force facility in some representative's district. That's politics. At any rate it was some time in coming. I had graduated from high school and was on a trip to New Mexico with a friend when I got the telegram in early June to report to Colorado Springs on June 24th for induction.

June 22nd, 1959, I was on the 10:30 pm Union Pacific train westbound for Denver. The train arrived in Denver mid-morning on the 23rd. I transferred to a bus for the USAFA facility. On the 24th at 10:30 there were hundreds of cadet recruits on the Tarmac level at the induction station of the Cadet Dormitory building. These troops were wearing an assortment of civilian travel clothing, wrinkled from several days of crossing the North American Continent, to get on base with a variety of long hairstyles they were soon to unceremoniously lose. The base barbers were one level below sharpening their shears.

We were checked in by an assortment of enlisted men and gathered in groups to swear allegiance to the Constitution and the Flag of the United States of America. That accomplished, a hellish 11 months of Cadet Basic Training was about to begin. First order of business was a buzz cut in the barbershop on the lower level. The busiest man in the shop was the guy with the broom. Next we were lined up and issued ill-fitting khaki uniforms. They were to be tailored later. Much of the rest of that day was a fog of regimentation and drill, then room assignments.

My first roommate was Jim Martin from Port Arthur, Texas. We were part of a training squadron and were assigned there for two months that summer. We would run, jump, drill, and march all day. At the end of each day we all congregated for what was fondly called "shower formation." The entire squadron would form up in a brace position against the walls of the hallway in the dorm.

Exercises were assigned and completed until the upperclassmen determined that you had "worked up a sweat." When this occurred, you were sent to the shower and had three minutes to complete the process. I had the capability of working up a sweat just by standing in the brace position against the wall. As a result of this previously undiscovered talent, I was never less than sixth man into the shower out of a squadron of 36 Cadets. It saved a lot of exertion and time at the end of a day.

The training was tough. When outdoors we always ran everywhere. This was often with packs and rifle. One day I was invited to participate in a special detail. This was for cadets who had failed to pick up their clean laundry from the laundry room on time. I had picked mine up. The laundry inventory had occurred before that pick up, however, so I was still on the list.

We ran five miles with rifles out to Cathedral Rock and five miles back to pick up that laundry. Just another formation. We were so busy that the two months passed fast. After the basic summer we were assigned to our academic squadrons for the fall. Mine was the Fifteenth Squadron. My new roommate was R. Peter Hammerton from Michigan.

Now, I've never considered myself the smartest snickerdoodle in the cookie jar. I was impressed, however, when I discovered that Pete Hammerton went through his freshman year at University of Michigan on a National Merit Scholarship. He then gave up that scholarship to accept the Academy appointment. I now realized that I was up against some fairly incredible academic talent. Pete was smart. Could every other cadet in my class be mentally ahead of me too?

One Saturday afternoon when we were studying in the room, Pete said "Would you like a candy bar?"

I said "Sure."

He threw me a dime and said, "good, while you're down there buy me a Snickers Bar too." "Down there" was the cadet store. It was a quarter mile down and another quarter mile back. I knew I'd been suckered. I went anyway.

Freshman football gave me more to eat in the dining hall. We had all lost 20 pounds over the summer. We were eating 6,000 calories per day and had been burning 9,000 a day all summer. As it was football season we were now able to sit at a football table in the dining hall. The upper class football players knew we needed to eat more to put on weight for the season so they kept the "doolie poop" spouting at the table to a bare minimum. We first year cadets were called "Doolies."

They let us eat rather than verbally spout BS from our training manuals. This was great, but football season was over in three months and we had to return to the squadron tables after that. There was also talk that the squadron was looking for a "heavyweight" to put on the squadron boxing team. That was an assignment I absolutely did not want. To avoid it I went out for the freshman wrestling team.

The closest I'd ever been to wrestling was in the back seat of a parked car several times in high school. That lasted a couple weeks until the first squad cuts came. I was then back on the squadron tables and drafted for the boxing team. I have never been a fighter. I'd never been in a fist fight. At 6'3" and 200 lbs. in high school, I'd been able to avoid scrapes. Now I was stuck.

My first three fights went ok. I kept my guard up. In the fourth fight I was paired up against Bob Shaw who had won a Golden Gloves Championship fighting in Philadelphia. He was fighting above his weight class and he was good. In the third round he landed a right which staggered me back across the ring and when I bounced off the ropes, leading with my chin, Shaw was waiting with another right. I don't even remember the first right.

The next thing I do remember was two teammates walking me around outside the gym in the snow, rubbing snow in my face. After that, I next remember lying on my back on the shower room floor with cold water cascading down upon my head. I made it back to my room in the dorm and lay down until Pete called me to get to dinner formation. I marched to the dining hall and got to the table. Two of the upperclassmen noticed that I was not functioning at all. They stayed on either side of me and walked me over to sick bay. I was admitted and tested and put in a bed overnight.

When I was let go the next morning I had brain concussion and a light duty pass to keep me from running or marching for a month. I had trouble with studies for several months after that. I don't know to this day what effect that brain scrambling had on my academic performance, but boxing was over. The reason that 4th-class men (first year cadets) are always drafted for the squadron boxing team is that the upperclassmen are either too savvy or have squadron political connections that are too strong to allow them to be put on the boxing team. The grunts get that work.

At Christmas the upper three classes were on leave to go home. The Doolies had to remain at the Academy base. My folks did come to Colorado Springs to visit for several days. During this visit I got my first opportunity to go skiing. With the escort of our parents we were given a dining pass to accompany them and leave the base.

There was a rope-tow and a very short ski run at the Broadmoor Hotel in Colorado Springs. We all went down there and rented skis, boots, and poles to try our luck on the slopes. I'd never done this before. It was exciting to aim the skis downhill and feel the cold wind whistling past my ears. On that first run, toward the bottom of the slope, the lodge suddenly appeared. I was going way too fast.

I didn't know how to turn, much less stop. All I could do was to fall down and slide into the wall of the observation deck. I got up, dusted myself off and muttered (loudly enough for those in the front row of tables to hear) something about the slick patch of ice up the slope about fifty yards. Later on that evening I did learn a rudimentary turn using the old 'snow plow' maneuver. A stem christie it was not.

Before Christmas, that fall semester, I had flunked college algebra and trig. I had not taken senior math in high school and now deeply regretted it. I'd been too busy and too lazy to tackle that in high school, and that chicken was now home to roost. In hindsight, I took an Algebra and Trig make-up course and passed it.

The make-up course kept me out of calculus and I began calc in a remedial class after algebra and trig was over. Because of the make-up course I was to miss the first three weeks of the summer tour of Air Force bases around the country and then I was to come back in late July to finish the calculus course and take the final exam. In the meantime, and before the summer tour, the Class of 1963 was recognized and our doolie year was over. It felt good not to walk around in a brace all the time and kowtow to every upperclassman. I was now a cadet. My folks were out for June Week, Recognition Day, and the parade, and we all went out to dinner that night in Colorado Springs.

One of the Air Force bases we visited that summer was Hamilton AFB in San Francisco. While there, we were each given orientation rides in the F-101s. This was a twin-jet fighter with the

     DON MCGEHE

pilot in the front seat and one cadet in the rear seat. We flew out over the Pacific Ocean doing barrel rolls and flying faster than the speed of sound. As we went through Mach 1 there was just a brief shudder, then smooth air again.

At one point, while I was busy looking at the instrument panel, the pilot came on the intercom and said, "look up, Cadet McGehe, and you will see the ocean." We were, at that time, flying upside-down. I lost my lunch shortly thereafter. The cockpit in this aircraft was pressurized and it was a relief after we landed to have the canopy run back and experience the fresh air of Mother Earth once again. We were given an overnight pass in San Francisco; my classmate Frank Karasiensky and I found a cheap flop house hotel near North Beach and visited several North Beach clubs that night. We did not drink but we felt like fish out of water. Our civilian clothes were totally inappropriate and we resorted to just looking, listening, and learning.

Once back in Colorado Springs we had several weeks more of classroom instruction and the final. I was scared. I still didn't know or understand the calculus. The night before the final I was up cramming on the books until after 2:30 am. I still didn't know the stuff. I was worried. I wrote down some notes, including several formulas, that I thought I might need on flash cards. I knew this was wrong.

At the Academy, as at West Point and Annapolis, there is an honor code. It reads; "We will not lie, cheat, or steal, nor tolerate among us those who do." I knew those note cards were a violation of the code, but I also knew that I needed to pass the calculus. I finally got in bed for three hours of fitful sleep, if you could call it that. Next morning I went to the test with a portfolio in my hand.

I looked at the test and recognized nothing, but nothing, on it. What I had written down would do me no good. I used all the time allowed, even after the other three classmates in the group had left the room. When the instructor came back into the room, I handed him the test, picked up the portfolio, and the notes slipped out of the booklet onto the floor. The notes had done me no good. I had, in fact, gone into the test with the intention to cheat. The intention alone was the Code violation. I simply looked at him and told him that I would be going back to the dorm and turning myself in to the Honor Representative. Which I did.

Within two hours the Honor Representative gathered together a hearing of the Honor Board and I presented my explanation to the Board. It was cut and dried. I had broken the code and I was to resign. The following morning I was in the office of the Squadron Air Officer Commanding. He called my father on the phone and gave Dad the result.

I was in tears as I talked to my Dad and let him know that I would be on the eastbound Union Pacific that very evening. It was a long slow train ride leaving Denver after midnight and arriving in Manhattan some ten hours later. I was returning home again. I was 18 years old. I felt like shit.

I carried my suitcase up Poyntz Avenue three blocks to Cole's Department Store. I walked in the back door and saw my Dad. We let it go with small talk and I let him know I would catch a city bus up to the house to see my Mom. When I got home Mom had a big hug for me and a cup of coffee. After sitting for 20 minutes I took my suitcase down to the finished basement, where my room used to be, and reclaimed the space.

I had been wearing a uniform for a year and my civilian clothes were, for the most part, too large for me now. Even though I felt physically good now, I knew the weight might change after I got into a more sedentary life. It did feel comfortable being home. I knew I was loved and cared for. It felt the way home is supposed to feel.

CHAPTER 9

I HAD THIS FEELING, AT THAT MOMENT, THAT I HAD BEEN IN solitary confinement for a year. I wanted to get back down to Kite's, the local beer bar, and find some social life for myself. It wasn't even noon yet. That was a crazy idea until at least 8:00 pm or so. At the time, Kansas had a legal drinking age, for 3.2% beer, of 18. Places like Kite's were prime drawing cards for the university students.

But it was summer. School wouldn't start for five weeks. I made a couple of calls and managed to scare up several of my high school buddies to meet in the evenings soon. One of those early nights I dropped by my high school friend Molly Hoover's apartment to say hi, and met a gentleman she was dating named David Paul Rehfeld. He was a student at KSU, as Molly was. We talked fraternities for a while and Dave invited me to visit Delta Tau Delta during rush week. I accepted.

The Greek system was strong at K-State. It would provide a broad exposure to meeting new people when I got to campus. The Delts also had members in key roles in student government and activities across campus. I had already been to talk to A. Thornton Edwards, who was a family friend and Dean of Admissions at the University. He wired for my transcript and said he could credit 33 hours from my Academy records, even with the four hours of "F" in Calculus. There was real meat in that Academy schedule. So my KSU enrollment was set.

I was so eager to get out and mix in society that I doubt I spent more than one night at home in the next two weeks. I'd borrow Dad's car and leave the house before 8:00 pm to return at midnight or later. One afternoon I was sitting on the counter in the back room at Cole's Department Store, watching Dad unbox merchandise.

My Father never swore. He had a very quiet continence. He asked, "Are you going out again tonight?"

I replied "Yes."

He then looked at me quietly and said, "You know, Don, you are really pissing your Mother off!"

That was a mouthful for my Father.

I suddenly realized that I had really been screwing off since I had been home. I'd been drinking and thinking of no one but myself. I was trying to drown my crushed ego and mangled expectations with 3.2 % beer. I asked, "What can I do to make it up to Mom?"

He answered, "If you have nothing better to do, you could start by painting the house. It needs it. You could also stick around the house several nights and talk to your mother."

"OK", I responded, and I was in the car and down to the paint store.

It took me a week of 10-hour days to paint the house. It was rewarding to be doing something. Dad had also scheduled me to make a presentation on the Air Force Academy to his Kiwanis Club meeting in late August showing an Academy film that the Air Force had mailed out for just this purpose. Since the Honor Violation and resignation, my father was not sure if I wanted to go ahead with that presentation, or if, as program chairman, he needed to think up some other program option for that month's meeting. I swallowed what pride I had left and agreed to make the presentation. I later found out he was very proud of me for going through with that. For all that he had given me in his life I owed him a hell of a lot more than that. I made a point of remembering that in future years.

That semester I enrolled in a curriculum called "General-290" which was designed for the indecisive who had not yet chosen a major. I knew I wanted a liberal arts program but would wait until something hit me over the head with undeniable possibilities to make a choice among options. I did go through rush week and I was able to talk to eight fraternities. I was really drawn to the Delts and ended up pledging at their house with Dave Rehfeld as my pledge father. We had a strong bond. Dave had been in the armed forces for four years before coming to K-State in a secondary education curriculum with a sports training minor.

Because of his time in the military he was probably 22 years old at the time. He had been raised on the streets of Oakland, California, before moving on to Carlsbad, and had savvy beyond his years. Dave was a jazz lover and had been raised around the California clubs. That year he was responsible for bringing the Dave Brubeck Quartet to campus for a concert where I got the chance to talk to Paul Desmond backstage. I said to Desmond that "Brandenburg Gate," which they played that night, didn't sound anything like the version on their "Jazz Impressions of Eurasia" album, which I was familiar with.

Desmond took the time to educate me that jazz was an experience of the moment. No song ever sounded the same as the last time that they played it. I was now learning from a master. I'd never heard *live* jazz before. My entire exposure to music was on the radio where there is only one version of any song and they just play the same cut, time after time after time.

Along with Brubeck and Desmond, Gene Wright was on bass and Joe Morello was on drums. I really learned something about jazz that night. Another jazz performance was given at K-State later when the "Jazz at the Philharmonic" road show came to play the Field House in 1962. Everyone who was anyone in jazz played with that tour group.

Dennis Denning, my drama coach from Manhattan High School, had moved up to the KSU faculty in 1959 and he cast me in the part of Turk in the William Inge play "Come Back Little Sheba." This was my first participation in the Drama Department at K-State. Denning also shared with me a possibility of doing summer theater in an eight-week program that coming summer at Kansas State Teachers College in Emporia, Kansas. This was great theater experience. It was summer stock, where the troop puts on five performances of a new play each week. Summer theater had a six-week run and this was a busy, creative, expressive blast.

At KSTC I roomed with a group of U.S. Army veterans, all going to summer school, at a house across the street from the Elks Club in Emporia, Kansas. These guys were producing home brew beer on the back porch and bottling off 10 gallons each week in quart bottles. The brew was about 13% alcohol and cost $.07 cents a quart. Some bottles did explode. If you put it in the fridge before opening and poured off the clear beer on the top and left the dregs (which had settled out) in the bottom of the quart bottle you ended up with a fine, low-cost beverage in a pitcher for hot summer afternoons in Kansas.

Coming back to Manhattan, in September, two of my fraternity brothers from the Delt house had rented an apartment for the semester. I showed these two, Don Morton and Ronald Otto Kruse, how to brew beer. We set up a 10-gallon brewery crock in their apartment. It would take a few weeks to brew, bottle, and let the quarts settle out. One whole case blew up and caused quite a stink in their closet.

In the fall of 1961 my body chemistry was changing. I was experiencing insatiable thirst, significant weight loss, and frequent urination. I could not get through a 50-minute class period without excusing myself to go to the restroom. At the time I was working on back stage production for "Teahouse of the August Moon." I was busy. I had set an appointment with Dr. Cave in late October but canceled it due to lack of time. My body reached a crisis situation on my 20th birthday, Friday, November 3rd.

I took a date to a bottle club east of town for drinking and dancing. On the way home from the club I stopped, got out of the car and puked at the roadside. I drove my date to her sorority house and then went to the Delt house and stripped, took a long cold shower, dried and went home to bed. Beginning at 3:00 am I was up every 30 minutes with the dry heaves. This was early

Saturday morning. I was scheduled to work that day at Cole's. I told my father that morning I was too sick to work and continued with the every-half-hour dry heaves throughout the day.

I could eat nothing. Anything ingested would just come back up. Mother made me some shaved ice and that I could keep down. I later realized there were no calories in the ice. Lack of sugar was why I could keep it down. This condition continued through Sunday morning the 5th and the folks called Dr. Cave who agreed to a house call.

He came, took my pulse and diagnosed tachycardia (racing of the heart). He suggested calling an ambulance and going to the hospital. As I was being wheeled into the ward at St. Mary's Hospital I slipped into coma. Dr. Cave (who was in his 80s) handed me off to a younger intern who was on duty at the time, and who was also a neighbor of my folks on Oakdale Drive. This was Dr. William Durkee, who asked my folks if there was any diabetes in the family, and Mom said "no." Seeing that I had not been able to keep down any food for two days, he called for a sugar IV.

My folks went down to the administrative offices at the hospital to register insurance coverage, and as they were about to leave, Mom decided to look in on me one more time. She later told me that when she walked into the room I was "white as the sheets." She called Dr. Durkee back to the room and he then did a blood sugar test. The blood sugar results were 748. Anything over 700 usually triggers death. Durkee now knew he was dealing with diabetes and began an insulin regimen.

I finally came out of the coma on Tuesday afternoon. Once they had stabilized the blood sugar and balanced the calorie intake the body began to function more predictably. Saved by a vigilant and caring Mother. She just wasn't willing to leave without answers. I was in the hospital for another week to get my new routine balanced. When Kruse and Morton found out about the diabetes they quit drinking the home brew suspecting that it might be the cause of the disease. It was not.

The thought occurred to me, years later, that the onset of diabetes might have been the result of a deep-seated, desperate, and guilt-ridden psychosomatic attempt to justify leaving the Academy. Diabetes would have forced me out of the Academy and Air Force anyway. Back then I could not have flown with the disease. These thoughts are a long, long stretch. Even 96 years after the "discovery" of the hormone insulin, by Doctors Banting and Best, the medical community still doesn't know what triggers or causes the juvenile diabetic condition. Could it be a virus? There are no answers, yet. I am still sitting on that question, wondering when the answer will hatch. It is entirely possible that the answer will not be found in my lifetime.

After I came out of the coma in the hospital, I had a week of down time to learn how to give myself a hypodermic shot. The nurses had me practice by injecting distilled water into an orange. A quick jab through the skin of the orange and a push on the plunger; it was simple…with the orange anyway. The next step is to throw that sharp needle through my own skin. Here is where it got a lot more serious. The hesitation on that first shot was forever.

But it got easier every day. While in the hospital I also had time to analyze what had happened to me and what the future held. I knew diabetes was very serious, and fraught with possible complications. No one I spoke to was able to forecast what my future held. It was November, 1961. I was 20 years old. I made up my mind that week that I would be able to live until at least 35 years of age. That was my goal. So…here goes!

My body recovered from the diabetes crisis quickly. I had planned to go skiing with Don Morton, Ron Kruse, and John Arford in Colorado over semester break and I was on that trip. We skied all day and played a lot of hearts in the motel rooms at night in Colorado. I went to all the pubs with the guys but I did not drink. At the time I was trying a two-week course of pills that Dr. Durkee had prescribed; they were intended to stimulate my pancreas to make more insulin but I still could hardly eat anything, even though I was getting a lot of "sugar burning" exercise on the slopes. I was still losing weight.

 DON MCGEHE

When we got back to school, Durkee took me off the pills and put me back onto insulin shots. That was for the best. I just had no insulin being produced by my own pancreas. Every unit of insulin that I needed to use for transport of sugar into the cells had to be introduced by injection. The diabetes medical treatment was really embryonic back in 1961.

I would go in to the clinic at 8:00 am on a Monday morning for a fasting blood sugar test and get the results by phone on Wednesday night. On my 2017 regimen, that test takes five seconds. At the end of the test I know my blood sugar reading. I now test at least eight times a day. Each test strip costs $1.25.

This is not a cheap disease. A month's-worth of Lantus insulin costs just north of $345.00. But…if I had contracted this disease before 1921 (when insulin was first isolated), I would be dead within three years of the onset. As I write in 2018, I have been shooting insulin successfully for 58 years.

Somewhere in the college curriculum of most students there is that course that, when taken, has a deep and sometimes destructive influence on the dogma you were taught at church when you were a child in confirmation class. For me that course was in the English Department at K-State, and titled "English Bible 1." The focus of the class was the study of the Old Testament of the King James Bible from a standpoint of its content as literature and not as religious dogma. My good friend, Mike Davis, who was a Catholic, called the class "Heresy 1." I enrolled in this class to get insight on the Book of Job for background to play the character J.B. in the Archibald MacLeish play we were to perform in the spring.

The instructor of English Bible 1, Dr. Jones, used other concurrent writings such as the Nag Hamadi Library, and Qumran (Dead Sea) Scrolls to substantiate or repute the biblical stories as to their truth or falsehood. He also pointed out where, in the scriptures, there had been notes added by those who were hand-copying the earlier documents, and had subsequently added those notes into the body of the script, creating errors which were now within the text. Dr. Jones was also a deacon in the Presbyterian Church. Even though he knew that some of the doctrine that most churches include in their teachings was not historically correct, he was still a man of faith. That may be similar to being a Bible Baptist and yet recognizing the validity of some of the concepts in Darwin's Origins of the Species. The class led me to discount much of the dogma declared by religious faiths yet honor the love professed in the hearts of their faithful.

I returned to the stage in the spring of 1962, playing J.B. in Archibald MacLeish's play titled *J.B.* The production was performed in Danforth Chapel on the University Campus. It was likely the most significant dramatic material that I have ever been fortunate enough to play. MacLeish took the story of Job, from the Bible, and set it in modern day America. A character named Mr. Zuss plays the part of God, and Nickles represents the Devil. These two bargain, back and forth, for J. B.'s soul: one from a balcony; the other from the pit. It is powerful drama.

During my sophomore and junior years I was able to pull my grade point average up and even made Dean's List honors in two semesters. I was doing a lot of work with the Student Union Organizing Committee during this school year. In the summer between my junior and senior years I had the opportunity to attend the Delta Tau Delta Karnia nationwide fraternity convention which convened in New Orleans, Louisiana. I drove down to the Big Easy with three other delegates from my chapter. That was a blast. I had never seen New Orleans, or any of the Southern U.S. except Texas before.

In a small berg in the Delta of the Mississippi River, we even came across a pay phone one day that you could still use for a nickel. We saw many plantations and went over to the Pearl River between Louisiana and Mississippi to go water skiing one weekend. I also seem to remember being introduced to a cocktail called the Hurricane at Pat O'Brien's in the French Quarter.

At the onset of my senior year I was required to select a major. I had been designated into General-290 as a sophomore and a junior.

When I looked at my transcript I had the majority of my hours in the Speech Department of the School of Arts and Sciences. Working with Dean Norma Bunton I was able to arrange my senior schedule to complete all the hours required to graduate with a Speech major. During that senior year I was looking only at one goal: University graduation with a BA degree.

I had no thought of what I was going to do with that degree in the arena of life-work. I had conducted no interviews. I was not aware of if, or where, there was a "placement office" at the University that could, or would, help with this choice. I doubt that they had one. I imagine that that is the kind of thing a good faculty advisor could do. I had never been assigned a faculty advisor and I wasn't savvy enough to go find one for myself. I'm sure there was someone who could have helped, but I hadn't pursued it. My lifelong work history shows that this was not a wise choice.

My older brother Dave had been married at Fort Sill, Oklahoma, in the fall of 1962. There was a new car for him and his wife Leila Feriale Haikal (Lily) in the collection of wedding gifts from Lily's Mother Denise Haikal. Dave had been driving a 1957 MGA Sport Coupe for several years. He asked me to drive it back up to Manhattan to sell it for him. A month after I had it back at school someone stole the side curtains off the car. I couldn't afford new side curtains so I just parked it under the sleeping dorm overhang at the Delt house to keep the rain and show off of it. I did not drive it that much.

There was also a problem with the electric fuel injection system which caused it to stall, and that would require letting it sit for a half hour before you could get it started again. I kept a quart of wine and a blanket in the boot to relax with in good weather while waiting on the ignition to cool while out in the middle of nowhere. The Marine Corps had transferred them to Twenty Nine Palms, California, in the spring of 1963. I had advertised the car for sale but it had not sold. I now had in mind driving the car out to Twenty Nine Palms after graduation and leaving Dave the car and then going on to Newport Beach to do some "California Dreamin.'" In May I bought new side curtains and had the fuel injection system repaired in preparation for the trip.

The main focus of my extracurricular activity in the senior year at Kansas State was the responsibility as Producer of the University wide Y-Orpheum Show. For Y-Orpheum, male and female living groups were paired together and are asked to write scripts for skits which were submitted for judging. The winning six scripts were then presented in a two-night show in May 1963. The 1963 theme was "In the Beginning." (These were the first three words in Genesis.) The final winner on Saturday night was the Chi Omega and Phi Delta Theta skit "In The Bee-Ginning."

It was a clever take off not only on the theme but also on the "KenneBee's" (Kennedy) Administration in the White House in Washington D.C., at the time. All the actors were bees trying to protect their hive against an attack of killer wasps. The six-skit show involved over 1,000 student-participants campus-wide. Y-Orpheum, in 1963, raised over $10,000.00 for the K-State Student Union Activities Fund. In only six more months JFK would be shot and killed in Dallas.

I graduated from Kansas State University of Agriculture and Applied Sciences in June, 1963, with a BA in Speech. I was a Kansas resident for only three more days.

PART 3

COASTAL FAULT MOVEMENTS

June 1963 - February 1972

CHAPTER 10

I drove out of Manhattan, Kansas in June 1963 in my brother's '57 MG-A Roadster, top down, luggage rack on the boot, and hopes, in my wild imagination, of a once-in-a-lifetime "Route 66" road trip. My destination was Liberal, Kansas, to pick up Bruce Brauer. He and I had graduated from Kansas State University three days earlier. We wanted to emulate Martin Milner and George Maharis—seeking fun and fortune in Southern California.

The day was warm; it was typical Kansas weather for June. With the top down, the wind rush cooled the MG perfectly. When we got ready to leave Liberal, we had to make some decisions about what to take. There wasn't much extra room in the MG. I was reminded of advice from my Aunt Imogene Heitman when packing for a trip: "Take half the clothes you had planned to take, and twice as much money." We went light—there was really no choice; only beach clothes and all the money we had, which was damn little.

We struck out to the south to connect with Route 66 at Amarillo, Texas. The map told us we were in the Oklahoma panhandle for an hour, but it still looked like Kansas. In 1963 there were several stretches of new pavement on the route—complements of President Eisenhower's grand vision to turn it into Interstate 40—but much of the old Route 66 was still drivable. While on the road we kept looking around for the chase car, with the camera crew aboard, but we must have missed it (the camera crew members were obviously looking to film a Corvette, not an MGA). The mile marker cities followed Bobby Troup's lyrics; Amarillo, Albuquerque, Gallup, Winslow, Flagstaff, Winona, Kingman, Barstow, and San Bernardino.

One segment of Old Route 66, which was replaced by US-40 in 1953, was the stretch from Kingman to the California border at Needles. Old 66 used to run up into the Black Mountains to a mining town named Oatman, Arizona, and down the other side to Needles. Oatman's 1915 gold rush produced $2.6 billion at today's gold price. Clark Gable and Carole Lombard honeymooned in the Oatman Hotel in 1939. Their suite was 12' by 12', with the restroom located down the hall.

Oatman is now a ghost town with a year 2000 population of 128 (3,500 in 1916) and wild burros running through the town. Today you access the Old 66 "Oatman Highway" four miles south of Kingman on US 40 and drive west. If you're in Arizona, and you miss Oatman, you're missing some fascinating western history.

After San Bernardino we forked south through Santa Ana and Costa Mesa to the Newport Peninsula and onto Newport Beach, California. Our outfits were ready for Newport: shorts, flip-flops, and a tank top. The sun, surf, and beach at Newport, were ready for us. I smiled at Bruce, with a quote from Dorothy in the land of Oz, "We're not in Kansas anymore, partner."

The feeling was exotic. Just to step out of flip-flops and let your toes sink into the warm California sand was the trip culmination. Sixteen hundred ninety miles from the prairie to the pacific. Our entire world had changed in three short, top-down, wind-blessed days. We were here.

The Pacific is so much more than just sandy beaches. With apologies to the Himalayas, to me the Pacific Ocean is the real Goddess Mother of the Earth. The Pacific Ocean covers one-third of the Earth's surface, 64 million square miles, and holds half of our world's water. Water is what makes the earth…The Earth. All the water that fertilizes the vegetation and nurtures the sustenance of our planet evaporates from the ocean, rains down upon the earth, and flows back into the ocean.

The law of gravity reduces fresh water to its mother source, the ocean. The life of the earth came not from terrestrial rock forma-

     Don McGehe

tions and plate tectonics but from the seas. If you wish to return to your source, seek the ocean. Twenty-one years of my life were lived on the Great Plains. I had now reached sea level, and the source of all life. I intended to remain a coastal resident for the remainder of my days. Like The Pacific Plate, west of the San Andreas Fault, I was destined for movement up the Pacific Coast for the next nine years of my life. It felt like I was finally home.

We couldn't sleep on the beach or in the sport-coupe confines of the MG. So, what's next? One of my snow skiing buddies from K-State was an architect in the Newport Beach area. I looked up Jack Steven Miller from a reference I had and let him know we had arrived. Jack said, "It's about time," and let us crash on his floor and couch for several days. We had stuffed our sleeping bags into the MG. They were a necessity for being on the road.

Somehow we talked Jack into looking for an apartment down on the beach which several of us could rent and afford. Miller had a roommate, and the four of us found, in the local newspaper, a new construction home, across the street from the beach, to rent. This home was on West Oceanfront. The owners lived in the upper second floor level and they were renting out the lower two-bedroom apartment to help pay their mortgage. Either we must have looked like a group of clean-cut, upstanding, Kansas lads or they really needed that rent money bad.

Either way, two of us were not yet working, and four bachelors at the beach was never a very stable real estate combination. Our landlords were not, at this time, aware of either of the caveats in the previous sentence. They might soon learn.

The time to return the MG to its rightful owner was hard at hand. Bruce and I regressed back up to the high desert climb of the Marine base at Twenty Nine Palms in our trusty road warrior. I handed over those keys with regret, and with thanks for a great trip to the coast. My brother Dave gave us a tour of the heights, to the south, overlooking Palm Springs and the lower desert then drove us back to the beach in his Pontiac station wagon. As we parted Dave issued me an invitation to return to the high desert and join him, his wife Lily, and Lily's Mother for Thanksgiving several months away.

Back at the beach it was time to get a job. We scoured the newspapers. I also talked to friends and found that they were hiring car parkers at The Newporter Inn which had recently opened just south of Newport Beach on the Coast Highway #1. We hitchhiked down to the Inn and were hired on the spot. It seemed we qualified with; 1) a warm body, 2) a valid driver's license, and 3) a BA degree.

The parking boss, Ralph Frey, was a sharp guy. He understood his business model and had all the necessary insurance to run his scavenger crew. Ralph was also a people person and seemed eager to help his employees in any way he could. We would hitchhike down there each day and start work about five pm. Getting back up to Newport in the dark was a lot more iffy at midnight.

The tips in the parking lot were good. Being off work in the daylight hours gave us time to get familiar with the beach which was just across the street from our apartment. This was working well for me, but three weeks into the job Bruce ran a customer's car into a light pole in the lower parking lot. It was a short time after that when Bruce decided he'd had enough vacation and made plans to fly back to Kansas. He was willing to stay through the end of the first month rental on the apartment.

I was in an ongoing conversation with the parking lot boss, Ralph Frey, about getting more reliable and steady work in the area. Ralph had a lot of friends in Orange County and suggested that I go up and interview with John McIntosh who ran a chain of 13 restaurants called "Snack Shops." These were all sit-down restaurants with reasonable prices and coffee for 10 cents a cup. McIntosh was interviewing for "manager trainees." He would start a new hire as a dishwasher for six weeks to make sure they would show up on time. Once past the dish racks the trainees would go into the cook station and work up through the chef ranks.

The next step up was floor work and finally assistant manager. It was a six-day work week. They paid adequately, with health coverage, and it was a regular pay check. I was hired and given a 6:00 am to 3:00 pm shift in the Corona del Mar, California, Snack Shop washing dishes.

Now I needed a car. I had to be on time at work. That ruled out hitchhiking. I called my Father about the money I needed to buy a car. He knew that I would. My father co-signed on a Household Finance loan for me and I bought a 1953 Ford four-door sedan named "Big White."

I had a job. I had a car. I was beginning to feel more like a legitimate consumer and not a beach bum. The landlord upstairs was now convinced that there was entirely too much partying going on downstairs. We were robbing them of sleep. They asked us to leave after that first month's rental.

Bruce was going back to Kansas. Jack's old roommate was wanting to move closer to work. That left Jack Miller and me to go where displaced beach bums had always gone - inland to Costa Mesa. This was August at the beach and the rents were at high-season rates.

In Newport Beach, the weekly rent in high-season would equal the monthly rent between September 15 and June 15. As a result of this financial disparity, the beach crowd would typically move up to the cheaper bedroom community of Costa Mesa for the summer then back to the beach again for off-season. Jack and I spent only six weeks that summer in Costa Mesa. In order to keep the Costa Mesa place clean and neat we kept a rubber 55-gallon trash barrel in the kitchen.

Off-season, in a southern California beach community, is a gross misnomer. The Los Angeles area normally gets a week of rain in the fall and a week of rain in the spring. There are abnormal years. But with the exception of those two soggy weeks, the weather is traditionally sunny all winter long. It is also at least ten degrees cooler at the beach than in downtown L.A. People from the inner city would pay those prime time weekly rates just to get those cooler ocean breezes in August.

We lived at the beach. We worked at the beach. We could take advantage of the winter rates in paradise. You simply signed a nine-month lease in September and started the party. Jack Miller had a fundamental principal for beach living: "If you have more stuff than you can pack up and move in two hours, you have too many roots down."

At that point it was time to start throwing stuff out. The beach rentals were typically furnished apartments. The interior design styles varied from Early Zodys to Late White Front. Whatever discount store was cheaper at the time. The landlords knew the furniture would likely be trashed anyway. It was a cost of doing business in rental real estate.

In early September Jack and I found a furnished lower two-bedroom on the Newport Canal under the home of Neal and Phyllis Armstrong. Neal worked for the State of California on a fire boat. He and Phil were perfect landlords. If we'd not had a party in two weeks, Neal would come down to check to make sure we were still in good health and ask why. We had a great friendship with them that winter of '63 and spring of '64.

In August my six-week stint of dishwashing was finished at the Snack Shop in Corona del Mar and I was transferred up to the shop in Huntington Beach, just south of the pier. I was now in chef training. At this shop we had one of the first radar (microwave) ovens I had ever seen. Some of the bus boys, who were foreign born, were a bit leery of that oven and thought it could interfere with their testosterone production. For the most part they steered way clear of the radar range as the cooks just smiled.

That microwave was a handy device for heating up baked potatoes which were a commonly served commodity with the steaks on the menu. This shop had a clear view of the ocean. When we had Santa Ana Wind conditions, the wind would blow the crest off the waves rolling in, and blow that froth back out to sea. On a slow business afternoon that was an interesting phenomenon to watch in the surf.

       DON MCGEHE

My shift at the Huntington shop started at 11:00 am to prepare for the lunch crowd. One morning in that November of 1963, I drove up from Newport listening to pre-recorded cassette tape music in the car. As I got into the parking lot one of the waitresses rushed out and yelled to me, "The President's been shot." I had not had the car radio on and was unaware of the Dallas shooting earlier in the morning. It was eerily quiet in the restaurant that day. Normally they had canned "happy" music on the interior sound system. This day it was uninterrupted, commercial-free, national news broadcasts of the Texas tragedy.

We conducted business but there was a stunned silence to the crowd as the news from Dealey Plaza was broadcast and updated. Shortly after noon came the news of the death of JFK. That began the period of political assassinations in the country that extended throughout the sixties. It was a bloody decade. I was too young to remember Pearl Harbor. The Kennedy assassination was the first occasion of my life where people would ask, "Do you remember where you were when…" There would be far too many more of these occasions before the bloody 1960s ended.

In this Snack Shop management-training program two hours each week were dedicated to management training. In the remainder of the 48-hour week the chain was just getting dedicated, reliable labor out of the trainees while teaching them the business from the ground up. The approach was sound. Once through the program, you were able to do any of the jobs in the chain effectively. The assistant managers would jump in at a moment's notice and spell any employee for an emergency such as a bad knife cut and the shop would still run smoothly.

The profile of the managers and assistant managers was typically early thirties, married, stable, and with a goal of making excellent money. As I looked at this profile, I didn't see myself working into the typical mold. I just wasn't that dedicated to the money. I also had questions about my dedication to the restaurant business. It required long hours and tight financial control of both food costs and labor costs. Those two expenses ate up 70% of the gross. The manager carved out his cut from the remaining 30%. At 22, I was lacking the necessary enthusiasm. In truth, that really wasn't why I'd come to the beach.

The layout of this Snack Shop was an open cook station, behind the main counter, with a collection of tables, chairs, and booths for customers spreading out in three directions from the main counter. From the cook station, the chef could see, and even converse with customers at the counter. In early January 1964, two guys named Bud Sperber and Russ Silliman would come for dinner in the evening just after 7:00 PM. They would usually sit at the counter, and over several weeks I became acquainted with them. I would usually be finished with work by eight.

One night they asked me to join them at a table in the back and have a cup of coffee. Sperber told me that he was arranging to buy a wood-hulled schooner moored in the Miami River, Miami, Florida, and motor it back to the west coast, under power, through the Panama Canal and up to Newport Beach. He asked if I would be interested in such an adventure. It did sound like fun. He indicated he was not quite ready to move on it, at the moment, but invited me to keep in contact with him if I had an interest.

The more I thought about it the more interesting it became. Both these guys had great smiles and good humor. Russ was taller but both were on the slim side. Russ had a vest pocket poodle that was his constant companion. The poodle was left in Russ' pick-up truck when they came into the restaurant.

After several more weeks Bud Sperber told me he was two weeks away from putting the deal together. I wanted to go get this boat. If it was this close, I thought it polite to give two weeks' notice to the restaurant. When they got their notice they let me go on the spot. I now had two weeks free to do whatever I chose. I saw this as a perfect time to drive back to Kansas, see the folks, then drive back to Newport Beach and leave for Miami from there.

 DON MCGEHE

I did not have much money and I also had two bald tires on Big White. I checked with the White Front tire store but the needed tires were just too expensive for my budget. Big White had rear-wheel drive, so I put the two bald tires on the front wheels and headed east via the southern route. If you are going to have a problem on the southern route the place that it is bound to happen is the highest, coldest spot on the route: Flagstaff, Arizona. The left front blew on a curve on a four-lane near Flagstaff. It was snowing at the time and Big White ended up in the wide ditch between the lanes without any body damage.

I replaced that tire and managed to get the car back on the road. I stopped at the nearest service station and bought a new tire while putting the patched left front in the trunk as a spare. The snow dissipated in 50 miles and I was back on dry pavement without becoming a snowman. This was a long trip. I was getting quite sleepy in Oklahoma and was frequently opening the drive side window to stick my head outside to wake up. Eventually I turned on the heater to blast as much hot air into the car as possible, stopped at a turnout, shut off the car, and napped until I got so cold I had to start up again.

It was a seventy-five-minute nap. This was, after all Oklahoma, not the beach. I managed to make it into Manhattan and home about 7:00 am one morning and sat down to bacon and eggs with a very surprised mother and father. I was there for five days and then did the route in reverse. The return trip was uneventful because I managed to purloin another used tire at home with far more tread on it. Your guess was correct. I spent more money on tires on the road than I would have spent at White Front before I started out. I was now back in Newport Beach and thankful for the California warmth.

CHAPTER 11

After five more days at Newport Beach, Russ decided it was time to start on the drive to Miami. Russ was in phone contact with Bud but I never saw Bud after I got back from Kansas. Russ was the one who knew Bud and on this whole adventure I was just along for the ride. It would take us more than a week to drive to Miami and involved a stop in Louisville to spend several days with Russ's mom and dad. While he was there, Russ bought his father a new Ford automobile. It was one of the less expensive models but nonetheless a nice gift. His dad was in deep appreciation for what his son had done for him.

I got the feeling Russ owed his dad a favor and this repaid it. We slept in sleeping bags at the Silliman home. Russ had a pick-up truck with a hard cover over the back of his truck and we slept under that cover every night on the road. This was a save-every-cent-you-can type of trip. We even ate beans out of the can to get by. We would try to find a cheap smorgasbord for dinner each evening and load up on carbs. As I recall we would normally pay about $1.35 each for dinner. A buck went a long way in those pre-inflation days. Nine days on the road, and we had arrived in Miami, Florida.

On the second day in Miami Russ called Bud Sperber for details. There were none. Bud said he could not get the deal to go through yet. Stand by, please. We found a spot to park the truck, near the Miami River, beside a boat yard and bided our time for a week. We thought we were out of money and finally Russ called Bud, who said he would wire us some cash. We were to expect it the following day.

     Don McGehe

I remember to this day the expression on Russ' face when he walked out of the Miami Western Union office. He was holding the telegram and had a cock-eyed grin on his face. When I asked him what was going on he revealed that Bud had wired only $14.37. He was laughing so he didn't have to cry. A collect call to Bud gave away the fact that there was no deal and would not be a deal for any boat in Miami. We were told that we should head on back to Newport where Bud had gotten hold of a 250-foot tramp steamer moored in the San Pedro harbor.

In my dreams there is a universe of difference between a schooner and a tramp steamer. We had been caught in a storybook fraud. Russ just happened to have a stashed $100.00 bill in his wallet. He pulled it out and used that money to get us safely back to San Pedro, California. Ben Franklin traveled a lot further back then. You can't even get through a single check-stand at Walmart today with one.

In 1941 there were 3,000 residents of Japanese descent living in San Pedro, California, on Terminal Island. The Japanese fishing fleet was extensive there, and many Japanese also worked in the fish canneries. These citizens were forced into internment camps in February of 1942. Their homes were bulldozed and destroyed when the U.S. Government incorporated San Pedro into the greater Long Beach shipyard during WW ll. Russ and I drove back to San Pedro by the direct southern route where you spend one third of your time in Texas. It is a wide state.

On arrival we met with Bud Sperber and saw the 250-foot tramp steamer riding high in the water at the yard with an extensive coating of rust on her. Russ Silliman somehow managed to acquire a small camping trailer to park on the dock to use as a sleeping and eating facility. This was a necessity since Bud was still not paying us. We began sandblasting the rust coats immediately and painting behind us as we went along. We were using eye protection and respirators to keep the sand and grit out of our eyes and lungs.

It was early spring but still hot enough under the protective clothing to trigger buckets of sweat. Two weeks into the repair we picked up another worker, Mike Powell, who was my age, and had a great fundamental can-do attitude. Mike was 5' 10" and stocky, with a smile that caused everyone to light up in his presence. He could have fun in, or with, any situation we came upon. Mike and I would usually take Sundays off and drive "Big White" down to Newport Beach to keep our heads on straight for the rest of the week. After a month in San Pedro, Bud was able to come up with some cash, but not much. We were just getting by due to the dirt cheap living situation provided by the trailer.

By mid-March the weather was getting warmer and Mike and I were getting restless. Easter was coming up. We decided to take several days off that Easter weekend and go down to Tijuana with a couple of ladies we had been seeing who lived on Lido Island, which was an upscale community in Newport Bay with lots of fine homes. The lady who I had a date with, Cindy, had told me her family (father) knew the president of the race track in TJ. She had evidently met this gentleman on a number of occasions in her childhood.

We left San Pedro on Thursday, March 26, and bunked at Jack Miller's apartment in Newport Beach Thursday night. Friday morning we got an early start in order to make the first race at the track. We all got through the border without problems and were nosing into the crowded parking lot at the track, stopping at each consecutive row trying to spot an empty parking slot. Suddenly, from the left, a Ford Pinto came barreling down the row that we were inching up to, and ran into the left front fender of Big White. The impact was considerable. Fortunately no one was injured. The wheel and the axle were bent, the fender was crushed, and the car was not drivable.

We all got out. Cindy spoke Spanish, fortunately, and found out the driver of the other car was a Mexican priest. Of all the people to have a collision with in a Mexican parking lot, a Mexican priest was

     DON McGEHE

probably the worst. He claimed he had no insurance. We doubted that. Neither car could move so we just waited while Cindy ran up to the clubhouse and found the president of the track.

They returned in about thirty minutes. The track president got talking to the priest and discovered that he did, in fact, have insurance. This was the voice of authority we needed. The president made arrangements to get Big White fixed and wrote down for us the address of the repair shop he would use. With that all set, the car was towed away and we went into the track to watch the races. The four of us were between the proverbial rock and hard-place. We just had to have faith that everything would be handled as planned. This was, after all, Good Friday. The car was to be ready late Saturday evening.

In the fifth race of the day, Mike spotted a horse named Bud's Bad Boy. That name hit the bell for us. We put a win-place-show $6.00 bet on the horse. In the home stretch, the horse came from behind and won the race. Our pay-off was something like $170.00 and that bet paid for our weekend.

We caught a cab to downtown from the track and found a cheap hotel room in which all four of us slept in the same double bed. We ate tacos off the street vendors for dinner, had a few drinks, a lot of laughs, and didn't get much sleep with a bed full of bodies but it was a real experience and we honestly did laugh a lot. Saturday we did a self-led cathedral tour and saw the sights in downtown Tijuana, with most of our stuff in two large backpacks that we had pulled from the trunk of Big White before they towed her off to the repair shop. Toward sunset we hailed another cab and rode over to the repair shop. We waited until about 8:30 for the Ford to be finished and the paint to dry. It was a quality job.

We then piled in the car and returned to the border. I personally did not want to tempt fate in Mexico any longer. We got back to Newport Beach just after midnight Easter Sunday to discover that the largest earthquake in recorded American history had struck in Alaska on Good Friday, March 27 1964. The quake registered 9.2

on the Richter scale and triggered a tsunami which caused a tidal effect in San Pedro Harbor which fluctuated between, plus and minus four feet.

Weeks later Russ told us that he was stepping lively to keep the bow and stern lines on the ship adjusted for the water level fluctuations. Once we found out about the earthquake we didn't bother to go back to San Pedro. Bud Sperber had not won our trust. He had provided for us nothing more than the name of the lucky horse who had sponsored our weekend south of the border. Were we Bud's Bad Boys or what?

When I left for Miami, Jack Miller had recruited Charles Aimsworth Peasley to take my spot in the Armstrong's Newport Canal apartment. CAP, as we called him, was a friend of several other beach residents. We had known him for over a year. His dad had a food brokerage business in downtown LA called Fairbanks/Peasley Brokerage. They represented Sunsweet Prunes, Sunmaid Raisins, Mott's Apple Juice, Snow's King Crab Legs, and a dozen other grocery food lines in the LA supermarket business.

Mike Powell left for the San Francisco area and I made an arrangement with Jack and CAP to keep their apartment clean and to cook for them in exchange for room and board until I could find another job. Neal and Phillis Armstrong had a 17–year-old daughter named Denise who was a senior at Newport High School. We called her Denny. She would come home from school about 3:00 PM weekdays, dump her books upstairs and drop downstairs to visit. Denny was shy, as was I. She was 5'9", trim, cute face, wore glasses, and was just beginning to blossom as a young lady.

Neal and Phil knew where she was and trusted her. Neither of us had any money but we would both look for something to drink for our daily "happy hour." Without money the only beverages available were ancillary mixing tonics that were used in limited quantities in other mixed drinks. These were normally bought by the fifth, and were left over from past parties.

 Don McGehe

We would have Triple-Sec Tuesday, vermouth Wednesday, Cream de Cacao Thursday, or Bailey's Irish Cream Friday. If all else failed there was usually a can of Golden Grain Beer in the refrigerator. It was then selling at Market Basket Stores for $1.99 a case. Creativity was key, but alcohol was still the primary focus. By 4:30 it was time to toss Denny out to begin dinner preparation for Jack and CAP.

By the end of our lease in mid-June, CAP was married to Patty Stoner and it was Jack and I who went to Costa Mesa for the summer. One noted feature of the summer quarters inland was that it always had that same old standby 55 gallon rubberized garbage can in the middle of the kitchen. You know what they say, cleanliness is right next door to heaven.

CAP Peasley hired me in June to be the Fairbanks/Peasley representative in Orange County. I began calling on Ralph's and Von's, and all the other chain stores, stocking shelves and pushing raisins and prunes onto the produce managers' displays. The old-age and retirement community was beginning to grow in Orange County in the '60s, so the demand for prunes was a growth opportunity for the brokerage.

September of 1964 was our opportunity to sign the best 9-month lease available on the beach. This was a house with four available bedrooms right on the sand. It was on the ocean side of Seashore Drive, the last street before the water, at the head of the Balboa Peninsula. The house had a huge vaulted ceiling living room with fireplace and a kitchen alcove. Out the kitchen door was a concrete patio surrounded by a one-foot-high brick wall, with deck chairs on the patio. On the Pacific Ocean side of the wall was a full sand volley ball court and then 30 more feet of sand, at high tide, all the way to the water's edge.

We were on the beach, period. From my bedroom I could hear the waves pounding onto Newport Beach, lulling me to sleep at night. Outside this lower level bedroom was another small patio, with latch-gate fence, and street access between the houses out to

Seashore Drive. The landlord was off site. We simply mailed in the monthly check. This place was heaven. Jack Miller and I were on the lower level. Our friends Jerry White and Gary "Bruno" South were on the upper level overlooking the living room. To get to the beach you simply donned a bathing suit, wandered through the kitchen to grab a Bloody Mary, and stepped out the patio door.

Drinking and driving was already frowned upon, even as early as 1964. We were fortunate to have a convenience store a block and a half from this beach house. They had liquors and cold beer in stock, as well as pre-made sandwiches. The item we most often purchased from them, however, was "Fred's Fresh" orange juice. It mixed well with vodka, gin, and rum. An excellent source of weekend vitamin "C." One must maintain one's health.

And the convenience mart was close enough to walk there. In the fall and spring there was enough light to play several games of volley ball even on a weekday after work, but you needed to scare up a minimum of four players for a game. Mustering up those four participants was never a problem on weekends. We issued open weekend invitations to all the ladies we ran into in our beach contacts. When the ladies showed up, the gentlemen were never far behind. Food, in addition to their presence, was always appreciated from all of our guests.

There was a bar in Newport Beach, down by the pier, which was unique. It was a hole-in-the-wall called Sid's Blue Beat. Sid was an old timer down there and served a real price-performing barbecued chicken dinner with fries and warm bread that made it a go-to place if you had nothing in your refrigerator. I say "chicken," at least we all assumed it was chicken. Come to think of it, we never did see too many seagulls hanging around Sid's beach neighborhood.

After 9:00 pm Sid would present acoustic guitar and vocal artists to entertain. This place was one of Jack Miller's favorites. When I was working the 6:00 am shift at the Snack Shop in Corona del Mar, Jack would shanghai me to go down to Sid's and give me an honorary "gold star" if I would stay down there with him past 10:30

　　　DON MCGEHE

pm. I would sometimes try to get ahead of the game by taking a cat nap between 4:00 pm and 5:00 pm after I got off shift.

That winter of '64 was my first introduction to Warren Miller (no relation to Jack) Ski Films. This was the ski season opener. All the ski equipment vendors in the Orange County area would sponsor the Warren Miller Ski Film showing, and every ski bum on the beach would turn out to see it. From then, on through spring, we would schedule weekend trips up to Mammoth Mountain to ski the greatest powder snow in California. It was a long weekly haul to the slopes.

We would fight our way out into LA traffic on Friday night, leaving about 4:00 pm, and drive north towards Reno on US 395. The trip was six hours to Mammoth Lakes. Between Lone Pine and Big Pine you could always expect to see the "Ski Patrol." California Highway Patrol State Troopers lurking along the route, after dark, were eager to ticket skiers in an attempt to increase State revenues. It was a game. Sometimes a costly game.

One of the more popular cars with these week-end skiers was the VW Beetle. You could often tell who was in a Beetle that you were following, by the length of the skis sticking straight up from the rear bumper ski rack. If it was one long pair and one short pair, it was usually a couple. If there were two short pairs, that was the car you wanted to follow. Two shorts usually spelled ladies traveling together. If they noticed you, and you saw their car again in a parking lot up at Mammoth you could strike up conversations that might lead to social, après-ski, connections. So the ski patrol was not strictly limited to the CHP.

Entertainment on the drive to Mammoth could be found on AM radio listening to Wolfman Jack on 250,000 watt clear-channel station XERF from Ciudad Acuna, Mexico (across the border from Del Rio, Texas). At 250,000 watts it was truly radio broadcast-power inflation.

Mammoth Lakes is also in the Eastern Sierra volcanic caldera field. This provided hot creeks which were perfect for loosening up those sore ski muscles after a long day of moguls. Four miles down the valley, south of Mammoth Junction at 395, was such a creek. There was a hot spring on one bank of the creek that fed into the stream and provided hot water to sooth the sore thighs. A short move into the center of the stream furnished cold water to moderate that heat.

A gallon of Ernest & Julio's Rosé was often found gently floating in the current (pre-heated). A swim suit was seldom an optional item. One season I was fortunate enough to ski thirty-four days at Mammoth which included two weeks straight over Christmas break. That year I made it to the hot spring twice.

CHAPTER 12

After finishing out the lease on the Seashore Drive beach house, I moved up to Manhattan Beach, California. Manhattan was a different kind of beach. Closer to the city, built on a hillside, it offered better views from off the beach than Newport did. There were no homes on the sand here. A sidewalk, called The Strand, and a breakwater stone wall separated the residential housing from the sand beach.

I was becoming financially solvent and could now afford to rent an apartment on my own. Being closer to the City of Los Angeles, there were far more apartments in this community. Renters could live at the beach and drive into LA to work daily. No problem. You could find smaller, more affordable rentals here than down in Newport. The majority of rentals were singles or doubles.

From Interstate 405, driving north, the exit was onto Manhattan Beach Blvd. This road lead straight down to the Manhattan Beach Pier and to the heart of town. In that last block before the pier were three establishments of note. On the north was an open-to-the-sky beer bar called the Port of Entry. Across from the Port was the Beach House Cafe with an excellent beach view and great French fries. Two doors east was The Buccaneer Bar. The Buck was the first bar that ever offered me a charge account. That should have told me something.

The 'Buck' was the poster-child for NBC's "Cheers" show and 20 years before its time. The owner was Mike Grazanish. Mike's wife Carol was the bookkeeper who I settled my account with each month. Happy Hour was 5 – 7 pm daily, with mixed drinks priced at 50 cents each. There was full food service and a band playing 9:00 pm to 1:00 am.

This is where you went to meet all your friends. A weekly high point came every Tuesday night at 7:30 pm when the Batman show came on the TV above the bar. All eyes would follow the masked action for half an hour. The Buccaneer would close at 2 am on Saturday nights. At closing we would often organize an after-hours party at someone's apartment which would last until 6 am.

At daybreak everyone would then troop down to the Pier and throw over crab rings into the water. These crab rings had fish-heads tied onto the nets in the rings to lure the crabs onto the nets. We would then wait forty minutes, and haul in enough crab to take back to the party and boil up for a crab-feast breakfast with eggs. Crab omelets were also a favorite dish at these gatherings. After the crab feed it was home to crash. Well fed. Well-worn out.

In the spring of 1966, I called Jack, Jerry White and Gary South up from Newport Beach for a lobster feed. We all met on the beach at Rancho Palos Verdes. In the 60's there were still rock lobster in the waters off of Palos Verdes. The rock lobster looked just like the New England lobster but without the pincer claws. Fifty years ago they were still there. They have now been all fished out.

Gary South was the key to the success of this operation. He was an excellent free diver. He and Jerry White would put on their wet suits and masks and dive for the lobster while I got the fire going under about forty gallons of sea water in a huge aluminum kettle on the beach. This was no mean feat. It took more than four hours to bring the water up to boil with an open beach fire. We brought our own dry wood down to the beach along with kindling, corn, salad, drinks, plates, silverware, butter and a pan to melt the butter in.

Five hours later we would have boiled, cracked, buttered lobster with corn on the cob, salad, beers, and smiles all around. Open air beach luxury. Rancho Palos Verdes was six miles distant from San Pedro/Terminal Island, by crow fly, and a whole world apart.

In the late spring ski season of my first year in Manhattan Beach, I had one last, great, ski trip to Mammoth Mountain for that year. One of my buddies at the beach was named Tate Chesebrough. Tate

     Don McGehe

and I had shared a lot of French fries at the Beach House Cafe. We would season them with vinegar and salt and drown them with catsup. We loaded up Big White one Friday afternoon and headed north. The skis were inside, draped over the seats and resting on the dashboard. Tate asked to drive the first leg and he took Big White up to Lone Pine, California.

Just after I took over the wheel, Tate was sitting in the passenger seat and asked if it would be ok to smoke some weed. I had never personally experienced marijuana before. I asked that he not smoke it in the car because we were still in California Highway Patrol country. But I was curious. We got to our lodging about 11:00 pm and sacked out for the night. The next day we skied hard in the bright sunlight and corn-straw snow on Mammoth Mountain.

After we left the slopes and returned to the motel room we planned to drive just 10 miles south on US 395 to the McGee Creek Resort and Lodge for dinner. Tate pulled out a reefer and, being curious, I agreed. I was a cigarette smoker at the time so I was familiar with inhaling. Tate told me to just hold the inhale breath as long as I could. For some strange reason, each inhale did seem to take quite a long time. We finished that first doobie and since we were both ravenously hungry we got in the car and headed south to McGee Creek.

The moon was out and the snow was crisp under the tires. We had tunes on the radio and the trip to the Creek seemed to take a delicious forever. Entering the restaurant we drifted up to the bar and ordered beer and an ice water chaser. The environment was mellow and deliberate that evening. We said very little. Whenever we looked at each other, a smile would break out.

Just to drink in the scene of a healthy, heady crowd enjoying themselves with fine dining and ambiance was the experience of the evening. I was flashing back to an old theatre expression; "the roar of the grease-paint and the smell of the crowd." The sensory inputs of the evening were tantalizing and experiential. We ordered inch-thick braised pork chops, baked potato with sour cream and chives, salad, and iced tea. We ate deliberately and with savor. The evening was everything I had hoped it would be; thoroughly enjoyable. What an experience. The thought crossed my mind that that was a lot more fun than alcohol. We skied a half-day on Sunday and then enjoyed the leisurely six-hour drive back down U.S. Route 395 to Manhattan Beach.

As appealing as that marijuana experience was, I still had my main friendships with a bunch of fellow drunks down at the Buccaneer. Being new to weed I did not yet have sources to rely on. Besides that, I still had a charge account to access all the excess alcohol I could drink. Old, familiar habits are not easy to disrupt. Although we enjoyed being in each other's company, Tate and I ran in different cliques at the beach. I'd gotten in with the more raucous and noisy crowd and the more fuel we drank the noisier it got.

Drinking, like breathing, had become a daily affair. Let's get drunk and be somebody. I no longer opened bars at 6:00 am, as I had done on several occasions in Newport Beach, but after 10:00 am, on a weekend, the sun was over the yard-arm. Back in those days I could not think of any reason whatsoever why anyone would want to live a life of sobriety.

I had a romantic relationship in Manhattan Beach with Miss Bonnie McCarthy. She was working two jobs at the time when I met her. Her long term day job was with the Wall Street Journal in their offices downtown on Wilshire Blvd. On Friday and Saturday nights she also had shifts serving food and cocktails at the Buccaneer.

One weekday night when she was not on shift at the "Buck," but was in having a drink with friends, I bought her a cocktail. The bartender was Bob Wiggins (a co-owner with Mike Grazanish of the bar). Bonnie and Bob had been dating but I had heard their relationship had cooled off. Bob carried the drink to the table, slammed it down in front of Bonnie, and said "this is from McGehe," and walked off. Ooooh! (was Bonnie's expression). That exchange somehow got her attention.

 DON MCGEHE

Shortly thereafter we began dating. Her schedule was so busy, that often we were only able to see each other at the bar. Bob Wiggins had cooled down in a couple of days and we were once again friends. It doesn't pay to have your bartender unhappy with you. I would often stay after hours at the "Buck." This would be with the employees (and the date/spouse partners of the employees), after the closing hour at 2:00 am on weekends.

Mike and Bob would kick the customers out at closing, and the staff and friends would hang around until the clean-up was finished. These were always friendly casual get-togethers and drinks were free after 2:00 am (the cash registers were closed as per California Liquor Control Board rules). Everyone has to "wind down" after work, especially wait-staff personnel.

As the relationship with Bonnie progressed, we made an arrangement with Bonnie's roommate Nancy, for the three of us to share the rental of a house over the hill on upper Rosecrans Avenue. I had some interesting morning coffee experiences with them around that kitchen table. I would have my suit coat and tie on, with the coffee, and they would both be in front of their make-up mirrors applying business faces for the office. I had never had a sister before. This was almost like having a sister and a wife. We had a long driveway up to the garage at this house. One of the subjects that came up daily, was the mundane question of who had to move their car first so that everyone could get out of the three-car driveway and to work on time.

After a number of months Bonnie was interested in making some decisions about her future and presented me with the nuclear option, "Marry me or move out!" I wasn't that interested in change but I could see her point. My heart wanted the relationship but my brain wasn't ready for marriage. People don't go to the beach to get married. I voted with my feet. It was tough, but I was able to find another small one-bedroom, down closer to the beach, and moved out.

As with many relationships, however, it was not yet over. We had mutual comfort and familiarity with each other. Old ties are tough to break. Even living apart, we continued to see one another for months. It was like playing tug-of-war with Silly Putty, the chord just stretches and stretches until it gets so dry in the center that it snaps of its own accord. Silly Putty will dissolve with enough alcohol. I had that. Even in some marriages, separations are like this.

I left the food brokerage when I first moved to Manhattan Beach, and went to work as a salesman for Prince Matchabelli Cosmetics. I should have put "salesman" in quotes. The assigned territory was drug stores above Olympic Boulevard in LA, all the way north to San Luis Obispo. All these stores already had the line. My job was to increase business by urging the cosmeticians to stock and sell more. Yes, shelf stocking. Matchabelli would take returns for slow selling merchandise, but we were discouraged from doing so.

Matchabelli did offer a company car. I gave "Big White" to Gary South on some kind of a hand-shake agreement to pay me over time. He never did. I didn't chase it. There was a life lesson there. I'm really great at buying stuff. I'm lousy at selling it off. I never seem to be able to get cash at closing. I don't like to ask for the order. I never have. Someone could say *NO*. That should have been a neon stop light for my future in sales jobs, but I chose to ignore it.

People would tell me "Boy, you really look like a salesman," and I believed them. "Looking like" was only half the battle, "closing" was still the other half, where the rubber met the road. But this particular job worked fine for me. I really didn't have to "sell." I just had to stimulate more purchasing from the drug stores. I had gift stock in the trunk of the car to reward (read "bribe") the counter clerks. I tried to be a nice guy; smiled a lot. The car trunk stock was also useful in swapping with other reps out in the drug store parking lot, for razor blades, deodorant, shave cream, or any other personal needs merchandise.

The Prince lasted for just over a year. I had a friend at the beach named Bob Kashar who then referred me to another company

    DON MCGEHE

called Wright Line. Kashar was a good friend who was also a fine volleyball player and a surfer. He was tall, slim, with a great smile, twinkling eyes, and he had a prominent curved nose which gained him the nickname "Beakly." I've always been amazed that you can give a nickname like that to a man and he will own it with pride. Try that with a woman and you earn an instant enemy. Why the difference? (Rhetorical question, sorry.)

Wright Line sold computer punch-card files, disk and tape storage equipment, and computer supplies to the data processing industry. Here I had a territory quite similar to the one I operated at Matchabelli. The customers were already users of the products that Wright Line offered but often they bought from another vendor. They had a unique magnetic tape storage system which tripled the number of tapes that could be stored in a given area. This was my introduction to the computer industry in its early formation in 1967. Wright Line's headquarters was in Worcester, Massachusetts.

While doing the product training and orientation in Worcester, I had my first experience watching NFL Monday Night Football on the east coast. These games started at 9:00 pm Eastern time and were never over until after midnight. If there was overtime you could lose significant sleep watching 'til they ended. I seldom made it through an entire game. On the west coast the games began at 6:00 pm and were usually over by 9:00. Now, if you're on the east coast, and start drinking during happy hour, by 10:30 pm you are passed out and in bed at half-time.

July of 1967 provided an opportunity to fly to Kansas City to participate in the wedding of my younger brother Bruce Alan McGehe and Miss Elizabeth Gail Wartman (Betty Gail) whose home was Prairie Village, Kansas. Bruce and Betty Gail met while both were attending university at Kansas State. One of Betty Gail's sorority sisters fixed them up as blind dates after a KSU basketball game in Betty Gail's junior year (Bruce's senior). They both experienced remarkably sudden vision corrections, to 20-20 or better, and they were married on 29 July, 1967, in Prairie Village. After the wedding they moved to Fort Carson, Colorado where Bruce was stationed as a Lieutenant in the US Army. Bruce did a tour in Vietnam and on his return to the states they went to Des Moines, Iowa to live. Bruce was hired there by Hoffmann-Le Roche AG as a sales representative to call on physicians. They celebrated their golden wedding anniversary in July of 2017.

In the late 1960s we were broadening our skiing venues to include Colorado. This was a long drive from Manhattan Beach. We had also driven to Aspen once from Newport. Neal Kunst and I took off on the final trip on this route in late 1968.

Starting off on an evening after work, driving east, we made Las Vegas at about midnight. After Vegas it was a long, cold, dark drive through Utah in the early morning hours. If there was a full moon out, the Utah landscape would appear as if you were literally driving across the face of that moon. Grand Junction, Colorado would arrive about in time for breakfast. Beyond Rifle, Colorado we turned right off of Interstate 70 at Glenwood Springs and headed down Colo. Hwy. 82 to Aspen.

That year we stayed at the Aspen A's. These were A-Frame cabins just across the street from Little Nell ski lift. There was lots of snow on the ground when we arrived. They had a huge sauna at the A's. After spending forty minutes in the sauna it was a short jump into a four feet deep snow bank. With only our shorts on, this was invigorating.

Two sequences of hot-cold-hot-cold was about all you could take before it was time to shower and go to dinner. That year we had New Year's Eve dinner at the Limelight Lodge. Two tables over were the Kennedys—at least what was left of the family after their second tragic shooting, that of RFK in June of '68. They were a serious skiing bunch. They loved Aspen.

CHAPTER 13

I used the Wright Line computer industry knowledge to seek out the largest company in the industry at the time: IBM. The IBM division that I applied to was the Information Records Division (IRD) on Lincoln Boulevard, near LAX Airport. I drew the lucky straw the day I applied. The day that I interviewed, I was given several tests to complete. One was the PAT (programmer's aptitude test). I did very well on this test and was eventually hired by the division which sold computer supplies to the industry.

At this time in the business cycle IBM still strongly believed in intensive training for its employees. IRD had just announced a new product: a two-headed, web-fed, offset printer. This was IBM's first entry into the off-set printer marketplace, they had never called on print shops before. I went through the product training and was handed a territory south of downtown Los Angeles. There was already one unit sold in the territory to American Honda Motor Company. It was my responsibility to install this machine. Honda cancelled their on-order machine while I was at IRD sales school. The entire product failed to sell and was cancelled by IBM within nine months of its introduction.

My manager in the IRD Division made some inquiries and I had an interview with the assistant branch manager of the Salem, Oregon IBM office. Salem was looking for Systems Engineers in their Data Processing Division. I was hired by Salem and was then transferred (on paper) to the Salem office to fill this job. I was, at that time, still living in Manhattan Beach. Because of the necessity for training in three separate cities, I was allowed to remain in the Manhattan Beach apartment while I was in these schools for the Data Processing Training.

The first school was Basic Data Processing School held in Cincinnati, Ohio. The second was a four-week Manufacturing and Distribution Industries Application School in Los Angeles. The final school was Sales School for three weeks in Seattle in 1969. These were three unique schools. I'll detail them in sequence.

In Ohio, we were housed in a six-story, 100-year-old hotel structure that had not been refurbished or redecorated since it opened. The rooms had 12-foot ceilings, ancient wall-to-wall carpeting, steam heat radiators, and antique bathroom fixtures. The school started in January. It was cold. It was snowy or rainy depending on which side of 32 degrees the thermometer decided to reside.

We took city busses to the IBM offices where the classrooms were located. New hires from all over the country attended the school. Right across the street from the hotel was a classic eastern "diner" with a juke box that contained the number one hit single of the day, "Proud Mary" by Creedence Clearwater Revival. For the first two weeks I thought the name of the song was "Rolling on the River." Lyrics speak loudly.

We spent four weeks of education on punch card equipment, 402 and 403 accounting machines that were run by wired logic panels. This training was a total waste of our time. From January of 1969 on, IBM never sold another accounting machine to a customer within the U.S. market. But, we learned how to wire them nonetheless. Evidently IBM had not yet developed the new age curriculum.

Our second class, manufacturing and distribution applications was an enlightening school. A manufacturing and distribution company has need of a certain set of accounting procedures which can be beautifully run on data processing equipment. These include payroll, payables, receivables, inventory accounting, and bill-of-material processors among many others. A bill-of-materials is a listing of each and every part, sub-assembly and assembly which go into making up a final product.

     Don McGehe

When you want to produce 25,000 widgets on a given date, the bill processor will explode out all the parts necessary to have on hand to make the 25,000 widgets, down to the smallest 1/2" screw. You project all those parts out, then subtract the inventory that you have on hand, to get the net orders that must go out in a timely fashion (considering varied lead times on each individual item) to have all the parts on hand when needed to make the 25K widgets. Computer systems are designed to facilitate this complicated scheduling math. This school shows you how to work with the manufacturer or distributor to answer all these complicated forecasting questions in real time at the lowest cost.

Each of these school classes has a "case study" of the IMB Company (International Milk Bucket) which manufactures agricultural products for the delivery of milk to consumers. The students are asked to "invent" a new product for IMB to manufacture and show how computers will enable a smoother running company (with their use) in the production of this new product. It was a lot of fun. At one point during this school I ran out of insulin. I went to the IBM medical office to get a new prescription. They looked closely at my medical records on file.

When I had joined the company my medical review had been done by an independent lab in Santa Monica. This lab noted that I had type-1 diabetes in their initial report. Somehow that information was never transcribed to my charts at Western Regional Headquarters. The IBM doctor gave me the Rx and updated my records. This records update would come back to haunt me years later in Portland.

Sales School was sales school. You practice by presenting sales calls to instructors who represent users, buyers, and executives of typical customer types who you will eventually call upon in the field. It was during this class in Seattle that I first saw an anti-Vietnam war march coming up 5th Avenue on its way to the Federal Courthouse. We were viewing the crowd from the safety of the third floor of the building. They were angry. They were committed. They were serious.

I suddenly saw the depth and breadth of the deep-seated emotion against the war that was beginning to spread through cities across the land. It did not get as bad in Seattle as the 1968 Democratic Convention in Chicago, but Seattle didn't have a mayor named Richard J. Daley either. Sales School lasted three weeks. During the two free weekends several of us took time off to drive up into Canada to visit Vancouver, B.C. I shopped for, and purchased, my first First-Nation Cowichan Indian sweater on this trip.

One weekend we went to Stanley Park in Vancouver to marvel in the quiet spring beauty of this huge in-city park. We even had some BC Bud to enhance the deep greens and delicate fruit blossoms which were blooming in the park. Vancouver is a very modern city, but just 20 miles outside of the city you can experience what rural, and semi-rural, America was like 50 years ago. It had much the flavor of rural Britain with multi-color painted homes and barns and older steel farm equipment parked in farm yards. I loved the Canadians. The Canadians also respected the Yanks.

You might question why a Systems Engineer would be attending sales school. Fair question. In the late 1960s, IBM was separating the systems engineering function from the sales function and was beginning to charge for all system engineering services. The computer and the services had previously been bundled into a single packaged charge to the customer. Now they were separate. Being separate, the company felt you had to sell services the same way you sell systems. Hence, there was sales school, even for systems engineers.

At the end of this last school, I flew back to Los Angeles to pack up my goods and load up a moving van with furniture for transfer to Salem. When I got to Oregon my lifestyle changed drastically. In Salem, Oregon there were 105 churches and only four nightclubs. The emphasis in Salem was on the soul not the flesh. They did have liquor stores. Drinking at home was to become the new venue. After moving in, I began to feel that the town of Salem was a bit too small. Even though it was the state capital, it was still small-town America. I did keep my eyes and ears open for an alternative opportunity.

Within three months I was able to get a transfer up to Portland, Oregon. Portland had major city potential. This Portland position was to help staff a new small business effort that the company had developed in order to sell a small computer, the IBM System 3. The new job was as an instructor in the Basic Systems Center which was intended to serve all the new business development in the Oregon market. Some small business establishments were getting their first computer or were upgrading from punch-card accounting machines. IBM anticipated a large market growth with this new, less expensive, small business computer.

New business customers were to come to Portland to train for the installation of these new systems. At the Basic Systems Center we were to conduct executive sales seminars and technical training classes for user personnel. This was the position I had been waiting for. It developed into the best, most rewarding, and satisfying work experience I ever had with IBM. I was put in charge of the Executive Education program to train the small business company presidents and CEOs of new prospective clients for System 3 installations. I would get them for two days and even teach them some simple programming coding.

One of our class exercises was the "Indian Problem." We asked them to calculate what the interest would be on the original $24.00 worth of beads that the natives were given for Manhattan Island, in 1626, at 1%, 2%, and 4%. We helped them code and compile the program, and to print out the results on a System 3 computer which was similar to the ones they had purchased. Some of the students were asked to round off the yearly calculations and some were asked to just drop the remainders. When comparing the answers the next morning, there were thousands of dollars of difference in these two results. This pointed out the need of the executive to monitor even the smallest of details in the implementation of their new systems, and to establish control systems. This dollar difference was caused by one entry, in one column, on one coding sheet. Small details are not only important, they can be critical.

I got to know, and thoroughly enjoyed, the company of a core of fellow IBM-ers in this branch office. A group of four of us, Terry Hendricks, Per' Bjerkman, Bob Price, and I rented a cabin on Mount Hood at Rhododendron, Oregon each winter for skiing. We would all troop up to "Rhodie" every weekend during the winter to enjoy skiing, partying, snow play, country breakfasts, and contract bridge. Terry would bring his family with children, Bob would bring Sharon Tipton, and Per and I would bring up a date if we had one.

Within one hundred yards of our cabin was a bar/restaurant called the Log Lodge for dancing and entertainment. This cabin rental happened every winter for three years. I had never in my life experienced a more tight-knit group of friends than this. At Mt. Hood I also met a couple who became life-long friends, Marjorie and Keith Yokum (44 years, so far for Marge. Keith passed away in 2013). The Yokums lived on the mountain and commuted to Portland daily to work. Keith drove a Porsche 911 and I'd just purchased a new Porsche 914 in Portland so we had car enthusiasm to share as well.

The primary residence I occupied in Portland was a two-story apartment in the West Hills above Portland State University on SW Hoffman Ave. The West Hills rose quite steeply below the apartment with an ascent of 130 feet between the next street down (SW Broadway Drive) and SW Hoffman Ave. As near as I can recall the address was 2320 SW Hoffman Ave. This apartment had a super-territorial view out over the Willamette River and Southwest Portland all the way to Mt. Hood. On the two story facade of the east exposure we wired up an illuminated martini glass which, when lit up at night, could be seen from two miles away. When the martini sign was lit, the party was on.

Per' Bjerkman and I had this place for over a year until he got married to Nancy Corwin and I had to rustle up another roommate. I could walk to work from this place. Downhill was easy. Getting back home was a healthy climb, however. When I finally left the West Hills I found a single apartment on SW Marigold St. at 32nd Ave. I had a patch of Himalaya blackberries ten steps from the door to this apartment.

That is one of the things I love most about the Northwest. In August each year, when the blackberries are ripe, you have free fruit for the picking nearly everywhere. Coming from Kansas, where we had to purloin watermelons in the dead of night, free food was a blessing. Homeowners detested the Himalaya blackberries. They were nearly impossible to kill and had to be hacked back, or cut out, each year to keep them from taking over everything. But, I had never experienced ubiquitous free food. I just love blackberries.

In order to enjoy the Himalaya blackberries, you should equip yourself with a pair of throw-away garden gloves with the thumb and index finger of each glove cut off half way. Thumb and index fingers pick the berry and the other fingers (still protected) avoid the thorns. A plastic pail, on a taut string around the neck, facilitates picking with both hands while still retaining a depository for the berries to drop into.

I was already consuming a lot of wine while living in the West Hills. After I moved to the Marigold Street address, I was within three blocks of a Fred Meyer Supermarket. I would use the Fred Meyer store as a weekend bank. On Saturday morning I'd cash a check for $50.00 and that money would last me all weekend. Food, wine, and entertainment all came out of this withdrawal. There was at least one case of rosé (four one-gallon jugs) in that Saturday morning buy.

At that time I was consuming a gallon of rosé a day on the weekends; a quart a day during the week. Saturday and Sunday would start with the first glass of wine with breakfast. "Here's looking at you, MaGoo." By 4:00 pm I'd be ready for an hour-and-a-half nap. This consumption level was becoming a regular habit. I seemed to be able to tolerate it. I did not have much social life at the time. I've always been a loner. Drinking alone was nothing new. It was just something that I did. Each Monday it was back to the office. Work is…the curse of the drinking class.

My first roommate at the S.W. Hoffman Ave. apartment, Per' Bjerkman, introduced me early on, in Portland, to Rupert J. Marks.

Rupert was our age, a native Portland, Oregonian, and soon became a running buddy. His father Arnold Marks worked for the Portland Oregonian newspaper and Rupert was a gentleman about town who loved to party. He belonged to the Schnee Vogeli Ski Club and had a condo up on Mt. Hood. We would often visit on weekends at our cabin or his condo. Another of his affiliations was as a member of the Portland Bachelor's Association. Rupert invited us into this group.

The Portland Bachelor's Association was a loosely held group of local gentlemen who held two major functions each year. In early December they organized the Bachelor's Ball. The Ball was a formal dinner-dance at a local country club. For the Ball we would each buy a reserved table for the dinner-dance, and then invite three friends and their dates (or wives) to join us at our table. It is the height of pleasurable decadence, during the Christmas Holidays, to feast on a half-pound steak dinner, drink, and dance all night in a rented tuxedo with a bright red cummerbund. All this with a tableful of your best friends in a banquet hall filled with 25 other Bachelors and their guests.

In the summer, the sponsored event was the Bachelor's Beach Ball over on the Oregon coast. The group would charter a resort, set up sand court volleyball, initiate raw egg tossing contests, swim, build sand castles, and just play in the sun for two days. There was often a question of which would run out sooner, the wine coolers or the sun-tan lotion. (After I got up to the Seattle area, later in 1975, I got a phone call one day at work from my friend Bernadette St. Onge. The first thing that Bernadette asked me was, "Are you sitting down?" I should have known that bad news was about to be fired down that phone line. She then told me that Rupert had just died of heart failure. He was 32 years old. I was able to attend Rupert's memorial service and also had a memorable reunion with Bernadette that weekend up at her cabin on Mt. Hood.)

One day in the spring of 1971, I was at my desk in the IBM offices in Portland and was overcome by a severe insulin reac-

     DON MCGEHE

tion. This reaction hit me so fast that none of the usual tell-tale signals that I normally experience were presenting themselves. In this instance I had too much insulin in my blood system, and not enough blood sugar for that insulin to work on. As a result the insulin starts to attack brain cells and causes blackout. Forty percent of the body's blood sugar supply is typically in the brain. The human brain has its own priority system for where this sugar is best utilized. Frontal-lobe consciousness is often the first to go in a crisis. The very last are the functions of the autonomic nervous system such as heartbeat, blood flow, breathing and digestion.

The secretary in my office had been attempting to contact me by intercom and was not getting any response. She left her desk and walked back to my office and opened the door. When she found me, I was slumped atop my desk and unresponsive. The 911 crew was called. I remember just sketchy moments of consciousness on the way to the hospital. I was wearing diabetic wrist identification so they knew immediately what to do in the emergency room at the hospital.

I had not been smart enough to educate my fellow employees on the procedures to follow in case of that type of emergency. I was soon revived. When the hospital recognized that they had an IBM, health care-insured gold mine on their hands they figured out a way to keep me in the hospital for a week of "rest and rehabilitation," with education on how to prevent this from happening in the future.

While I was in the hospital I was visited by Christie Lee Caufman (the daughter of my good friend Marjorie Yokum. Christie changed her name after the turn of the Century to Lee Erickson to honor her Grandfather) and her father Robert Wesley Caufman. I was impressed to think that someone cared enough to visit the "sick" (actually just on R & R) and bring a little cheer into another's life. I was touched. I remembered that visit. I vowed to repeat that giving experience many subsequent times, over the years, whenever my friends were in hospital. From Matthew: "I was sick and ye visited me, I was in prison, and ye came unto me." Been there. Known that. Thanks!

When I got back to the IBM branch office I was informed that from that time forward, whenever I wanted to go out to visit a customer, I had to either ride with another IBM employee or take a taxi. With diabetes I could not drive on company time (company insurance requirements). My God, was it still the dark ages? I now knew how the elderly feel when their driving privileges are taken away because they are too old to drive safely (by whose judgment?) or can't remember where the key goes in. Not everyone lives in New York City.

No urban area on the west coast has decent public transportation. I could not believe IBM was that backwards. At about this same time IBM was de-emphasizing the Basic System Center approach to dealing with the new business customers. They wanted to make me into a regular systems engineer (crippled or not) calling on the trade. As often happens in life, when one door closes, another opens. What came open was not necessarily a better door—only a different door.

Richard E. Funderburk was, for years, a top IBM computer salesman in Seattle. He and I had worked together on new business sales conventions over the years. Our best show was a three-day seminar at SunRiver Lodge in Bend, Oregon. He had left IBM in late 1970 to work with a new travel club concept called Jet Set Travel Club. I had put up some investment money in the project, on the fly, in late 1970. Rich was a good salesman. He came to Portland to see me close to Christmas 1971. He asked if I would be interested in coming up to Redmond, Washington as a branch manager for the Jet Set Travel Club. I was disillusioned with my IBM future after five years and still angry about the diabetes decision which excluded driving on company time. I drove up to Redmond one weekend to look over the set-up he was formulating.

Jet Set Travel Club was only a startup. The club plane was out on the runway at Boeing Field. It was, in fact, a Lockheed Electra. Only a prop-jet. The marketing plan was to use direct salesmen, in the home, and charge an initiation fee ($295.00 per family, payable at the time of sale or financed, if needed) and yearly club dues. This would allow a member to fly on Club scheduled trips at will.

     Don McGehe

An example of a weekend two-day air fare was a round trip Reno for $49.00. The hotel package was extra, but by booking large blocks of rooms the Club could get the room rates down to $95.00 per person which included air and ground for the weekend and two buffets (gambling and shows not included). That all sounded good. The excitement of vacation travel was also part of the emotional appeal of the Travel Club.

The first air travel club in Seattle was formed in 1971. It was called Club International and was founded by A. Joel Eisenberg who bought a Boeing 707 from TWA and leased it back to the travel club. In the summer of 1972 he was flying weekly trips to Hawaii for $125.00 round trip. The Jet Set concept was to fly shorter weekend trips to popular vacation destinations in the Western US and Mexico. The first Jet Set flight was in July of 1971 on the Lockheed Electra. Jet Set was a nonprofit corporation, organized under the laws of Washington in 1970 for the purpose of owning and operating an airplane in order to provide vacation travel for its members. The founding money was provided by Ben and Fred Sessions who were previously involved in health clubs in Washington.

Rich Funderburk was slick. As mentioned before, he was a good salesman. I bought the pitch. In order to test out the travel club idea, and get a good feel for the Jet Set organization, I asked for a six-month leave of absence from IBM. The purpose of the leave was "to rebalance my insulin regime and repair my health." The leave was granted with the understanding that it was to be taken without pay. My final day on the payroll at IBM was to be February 15, 1972.

I had a lot of moving activity to accomplish to get the contents of my apartment onto a moving van and up to Redmond, Washington. I called the Sixty-01 Apartments in Redmond to reserve a one-bedroom apartment. I had been through their facility on my scouting weekend earlier. This was a beautiful complex of 770 apartment units, in many separate building blocks, including several high rises, gyms, pools and a clubhouse with a bar.

Somehow I accomplished the move within one week. This was the next leg of my Coastal Fault Movements; north up the Pacific coast of North America. I drove the U-Haul van up Interstate 5 to Redmond, Washington and arrived on Washington's Birthday, February 22, 1972.

PART 4

PRE-MED

February 1972–July 1982

CHAPTER 14

The U-Haul Van, visually-impaired head teamster Mr. Magoo at the wheel, motored up to the Sixty-01 Apartments in Redmond, Washington on February 22, 1972. This was a holiday in Washington State commemorating the birthday of George Washington. It had been a national holiday since the US Congress voted it so in 1878. The State of Washington entered the Union as the 42nd State in 1889 (on the 100th anniversary of Washington being sworn into the presidency for his first term).

In 1968, Congress passed the Monday Holidays Act, which moved the official observance of Washington's Birthday from February 22 to the third Monday in February. Ironically, the third Monday of February can occur only between February 15th and February 21st. So it can never fall on either Washington's or Lincoln's actual birthday. Some in congress had wished to change the name of the holiday to "President's Day." That idea was rejected by the Congress. The holiday, therefore, remains officially "Washington's Birthday." Because of this name identity, Washington State has always celebrated this day as a holiday, and most business firms are closed.

Waiting to unload the van were my new boss Rich Funderburk, his son Bruce, and another lad who Bruce had recruited from his neighborhood to help. The new apartment was at 6001-140th Ave NE #105, Redmond, Washington. This was a large one-bedroom, one-bath, apartment, with vaulted ceilings, deep-blue-pile wall-to-wall carpeting, and a view of the main 6001 lake. Deep, in this case, referred both to the shade of blue and the depth of the shag which was over an inch thick. This unit had been the show model one-bedroom, for the complex, when it was first opened for renting several years before.

The unloading consumed three hours and I rewarded Bruce and his friend for their help. Because of the need to bring the U-Haul up on Tuesday, I had driven to Redmond in the 1970 Porsche 914 the weekend before, parked it in the reserved stall at the apartment, and flown back to Portland by commercial airline. The Sixty-01 complex that I was moving into had won design awards when it was first opened. It contained 770 units which surround two man-made lakes, and was a 24-hour gate-guarded community. The pool, east of the clubhouse, was the social-life center of the complex on sunny summer weekends.

When I first moved to Redmond in 1972, the town still had a rural atmosphere. Seattle itself was experiencing an employment identity crisis due to a four-year reduction in Boeing employment from 100,800 in 1967, down to 38,690 in 1971. Bob McDonald and Jim Youngren, two real estate agents for Henry Broderick, Inc., paid $160 in 1972 to post a billboard near Sea-Tac Airport reading: "Will the last person leaving SEATTLE – Turn out the lights." Theirs was a spoof on the gloom and doom scenario of the Boeing Bust.

In Redmond there was only one, lonely, stop light at the time. It was located at the corner of Leary Way and Redmond Way. Even this one stop light switched to blinking yellow on Redmond Way and blinking red on Leary Way at 11:00 pm each night. This was all before Microsoft came to town. As I recall, salmon may even have had the right of way any place where a highway bridge crossed the Sammamish River.

Since the Washington Birthday Holiday fell on a Tuesday, the first day to report to the Jet Set Travel Club office in Bellevue, Washington was Wednesday, February 23. The new office was on the lower floor of a four-story building in downtown Bellevue. This was the membership sales office for Jet Set. The Jet Set corporate office was on the fourth floor of this same building. The first person

I met at the office was Rich's secretary/office manager, Patsy Montgomery. She ran the office. She was fiercely loyal to Rich and was an excellent office administrator.

The sales personnel that Jet Set hoped to hire were those who had been successful in direct (to the consumer, in the home) sales. They were a special breed. Several companies who employ direct sales representatives are Avon, Amway, and Mary Kay. The Direct Selling Association says that the median income for a direct seller is $200 a month or $2,400 a year. Jet Set intended to pay the sales force no salary, only commissions on sales.

Generally an office would have one or two star sales people. It was an 80-20 rule situation. Eighty percent of the sales were made by 20 % of the salespeople. We were attempting to find those select people. The sales leads came in from "take-one" cards, which were displayed in small cardboard kiosks, distributed around the area in the business community on cigarette machines, counters, and at obvious high-traffic locations.

The signs would advertise "Fly Reno Holidays for $49" and invite the viewer to "take-one" card, fill out their name, address, and phone number, and mail it back to Jet Set free of charge. The Club employed female appointment-setting callers to phone-contact the people detailed on these returned cards and set up appointments to have a "club member" call on them, in the home, to explain the Club. Once an appointment was established, the card would be given to a sales representative to see the prospect, in their home, on the evening of the appointment. The success of signing up a new member was a direct result of the salesmanship of the representative who was in the home. Jet Set was selling a dream of low cost, convenient, weekend, vacation air travel. The salesperson had to convey, with enthusiasm, the excitement of this air travel plan, with friends, to popular resorts, and get a commitment (a check or signed payment contract), in the home at time of first contact to be successful. Some could do this. Most could not.

Many prospective new salespeople could get very excited about the prospects of the travel club and their hopes for personal vacations using the club. When facing full time dedication to direct sales, however, many were reluctant to give up a day job that put steady bread and butter on the table. If we could find a prospective employee who had had success in direct sales, these folks could be very eager to adapt to this new, exciting travel program to sell. But as mentioned before, they were rare and difficult to find. Another source of salespeople were spouses who loved the concept but also had a steady breadwinner, already in the family, to support them in the early days when they were still learning the direct sales approach.

Whenever I saw a sale come in, made to a single person aged 18 to 20 on their first job, who financed the membership on monthly payments, it would make me feel sad. Often this person had been sold the excitement and joy of vacation air travel, but they still lacked the personal finances to get on that first trip. If they had to finance the single membership price of $149.00, coming up with the extra $98.00 for the first Reno weekend trip, with ground package, might have to be postponed for several years. As long as the credit was good, however, their membership was accepted. If it were a financed family membership, that first trip for the couple would be a minimum of $196.00 (gambling gains or losses, stage shows, and walk around money not included). People buy for lots of reasons. As long as we made our sales goals and kept the club financed, they would have a club to fly with when they could afford to take advantage of the half-priced airfares we offered.

As expressed earlier, in the Coastal Fault Movement section, I was never a successful salesman because I didn't like to ask for the order. Now that I was involved in management of direct salespeople, the dichotomy of my attitude towards, and willingness to make, direct sales and the necessity of making those same sales presented a disorder of purposes. Several of the other branch managers promoted competition between their own personal sales and the sales

     Don McGehe

of their top producing salespeople. This often presented a challenge within the salesforce and stimulated overall branch sales. I did make occasional personal sales of memberships. As an everyday practice I just passed on all leads to my top salespeople. It was always my policy to distribute as many "take-one" posters as possible and to urge the entire sales force to do the same. With enough leads to work with, it all becomes a numbers game.

It was early April, 1972. I was doing paper work in the office on a Tuesday morning. I heard male voices in the outer office (my office door was open but the wall to the outer office was opaque Plexiglas so I couldn't see who was there). They were asking for Rich Funderburk.

Patsy said: "He is not in the office at the moment."

The questioner asked, "Will he be back soon?"

"I don't expect him until this afternoon," Patsy Montgomery replied.

Thinking I might be of assistance, I stepped through the door to my office and stopped at Patsy's desk. Looking me in the face were three IBM representatives out in their territory, looking to scare up some new business. They had stopped by, knowing their old friend and former fellow employee, Rich Funderburk had an office in this building, and they were going to say hello. There were two salesmen and one systems engineer. I knew the SE very well. We had worked together closely in IBM even though he was in the Seattle office and I was reporting in Portland.

We exchanged pleasantries. I explained that I was up here trying to help Rich out setting up his new office. I also told them that I was sure Rich was not in the market for any new computer equipment at the moment, but it was kind of them to stop by and say "Hi." We shook hands and they left. I returned to my office and sat down. It had been a major blunder to step into that outer office. I could recall what curiosity had done to that cat in Elizabethan fable. I also knew that this accidental meeting would get back, within a day, to the Branch Manager of the Portland Office.

I suddenly realized that I would not be able to come back to IBM, after the leave of absence, and resume my old duties. My employment with IBM was now finished. At the end of August I returned to the IBM office in Portland. The six month leave of absence was over and I wanted to check in to wrap up the relationship and inquire about the possibility for severance. Severance was denied and I returned to Redmond the same day.

In the fall of 1972 Patsy Montgomery was curious about my social relationships. I was not dating anyone in Redmond. I did have several female friends who would visit from Portland who I enjoyed being with. On long weekends I would invite Oregon guests to come visit in Redmond. I had made a decision, years ago, not to date anyone in the work force in which I was employed.

This had been a hard and fast rule in my life for my entire working career. I had seen the problems involved in forming in-company relationships over the years and wanted to avoid those ties. One of the branch office salesmen who worked for me was named Tom Winters. Tom and Patsy both knew a lady, socially, who lived at Sixty-01. Her name was Sherri. Tom and Patsy both thought I might enjoy meeting Sherri. I agreed.

I was thinking of a way to initiate this meeting and came up with a plan. I went to a meeting of the Young Republicans Organization in Bellevue. Richard Nixon was running for his second term as President in 1972. I'd been a Republican (recall those Kansas roots) all my life, and saw fit in this election to join the campaign for his re-election. Nixon was up against Senator George McGovern who was running an anti-Vietnam war campaign against the Republican President. McGovern was somewhat handicapped by his outsider status, by limited support from his own party, and by the perception of many voters (fostered by Republican Party advertising) that he was a left-wing extremist. There was also the scandal that resulted when Thomas Eagleton, U.S. Senator from Missouri, was forced to step down as the Democratic Vice-Presidential nominee.

 DON MCGEHE

I volunteered to canvas the Sixty-01 Apartment complex for the Committee to Re-Elect the President. I knew the apartment Sherri lived in. I envisioned knocking on her door and meeting her under this political ruse. Little did I know that I was a west coast envoy of the organization that, two years following the June 17, 1972, break-in at the Watergate, would bring about the first resignation of a President of the United States.

When I went out to canvas, I dressed in a white shirt, tie, and suit, with well-shined shoes. On that Tuesday evening in October, I knocked on the door of Sherri's fifth floor apartment in a Sixty-01 high-rise and there was no answer. I thought my plan had failed. I slipped a flyer under the door and continued on my rounds of the building. Little did I know, at the time, but I had seen her when she had come out to the door of an apartment on the second floor of that same high-rise earlier in the evening.

I'd knocked at this second floor suite and an older gentleman had opened the door. I later found out that this unit number was a veritable den of Democrats. The apartment owner laughed when I stated my business. His name was Gordon. I found out later that Sherri was a good friend of Gordon.

Gordon then called everyone in the living-room to come to the door to be witness to the raw politicking that was being perpetrated in his building. Everyone, including Sherri (who came to the door with the group), thought this was the most humorous thing they had heard all evening. They let me know that I was not representing the candidate they would likely choose in November. I smiled, thanked them for their time, and wished them all a pleasant evening.

A week later I called Sherri by land line phone and introduced myself, using references from Tom Winter and Patsy Montgomery. After a friendly conversation, she agreed to a dinner-date the following Friday night. We went to dinner that evening at the El Gaucho restaurant in downtown Seattle. I was personally impressed with the elegant ambiance of the restaurant and its waiting staff. I felt that we were both a little nervous in this first meeting. At that time we were both cigarette smokers. This was years before smoking was banned in indoor public areas, including restaurants.

After we ordered drinks we both drew out our cigarette packs and lit up. Smoking was good casual business which alleviated the anxiety we both felt. I managed to take cues from the wine steward and ordered an appropriate vintage for the table. Once I get past Ernst & Julio Gallo on any wine list, I'm in way over my head. A delicious dinner was then ordered and enjoyed. We had another cigarette after dinner.

In the excitement of a successful dinner, lubricated by a good wine, I managed to light two cigarettes at the same time. I had done this before. It was usually done in a dark bar. I suddenly realized my error and made every move I knew of to cover this faux-pas. It did not work. Sherri saw the confusion and had the good grace to laugh quietly at the mistake and it gave me the excuse to admit that I was somewhat nervous. I snuffed out the second Benson & Hedges, we both smiled, and our conversation continued from there. The evening ended up being a great first date.

Sherri was raised in a Reformed Jewish Traditional family in Minnesota. She was the first person of this religious persuasion that I had ever dated. I was fascinated by the holidays and traditions of the Jewish People and was eager to learn everything I could about their customs. Sherri's grandfather was the first of her family to emigrate to the United States. He held the freedom and opportunity of the American way inviolate. He was honored to pay his taxes. He considered income tax a small price for the freedom that being an America afforded his family. In the midst of his success in America, many of his former friends and family who remained in Europe were perishing in one pogrom or another—some of this even before the Holocaust perpetrated by the Nazis in World War II.

I found Sherri to be an exciting, smart, fun person to be around. I considered her to be smarter than I was. This I liked. It offered a consistent challenge. As I look back, the ladies that I have often

    DON MCGEHE

found most endearing were those with sharp, quick minds and often acid tongues. That is, as long as they could spit those lightning bolts out through smiling lips. Sherri was also wise in the ways of the world.

Her family had raised her to respect elders and to develop friendships with people of all ages. Her choice was always to develop intimate friends spread throughout a spectrum of generations. This way, in old age, you can avoid a sudden die off of same-age friends. She had no children from her previous marriage but she loved kids and thoroughly enjoyed being around the children of her friends. Sherri had earned teaching credentials in the Bellevue School System and had been a substitute teacher in the elementary schools, in previous years. Sherri was five foot five inches in height with long dark hair; she was quick to smile and laugh, had a sharp wit and a very positive outlook on love and life.

By mid-November, after Thanksgiving of 1972, we had formed a solid dating relationship. The next holiday on the Jewish calendar was Hanukah. The 1972 celebration began on November 30th. Hanukah is the commemoration of the restoration of the Holy Temple in Jerusalem in the second century BCE. It is observed by the lighting of candles in the Menorah, a nine-stem candelabra with place holders for the eight days of the celebration and one slot for the shamus, or service candle.

Each day, after sundown, one additional candle is lit on the Menorah. On the eighth night all nine candles are burning, adding celebratory illumination to the otherwise darkest season of the year. It is called the Festival of Lights. Children celebrating the festival are rewarded by gifts of Hanukah Geld (gold-foil wrapped, coin shaped, chocolate medallions) for guessing which of the lit candles will extinguish itself last. This tradition can hold the attention of everyone in the family during the typical 45 minutes in which the candles burn.

Before the candles are lit each evening a blessing is said in Hebrew. I became so enthralled with this blessing ceremony I asked Sherri to write it out for me. I memorized it. From then on, each year, I recite the Hanukah blessing for the lighting of my own Menorah: "*Baruch atah, Adonai Eloheinu, Melech haolam, asher kid'shanu b'mitzvotav v'tsivanu l'hadlik ner shel Hanukkah.*" It has now become an annual personal journey. Tradition!

On December 7th, we packed away the Menorah and cleaned up the living-room. The apartment suddenly looked boringly bare. Holidays do add a note of festivity to a room. That must be why we celebrate them in those dark months of the Northwest winter. Hanukah was now over.

What about Christmas? I proposed the possibility of a Christmas celebration to Sherri. After a surprised moment of thought, she responded, "Sure, why not?" The following weekend we trooped down to the Kiwanis Christmas Tree Lot in Redmond. It was a cold evening and felt like it could very well snow. Sherri had seen tree lots before but had never had the opportunity to choose a tree from one. She seemed excited. We purchased a noble fir, about six feet tall, and tied it onto the roof of her Monte Carlo.

Now we needed decorations. We had none. Many folks keep a deep box of Christmas decorations stashed in the garage some-where. Since I had left home in Manhattan, I had only celebrated this holiday when I had someone to share it with. That had not been often.

Many years I had just taken off for the ski slopes for the week including Christmas and New Years. The only trees I'd come in contact with then were the ones I'd run into on skis or stopped beside to create the marvel of yellow snow on the slopes. So Sherri and I needed to go shopping again. We arrived at Bellevue Square and took home tinsel, sparkling lights, extension cords, silver bells, silver balls, popcorn to string and a tree stand. We seemed to grab everything except a tree-top angel and a baby Jesus ornament. As Gary Larsen might have pointed out, "That's just a bit too 'Far Side' for a lady with a more ancient holiday tradition."

    Don McGehe

The living-room was re-arranged to provide placement for the tree in the southeast corner near the wall plugs. A Sunday decorating ceremony followed. By mid-December the elf adornments were complete. We then began to stash our wrapped gifts atop the white cotton "snow" surrounding the tree. One of the presents was an alarm-clock radio. The tag read: "To Sherri & Don, From Santa & Mrs. Claus."

I had been growing impatient with the wind-up alarm clock Sherri had on the night stand. The tick-tick was driving me batty. I thought it should be replaced with an electric clock-radio. So… that's what I did. She was somewhat alarmed when she opened the package but said nothing further for several days after the holiday.

Then one evening she was sitting at the dining room table with the most halting, quizzical expression on her face. I asked her what was up. She explained that she didn't quite know what to write in the thank-you note to my parents for the clock radio. I smiled, held her pen hand, and responded that the radio was "From Me, To Us," and my parents didn't have anything to do with it. I had just used the: "From Santa and Mrs. Claus" on the gift card to distribute the gift giving responsibility around the universe a bit more widely. She was much relieved. I can understand why, after I thought a bit more about her misunderstanding of the source, and the bedroom environment the gift was to reside in.

CHAPTER 15

We both experienced the usual after-Yule let down which normally follows New Year's Day. The tree dries out from lack of watering. The wrapping paper is ripped up and thrown out. All the opened wine bottles have gone flat and can only be used for cooking. We'd gone through all the Hanukah and Christmas chocolate and were wearing that beneath the belts. KPLU was playing "January Blues" on the jazz station. We threw the tree off the fourth floor balcony and retrieved it below for dumpster disposal. Life was back to rain, wind, and chilly forecasts.

One Saturday in early January we were having morning coffee with Russ and Andrea Stutz who lived on the second floor of the high-rise. Russ was bored, and in a sudden stroke of inspiration said:

"Hey! Let's just go up to Goldmyer tomorrow."

I questioned this with "What's Goldmyer?"

Russ said: "It's a hot spring up by the Middle Fork Snoqualmie River, on the Pacific Crest Trail, north of Snoqualmie Pass."

That sounded so good, on that cold January Saturday morning, that we made a traveling agreement and immediately began planning the logistics to crash that party the next day. The road to Goldmyer ended up being a substantial auto trek and a short one-mile physical hike. We packed a lunch bag with sandwiches and snacks, brought water and a gallon of vin rosé, stuffed in towels and a map into our backpacks and left Redmond at 8:00 a.m. on the Sunday morning. Russ and Andrea had a 15-year-old "hippie-mobile" that provided perfect conveyance up that rutted, washed-out, Middle

Fork Road. If that car had any shocks left in it they were severely tested by the experience on that road.

Our route took us east on I-90 to a left, off the interstate, at Exit #34 (Edgewick Road) just past North Bend. North of the I-90 here, there is a large truck-stop on 468th Avenue SE and we then needed to turn right onto SE Middle Fork road (NF-5600). We followed NF-5600 for over eight miles up to the Middle Fork Campground. Just past the campground and over the bridge is the connection to NF-110 where you veer off to the right. In 1973 this road (now known as NF-110 or NF-5620 as it was called further southeast) took you all the way to a parking lot next to Burnboot Creek.

At the west end of that parking area we crossed Burnboot Creek, carefully balancing ourselves and our gear across a five-foot-diameter fallen log over the water. From the west bank there was a clearly visible trail down which we hiked nearly a mile to the Goldmyer Hot Springs. On that first trip up, there were not any washouts on the road, and we made it in Russ's ancient, beat-up Chevy all the way to the parking area. In many subsequent years, after heavy rains in the area, that Middle Fork Road could be washed out all winter long and the Forest Service could not get in to repair it until late in the following spring. Much later, in June 2007, the U.S. Forest Service installed a locked gate at the Dingford Creek trailhead, blocking the road to Goldmyer and increasing the one-way hiking distance to 4.5 miles.

Once you get up to the hot springs there is another cold water creek running just 10 yards south of the hot springs outflow called Burntboot Creek. These two creek names are quite similar and are easily confused. The only difference is that the creek next to the springs is the past tense of the first creek encountered, and crossed, at the edge of the parking lot. The two creeks do conjoin several miles further on in the water-shed and are named Burnboot once again. If you are confused now, just wait until you are up there and experience all this with a wine soaked mind.

Goldmyer Hot Springs flows out of a five-foot-high and ten-foot-wide hole in the side of the sheer rock wall. At the base of this opening there is a narrow stone wall built up to a three-foot level which forms a pool behind the wall extending back into the hill about 13 feet to the source of the hot mineral spring. As the water flowed out a notch in this wall it rippled into a tub placed beneath the output spout on lower ground. Water leaving this tub trickled down a twenty-foot shallow runnel into the cold flow of Burntboot creek. The hottest water is found in the dammed pool inside the cave.

The tub water is just slightly cooler as it is tempered by the colder air outside the cave. Bathers will typically carry a stubby candle into the cave and mount it on protruding stonework on the cave wall to provide atmosphere and illumination. A gallon wine bottle will characteristically be floated on the surface of the pool, in the cave, to provide warm adult-beverage refreshment for the relaxing bathers. Goldmyer: a virtual paradise in the quiet Cascade wilderness.

That first trip up was on a cloudy, misty, January day. There were maybe twelve people at the springs. Many hot springs occur in the Northwest. Most are accessible by paved roads and parking lots. With pavements and parking lots, you get families and tourists with children. These "normal" hot-spring type visitors did not go to Goldmyer. It is just too remote. It took dedication to get there.

If you felt that you must, you could wear a bathing suit in the springs. Few did. No one cared. We all just stuffed our clothes, boots, and dry towels into black 30-gallon trash bags, to keep them as dry as possible, and waded in. Modesty quickly evaporated like hot mist into a cool breeze. These were the 70s. Our generation was still mellowing out from the raucous 1960s. We yet had abundant "hippy" blood coursing through our veins. This was our element.

The cave pool was quite warm. After twenty minutes in the cave you needed to get out and let the body air-cool, or walk the 20 feet down to Burntboot Creek, on the smooth slick-rock, to splash ice

     Don McGehe

water on your body. This provided the classic Scandinavian hot/ cold, hot/cold, thermal transition for refreshing mind, body, and soul. It worked. After three hours we were wrung out. Thank God for dry towels. We shoved everything into back packs and eased our way down the mile-long trail to the car.

Goldmyer Springs was open and totally unsupervised until late 1976. The property owners, the Vieda Morrow family, formed the non-profit Northwest Wilderness Programs in 1976 in response to the abuse the springs had suffered during the 1960s and 1970s. The Morrow family donated the land to NWWP, which continues to manage the property today. Access to the springs is now available through www.goldmyer.org by reservation and fees. Currently, access to the springs is limited to 20 people per day on a first-reservation basis through the phone number listed on the web site above.

When we first met, Sherri was working as an office manager for Global Plastics, a small plastic rotational-molding company producing custom storage containers for the agricultural and fishing industries on the west coast. They had a very small office attached to their large production/warehousing plant in Kirkland, Washington. Her boss was the co-owner of the firm; his name was Peter Byron McRae, and he was the manager of the Kirkland plant.

From Sherri's description of the business plan it appeared that the company consisted of herself and Peter McRae with six sales reps in the field and production technicians to fill three shifts in the Kirkland plant. Peter spent much of his time in the field, as the lead sales representative, and Sherri effectively ran the office for him. Sherri spoke very highly of McRae and was unquestionably loyal to him as an employer. I thought it might be a good idea to go out and visit the office to see what this was all about.

The Global office was open Monday to Friday, 8:00 am to 5:00 pm. That was Sherri's schedule. One Saturday we drove up to the office, and having a key, Sherri opened the door and we entered. All I could see was a coat rack, a couple of filing cabinets and several Boeing-surplus desks and chairs. Sparse was the word that came to mind. Sherri had applied decorative wood-grain shelf covering to the desks but they were still Boeing-surplus. Functional. By no stretch-of-the-imagination plush.

Since Peter's car was out front, Sherri opened the shop door and called him out to join us. He came through the door several minutes later wearing dirty jeans, a blue cotton work-shirt, and industrial orange rubber gloves. He looked to be covered with plastic grinding dust. Covered, that is, except for around the eyes, from where he had obviously just removed his eye-protection goggles. Peter was of solid build, medium height, about five years younger than me, and with a broad and rather mischievous winning smile.

He had been in the plant that morning training production workers. He evidently relied on Sherri to run the office, answer the phones, organize the paperwork, and act as a sounding board when he got a good idea. She also kept things moving in the office so he could focus on selling the product in the field. He was, however, still a people person. He liked to verbalize his ideas, by sharing them with associates. By so doing, he could clarify the details of his plans in his own mind. When finished with those conversations, those plans would be nearly production ready.

As we drove home I judged that the situation at Global was strictly an employer-employee relationship and that I had little reason to be concerned that it was anything more personal. At that time I wasn't able to see that far into the future. Sherri and I were not destined to remain in our relationship for more than several years. Peter McRae is still one of my closest friendships, continuing as of now, for more than 45 years.

The calendar for 1974 was crawling into April. I was spending many of my off-work hours with Sherri. Normally this was at her apartment in one of the high-rises. Rents at The 6001-Apartments were going up. It was a popular, in-demand, residence. In order to save rent money I talked to one of the rental agents about relocating within the complex. After touring several of the options, I chose the least expensive which was a studio. These were limited in number

     DON MCGEHE

to 96 of the 770 units within Sixty-01. Each was 452 square feet in size but well laid out.

The studios were situated below two-bedroom uppers which insulated them to keep them warmer in the winter and cooler in the summer. The one that was available was Unit # 9. It was my choice. I had a very skinny assortment of furniture so this move was about an 800-yard, two-man tote. Provided, of course, that that be done when it was not raining. Sherri's high-rise was just to the left of the guard gate. My studio was just to the right—a short walk. It was important to me to maintain my own personal housing unit. I felt my independence to be inviolate. After May 1, 1974, my new address was 6001-140th Ave NE #9, Redmond, Washington 98052.

By the fall of 1973 the United States was beginning to experience the OPEC oil embargo. Suddenly, as if overnight, gas prices at the pump jumped from around $.26 per gallon to over $.50 per gallon. Culture shock set in. Gas lines formed all across America. Some states initiated even/odd days to purchase gas depending on the last digit of one's license plate. If you had an even last digit, in a 31-day month, you could buy gas on the 30th but have to wait three more days to refill until the 2nd of the following month. President Nixon signed legislation on January 2nd, 1974 to lower the national speed limit from 70 mph down to 55.

In the summer of 1974, Sherri and I were able to take our first trip on the Jet Set aircraft. We booked the scheduled one-week flight to Denver, rented a car, and drove east to Manhattan, Kansas so that Sherri could meet my folks. This was the first long trip I had had to test the new national speed limit. It seemed even slower due to the monotonous nature of the landscape. Miles and miles of miles and miles. It's all the same in western Kansas.

This trip was an interesting experience. Sherri got the master bedroom at home and I bunked in the basement where I had always slept. We did maintain strict decorum. The second morning we were there I overheard, from the basement, a conversation between Sherri and my Mother. Dad had always awoken me in high school by just pounding on the heat registers and in a normal voice saying: "Time to get up." I mention this to demonstrate the ease of hearing between these two floors.

The gist of the conversation centered on my Mother's concern about the future of the relationship between Sherri and myself. The subject of religion was at the heart of this concern. I'm sure my Mother had never known any Jewish folks. Sherri handled the conversation beautifully. I sped up my dressing to get upstairs to join this exchange of views as soon as possible. By the time I got up there they were both very cordial.

Mom had some family mementos that she had set out to show us on our visit. In a wise, and cleverly artistic, desire to please, Sherri used her interior decorator skills to arrange many of these artifacts on a totally blank wall in the living-room behind the sofa. We went downtown, purchased some wall fixtures, and redecorated that wall for my Mother. Mom was overjoyed. She left the wall untouched in that home for the next 25 years. After my Father died and we moved Mom to a retirement community, we had to take the items on the wall down and rebuild it for her at her new apartment in the rest home. Sherri was good. She won them over.

In the fall of 1974 I had another opportunity to fly on a club trip. Mazatlan, Mexico was the destination. The club had given away a free membership and a free Reno trip in a drawing at the Fan Appreciation Night for the Tacoma Rainiers Baseball Club in early September. I went to Tacoma and made that presentation after the game on Saturday, September 1.

The following day the Jet Set flight left from Boeing Field for a fuel stop in Los Angeles and then on to Mazatlan. This was a dream trip. I assisted the cabin attendants in the galley on the flight down and back by making mixed drinks, to order, for the passengers. I was fueling myself as well as the passengers. Possibly better.

The Club had reservations in one of the best hotels, right on the Pacific Ocean beach. I had a large single room on the land side of the hotel which could be opened up to let in the free flow of tropical air in the evening. It overlooked the old city from the fourth floor. I made some friends among the members on the trip and had a great time running around the old market in town.

The meat market was indoors, but totally devoid of any refrigeration or air-conditioning. You had to fight the flies to get to the meat. We didn't bother. We had two meals a day in our plan at the hotel and often ate or snacked down at the market. I used the excuse that since we couldn't trust the water, we were forced to drink Dos Equis (XX) whenever in town.

I had not been swimming in the Pacific Ocean since I'd lived in Manhattan Beach, California in 1969. I got a wild (read "dumb") hair in my brain, one night about 11:00 pm, and decided to go body-surfing at the next beach down from the hotel. I hadn't done that since California either. The ocean was warm. No wet-suit was needed; swim trunks were fine. Even at night the water was near 80 degrees. My personal proof was near 96. Those two really shouldn't mix. That night they did. Successfully. Thank God.

On the last ride I skinned up my chin on the sand as that last wave was washing up my back. I was smart enough to quit and go back to my room. No damage. Next day I just lay around the pool. You'd think I was getting smarter. Maybe? I doubt it.

On the return trip the Lockheed Electra touched down in Los Angeles once again, this time for both fuel and a customs inspection. We delivered the passengers back to Boeing Field and met with some Jet Set personnel at the terminal. They spoke of some bad feelings between my boss Rich Funderburk and the senior management/ownership of the club. I'd hear the other side of that disagreement soon.

One of my pastimes at university was playing bridge. My folks had taught me the game. They belonged to a bridge club that met once a month for nearly 40 years. They would lose a membership couple occasionally from the club, to death or transfer, but always found replacements. Sherri had also adopted the game. We would play with other couple-pairs who lived in the Sixty-01 complex and also at an occasional duplicate tournament held at the Sixty-01 Club House.

Whenever possible, with other couples, we played the men against the women. That way you could avoid the "why didn't you lead into my void in hearts" conjecture that may have caused a disagreement when the game was over. These were social games. I always played serious bridge. Sometimes these two gaming philosophies did not mix. When you play to win, that is often not the wisest choice in coupledom.

My branch sales were not up to the other branches. My alcohol consumption was increasing as the branch sales were decreasing. It was becoming a problem. I was beginning to feel like Willy Loman near the end of his sales career. I wanted an answer. It had to be an answer other than that given by Arthur Miller for Willy. Suicide was absolutely out; things were not near that bad. So I just drank more.

Something happened within the Jet Set organization that caused a feud between the ownership of the club and the marketing arm. From the writing distance of 40 years now, I no longer remember what that conflict was. It was of such magnitude, however, that the sales force was choosing sides and separating into two factions. I maintained my loyalty to Rick Funderburk. Nearly 80% of the force was also with Rich.

Rich was looking around for another company who would take his marketing arm and employ their talents. That company was the local rival travel club, Sunfari Air Travel Club. Sunfari also flew out of Boeing Field. They had a jet; their club flew a Convair 880. Over a weekend, Rich rented another office in Bellevue, Washington and we were now the sales arm of the Sunfari Air Travel Club.

The Sunfari arrangement lasted about seven months. I never flew on the their jet. One Monday morning we were all in the Bellevue office for a sales meeting and Rich announced the dissolution of the marketing arm. Rich Funderburk did his best to find replacement positions for as many of the employees involved as he could. I personally signed on with a computer service bureau down in Burien headed by a friend of ours, John Bevin. Most of the work done by this service bureau was coded in Cobol. I did not have that

　　DON MCGEHE

language background. They had some limited clientele who were using the RPG II language with which I was experienced, but both John and I soon realized that I was in over my head. Over a beer one Friday night he let me know that I would soon be unemployed.

The following Monday I was in the unemployment office registering for benefits. There was a two week waiting period to draw benefits. On Tuesday I called Snelling & Snelling Employment Services office and signed up to have them find me a new job. The arrangement with Snelling was for a client to pay the commission placement unless the new employer would pay the fee. They got me an interview that same week. On Friday I talked to Computer Systems Incorporated (CSI), a wholly owned subsidiary of the Seattle First National Bank. They had a unique assignment, which involved both sales and systems work. They offered me a job but would not pay the employment fee. Fine. I needed the work.

One of CSI's clients was Washington Physicians Services. They ran the Medicare and Medicaid service bureaus throughout Washington State. They wanted a systems engineer (read "chauffeur") to accompany their Medical Director around all the county medical bureaus to transition over to a new Medicare backup system they were installing (which, incidentally, would cause the replacement of CSI as their vendor). This involved overnight trips to many remote cities across the northern half of Washington State as far east as Spokane. In the first four months on the job we had completed all of these trips. The Washington Physicians Service was now finished with CSI.

It was shortly after the ides of March, 1975, on a Sunday night that spring. I had just run out of wine at about seven in the evening. I was at Sherri's. I told her I was going to the store to get some more. She asked me not to go. We had had this discussion several times before. She did not seem particularly angry when she said it. Just resolutely firm. Her words: "If you go out for more wine…don't come back." She sounded like she had had it with my drinking. It was a wine-or-me choice. Which is more important? I was already half tanked. I left.

When I got back to Sixty-01, from the store, I went to my own condo. It looked like the relationship was over. The finality of that separation had not yet hit me.

CHAPTER 16

At CSI in my first week on the job I had spoken with the sales department manager and impressed him with my knowledge of both systems and sales. I was transferred over to sales and at first did research on their customers and helped to develop a new marketing plan for CSI. This project wrapped up in several months and during that time the manager said he was appealing to the board to add one more sales person to his staff. There was a normal business recession in the Seattle area in early 1975. These recessions appeared to be far too normal. The board did not ok that extra position.

About a week after I had left the relationship with Sherri, the CSI marketing manager asked me to have lunch with him on Friday. I should have been smarter than to accept this invitation. These things always happen on a Friday. We went to a sandwich shop about a mile from the office. I ate a pink-slip sandwich special for lunch that day. It was really quite rare. Bloody in fact. Why do they always choose Friday for these notifications? Sorry; just another rhetorical question.

This was my second layoff in seven months. I still had six months to pay on the employment contract with Snelling & Snelling who had got me the job. Now I had no job. I reduced that payment to $20.00 per month, and eventually paid the contract off. I was now without a pay check. Suddenly I realized I could no longer afford to drink. This was a realization that was not without its rewards. What a waste of time, money, and life that habit had been. I was now ready to quit anyway.

I drove home from Southcenter very slowly that evening. The homebound stretch of I-405 North was always slow at 5:00 pm—tonight more so than usual. My common habit had been to stop by the mini-mart, just before the freeway, for a cold quart of wine for the drive. Not tonight. The Porsche 914 was a 5-speed stick shift. In that 405 slog the clutch was the most effective device on the car at 17 mph. The fragrance of the ozone overrode the absence of the alcohol.

The following weekend was my opportunity for self-reflection. I holed up in my apartment. My 452-square-foot refuge. I felt like a physical, mental, and emotional wreck, just looking for a place to happen. The real battlefield was not in the apartment. It was between my ears.

The innate serendipity of Sherri's ending the relationship and my decision to stop drinking, both within a two-week span, did not escape my reflection. But there was no going back to that relationship. It was over. Being suddenly sober meant an end to denying the problem even existed. That had been a crutch I had used to prop up my life for the last 13-plus years. I now realized that denial had been a willful act for me. Not just an African river.

A guy I knew at Sixty-01 was in Alcoholics Anonymous. I called him. We went to five meetings in the next week. When I was first recognized, in that initial meeting, I introduced myself and admitted that "I am an alcoholic." That was obvious to me. It was still tough to fess up to it in front of the group. It was necessary to do so. Denial was over; I was now committed to sobriety, one day at a time.

The separation from the relationship was not any easier for Sherri. She called the following week to tell me she had severely wrenched her back and was in Overlake Hospital in Bellevue, Washington under care. I went to see her in the hospital. She had some items at the apartment that she needed me to bring over to the hospital. I was able to go get this stuff and bring it back to the hospital room for her.

Even when you know it's over, you sometimes still rely on what is familiar in your life. I did this as well. It was good to see her again. We had shared a lot. I did not mention the sobriety to her. That was something that I would need to show. Not just to tell.

Sherri's Mom came out to Redmond from Minnesota to help her out in the recovery from the wrenched back. I had never met Mrs. Osmond. Sherri used to call home to check in with her parents every Sunday morning. I had later adopted this communication strategy with my parents. I was always perfectly quiet during these calls. She had never mentioned my presence in her life to the folks.

They had always had high hopes for Sherri. She was the first-born daughter in their family. They had not even approved of her first marriage to a "Jewish lawyer" husband. They'd lived with it because they had no choice. It was my guess that Sherri had arranged that first marriage in defiance of her parents—possibly to assert her independence. She could be strong willed.

I had known that Mrs. Osmond was in town. One morning I had something to take over to Sherri's and did not call first. When I knocked, Sherri let me in and introduced me to her mother, who was sitting in the front room. I'd just placed the returned item on the kitchen counter and saw her through the pass through bar into the living-room. She looked calm, very well dressed, and rather haughty.

Not expecting to see her, I was rather sloppily dressed and of no mind to make this acquaintance at this time. I was still in alcohol withdrawal. My complexion was blotchy, my hair askew, and I felt weak. I made the quick assessment that this was no time to be applying for the position of Golden Goy to the matriarch of the family. I mouthed a polite "Nice to meet you, Mrs. Osmond," and made an exit. It was over anyway. What Sherri elected to tell her Mother, about me and our relationship, was up to Sherri.

Sixty-01 Apartments had a Recreation Manager. She had an office in the lobby of the club house. Often I'd go to the club house on Sundays to have a cup of coffee and read the Sunday Seattle

Times. I was a fan of the New York Times Sunday Crossword puzzle, which appeared in the Seattle paper, and could photo copy it at the club house to work it on the weekends. At least start it on the weekend. I'd never finish it until the answers came out the following Sunday. That's how tough the puzzle was for me. Over my years in residence I was on a first-name basis in the rec. office.

At the north end of the club house was a fully equipped wet-bar with a refrigerator under the bar for a beer keg and its tap. The rec. office was then discussing starting a Wednesday night open bar for all residents and guests. This was to be a mid-week social session. I emphasized to them my recent sobriety (wouldn't be tipping at the tap) and willingly applied for the job of bartender at this new open bar. I got it. I wasn't the least bit concerned about the temptation of being around alcohol, I was very firm in my abstinence.

That open bar became a very popular weekly occasion at Sixty-01. There were a lot of singles and young adult couples with apartments in the complex. Many were evidently seeking a mid-week opportunity to meet their neighbors on a very casual basis and expand their friendship circles. It was Facebook without the computer, 29 years before the Winklevoss twins or Mark Zuckerberg. It was a real hit.

A year after the start of open bar the Seattle Seahawks came to town. Many of the rookies who were on the inaugural year team rented apartments at Sixty-01. In those initial years the Seahawks training facility was very close to Redmond. It was in our neighbor city of Kirkland, Washington. They were all over in Cheney, Washington in August for training camp.

Word got out in training camp about the Sixty-01 apartments. Most of the rookies were looking for a 'singles' complex with affordable rent. Many did not know whether they would make the team or not. They still needed a place to live. Come September of 1976, those who were signed to the team would show up at the open bar on a weekly basis. These were not the veterans; just the rookies. They did add some considerable excitement to the open bar crowd.

I met some life-long friends as a result of running that open bar. David Huls from Nebraska and Pete Juvet who worked for 3M Corporation were two such friends. Another gentleman I met was named Mel and he also lived in a studio apartment on the north side of the complex. One Wednesday he showed up early and before the bar got busy; we had a long chat across the bar. Mel knew Mary Jane and he agreed to re-introduce me to her. I'd met her a couple of years before, through Tate Chesebrough, and was looking forward to being re-introduced.

Another advantage of being in close contact with the activities staff at Sixty-01 was that I got involved in the functions each summer. One summer the activities committee organized a Pig Roast. This was a two-day affair with camping out in the commons areas around the club house. The main focus of the weekend was to bury the pig in a hot coals bed on Saturday, let it roast over-night, and serve a huge roast pig dinner on Sunday afternoon. It was a great weather weekend; the campout was a well-attended success. Everyone who made it through to Sunday morning was awarded a campaign button that stated, "I Slept With A Pig." I still have mine.

We had one gentleman who was called our "master chef." His experience was in the food service industry and we needed that experience. When we tested the pig early on the Sunday morning we discovered that it had not cooked. It was just on the warm side of raw. The chef quickly marshaled his resources and found a friend with a very large industrial oven in Bellevue. We hustled the pig out in a truck before anyone awoke and shoved it into that Bellevue oven. Somehow we managed to keep it there for seven hours and when we got it back to the club house it was medium well done. Luckily we managed to serve 120 dinners off that carcass. The Pig Roast was a success.

While serving up the pig that afternoon, I saw a lady who I thought was quite attractive. I found out later that her name was Julie Rock. Julie was the date of a fellow resident who I knew only casually. I had no job at the time and very little personal pride. I just logged Julie's name in the back of my brain and thought about it for the next 10 months.

Talk about slow on the up-take! Finally I got up my nerve and phoned her for coffee all those months later. Turns out we had a great time. Over the years Julie became a very close personal friend and a sometimes dating relationship. She taught sixth grade students in a Duvall, Washington grade school named Cherry Valley School.

Sixty-01 was a close community. You naturally meet your neighbors going back and forth between apartment, car-port, and laundry room. There were several swimming pools in the complex. One small pool was right across from my apartment. Not much swimming was done there but it was a mecca for absorbing rays from the summer sun; another place to meet your neighbors.

A young guy named Gary Edwards lived in Studio Apartment #1 on the end of my row. Gary was attending Bellevue Community College and working at a lumber yard after school. He had put together a cleverly-designed loft in his studio. Above the 8' x 8' sleeping alcove there was open space that extended well above the ceiling of the remaining studio. Gary had built a platform above the sleeping alcove with stairs going up on one end, by the window, and installed a double bed in the space above the ceiling. Mel knew Gary, so Mel also built an identical loft for himself in his studio apartment.

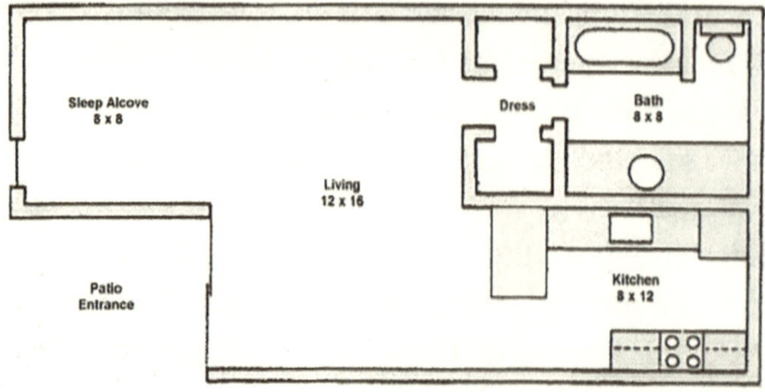

     Don McGehe

By placing the bed above the loft, it created an auxiliary 64 square foot room to use however you wished. Shortly after I first met Gary in 1976 he was preparing to move out to join his family (mother, father, and sister) on an around-the-world sailing trip. His older brother Larry M. Edwards was scheduled to join them on the cruise, but Larry backed out at the last minute due to business reasons. Since Gary was moving out of his studio he sold me the loft and I installed it in my unit before he left. He also had no use for his 10-speed bike so he gave it to me. He moved out to go on the South Pacific cruise in 1977.

We heard nothing of Gary for months. Then in late 1977 word came in the news press of a tragedy that had occurred aboard their ship *Spellbound* on the trip destined for French Polynesia. When the boat finally reached the Polynesian port, Gary informed the authorities of the deaths, at sea, of his father Loren Edwards and his mother Jody. The FBI reported Gary as the prime suspect in its murder investigation.

Federal prosecutors never indicted him, leaving the case unsolved. Later Ann Rule wrote a true-crime book about the case with the title: *But I Trusted You*. Larry M. Edwards wrote his own book in the spring of 2013, titled *Dare I Call it Murder?* to clear up some of the claimed mis-statements made in the Ann Rule book. We had a USPS mail contact with Gary in the 1980s but neither Mel nor I followed up. Until the Rule and Edwards books came to press little was known about the details of this tragedy at sea. Much of it, as yet, remains a mystery. I personally do not think that Gary was the kind of person who could have done what the FBI accused him of doing. Obviously others have had the same doubts. He was never even indicted.

I experienced a long period of unemployment from the fourth quarter of 1975 through to the June of 1976. Studio #9 was sill home. That apartment was as economical as I could find. My long period of unemployment insurance was running out. A neighbor named Larry Adams lived in apartment #11, two doors down. We knew each other socially as well as living in the same block.

Adams was working for Royal Typewriter Company. Their office was in downtown Seattle near Momma's Mexican Foods Restaurant. Larry was selling photocopying equipment as well as typewriters. He mentioned to me one day that his office was looking for someone to sell a new word-processing machine. I had been familiar with this type of machine since being with IBM in the late 1960s.

I wasn't excited about trying another sales job but I desperately needed a paycheck. When I say I wasn't excited, that was far too mild. I was terrified. But I still needed a paycheck. I thought I could try it for a while and see. Apparently the only thing I could still sell was myself. Either that or they were desperate; I got the job.

Royal sent me back to Hartford, Connecticut, to their home office to train: another east coast trip. The east coast did have something that I found fascinating: it had history. While in Hartford I visited several early cemeteries that had grave stones dating back to the late seventeenth century.

On the west coast of the United States, history seems to have begun with Lewis & Clark. European settlers were more than happy to ignore the fact that the Coastal Salish peoples had been in situ around the Puget Sound since the end of the last ice age. Hartford was nearly 165 years old before Lewis & Clark ever left St. Lewis. But, then again, you will run into expressions about the east that defy their history. Like "Newark, New Jersey: three hundred years of tradition, unhampered by progress."

Back in Seattle I would get into the office early every day. I'd do some paperwork, make several phone calls, and go to coffee with someone from the office staff. I'd leave the office about 9:15, operate the territory until 4:00, and get back to the office to wrap up and get to the freeway by 5.00. I'd put in the time, but I didn't make many sales calls. It lasted for six months before I was fired. It was a relief to be gone. I felt that I just had to find something that I could be good at, and enjoy working again. Sales was definitely not it.

At this time there appeared, on the Seattle horizon, a pick-up in the area's business climate. In response to this I contacted a former

IBM employee who I knew, and who was now with a professional job-search agency and applied for placement with his agency. His firm only placed employees with companies who were willing to pay the placement fees. There was, on his desk, a request for a systems engineer to help a small electronics manufacturer to move up into in-house computing. The company was Melco Labs in Bellevue, Washington. Melco made telephone switching equipment which they sold directly to the various major telephone companies.

In late 1976 I went through several rounds of interviews with Melco Labs and was hired for the systems engineering position. Melco was already talking to IBM small business representatives about the possibility of purchasing the very type of system that I had previously been supporting while with IBM. This was a welcome fit for me. I felt strong going into this job. I began immediately to focus on getting the Melco and IBM personnel on the same path toward the goal of integrating the business flow and procedures into the discipline that was necessary for successful data processing. This became difficult. I'd forgotten just how hard it was to get years of manual business procedures not only identified and flow-charted, but smoothed into the required flow that was adaptable to data system functioning.

The early months of 1977 were rife with rumors of the eminent plans, by the Sixty-01 owners group, for the selling of the apartments at Sixty-01 to the public. The scuttlebutt also had it that current renters would be offered very special rates. The months dragged on and still there was no special announcement. I now had a good job. That job would qualify me to get a first loan. I was becoming eager to make my first real estate purchase and get into the housing market.

For all of the 14 years since university graduation, I had lived with only one housing philosophy. That credo was: married people buy homes, single people rent apartments. I'd always thought that was the only way housing was done. I was, however, getting tired of seeing rents raised at the will of the ownership class. I was ready to buy—something; anything. My initial desire was to purchase one of the apartments at Sixty-01. Yet the ownership just kept procrastinating on the possibility of offering the apartments for sale.

Redmond was growing. New housing was beginning to be built. One Saturday in June of 1977, I went looking for a condo in downtown Redmond. I had hooked up with a real estate agent through my friend Nancy Johnston, who was a next-door neighbor to Sherri at Sixty-01. We met at the agent's office in Lake Forest Park that Saturday. I left my car at that office and we proceeded in the agent's car on our real estate scouting tour.

From Lake Forest Park we drove directly back to Redmond to tour an open house condominium. I must have been ready. The first condo I looked at, I wanted to buy. Was it that simple? It was a new construction at the 22-unit Ventrua Condominiums with the address of 8642 164th Ave. NE #106, Redmond, Washington 98052. This was right across the street from the property that would later become Bella Bottega Shopping Center. At the time there were just acres of Himalaya Blackberries holding the ground together in that valley.

Buying a home had to be more difficult than this. Before I made a final decision that day, I looked at the condo unit upstairs from #106 as well. This one was another $2,000.00 upgrade. In addition to the added expense, all the two grand bought you was another ten feet of vertical altitude: air space. The floor plans were exactly alike. And I didn't like the darker carpet upstairs either. So this was it, huh? They were asking $39,995.00 for #106. (In 2018, I would laugh at that price, but 41 years ago that was a lot of money. Times do change. Change is the one constant in the Universe.)

I looked at the agent and said: "I want it. What do we do now?"

The agent responded: "You write them an earnest money check."

I asked: "How much?"

Agent: "One thousand dollars should do it. Do you have your checkbook?"

I replied: "No, it's in my car at your office."

Agent's reaction: "Well, we could drive back up there to pick it up. Unless you can find someone else to write the check. The condo could be sold before we get back, however."

I thought about that for a second. Other people kept trooping in to look at the condo. Julie Rock's condo was about three miles down 148th Street. I wondered if she would write me a check? We grabbed several condo offer sheets, with pictures, and drove a block south to the 7-11 store which had a payphone out front. The phone call found Julie at home on a Saturday afternoon. She said to come on over.

In order to ask for a one-thousand-dollar check, I felt I needed to sell her on the condo first, and then to convince her that this decision was the right one for me to make. In so doing I knew I would either confirm my desires or squelch my own intentions. We drove to Julie's condo. She had made this same decision about two months earlier and was now comfortably settled into her new place. I showed her the flier and she said "Let's go look at it." I now saw that it was better to show her than to tell her. Sensory impressions count. We were soon back on 164th Ave. N.E.

Julie liked it. It had a great view out across the Sammamish Valley on that sunny summer afternoon. After agreeing to write her a reimbursement check on Monday, Julie wrote out the check and we presented it to the selling agent. It was done. Julie got a huge hug and my agent was all smiles. We drove Julie back to her place and then we headed north for Lake Forest Park. The decision had been made. The hard work was to begin now.

CHAPTER 17

I WENT TO APPLY FOR A MORTGAGE ON MONDAY. IN ORDER TO avoid the costly mortgage insurance, I asked my father to make me a personal loan, at the market rate of 8%, to get my down payment up above the 20% level. I told Dad that I would save the second bedroom for him and Mom, so that they could visit any time they could come out. They made a point of doing that the very next summer. That was the fastest real estate decision I ever made. It turned out to be a good one.

I held onto that condo through thick and thin for the next 30 years. I paid off the second mortgage note to my father, and paid off the principal mortgage to a series of four separate financial institutions as the paper changed hands over the ensuing years. The condo was sold in 2007 to Piper Sather and Tyler Scalise. Piper was the daughter of my very good friends Tom and Susie Sather and Tyler was her soon-to-be husband.

The move-in crew for the new condo was organized by Julie Rock. She enjoyed the job because she had so much to do with the decision. Much of the rest of the crew were friends from the Life-Spring organization that I had been involved with in the previous months before the purchase. I felt that I finally had a place that I could call home. That felt good.

In the months before the move, Julie and I had been given some seeds from her hairdresser who had a styling shop down in Pioneer Square. We were soon to become raw, neophyte, dirt weed farmers. This had all started in Julie's old apartment down on Lake Sammamish. We got a standard grow-light fixture and installed it in Julie's bedroom closet. Starting the seeds in vermiculite, we put in a twenty four-hour timing switch, which turned the light on for eighteen hours and off for six hours each day, and watched with amazement as these seeds sprouted and grew into starts and then spindly marijuana plants.

We knew nothing about growing weed. All we did was observe, with wonder, as the leaves developed. We then clipped some off, put them on a cookie sheet in a very low 175-degree oven, and dried them into crushable material to roll into joints with Zig-Zag papers. I was still smoking cigarettes at the time. Jules was not. Inhaling was something she had to learn. It took a while. She was eager.

Jules had always been a curious soul. She could grin and enjoy living on the wild side even after mirroring model behavior, with the same grin on her face, for years in education. I liked this wild side in her. She could play society's game. What's more, she even enjoyed it. I still smile as I think back on those days.

At the time we both purchased our condos and gave up renting, Jules and I retired the grow closet. I could get supplies from other sources. Mel and I would make an occasional buy and get better weed in the process. After I quit drinking in 1975 this was my primary method for relaxation. The weed helped wean me from my dependence on alcohol. I know—sad, yet true.

We would occasionally get some bad dirt-weed from Mexico. It wasn't like shopping at Whole Foods. You took what you had heard was available on the market by word of mouth. Occasionally you hit gold. Sometimes you got burned.

After moving into the new condo in downtown Redmond, Peter McRae and I began to get serious about bicycle riding. We started out by riding up the Sammamish River Trail from Redmond to Kenmore and back. An extended ride would be a weekend tour up around the top of Lake Washington and down the west side of the lake to the University of Washington. Over the years, and through several bicycle upgrades, we got into the habit of riding nearly every Sunday morning, eight months a year. Our favorite route for that Sunday ride would be driving out to Duvall, Washington and parking the car downtown. We'd then unload the bikes and head north to the Cherry Valley Road and circle east-south around several back roads down to Carnation, Washington. From here we'd head west through Carnation Farms and back north up the West Snoqualmie Valley Road NE, and finally east across the Woodinville-Duvall Road, across the bridge, and back to downtown Duvall and the car. The round trip on this route was just over fifty miles. A good ride.

Over the years McRae and I got this crazy idea of doing the Mount Rainier Ride. We were scheduled to do it in, I think, 1978. We trained for months. Two weeks before the ride McRae got appendicitis (or something that sure looked like it) on a family bike outing and couldn't make that ride. I went anyway.

This baby was a three-day ride. It started in Enumclaw and rode south down to the Nisqually Entrance to the park on the first day. The second day was from Nisqually up to Paradise and then down to the Ohanapecosh Campground. The third day was north on Hwy, 410 up across Cayuse Pass and back down to Enumclaw. This three-day ride entails 10,000 feet of climbing over 150 miles of road. It turned out to be one of those "once in a lifetime" opportunities (I've had several). The reason for the "once," is that, wonderful as it was, I'm happy not to have to do it again. Once was plenty.

Through the late 1970s I was putting in a lot of hours at the Melco Labs job. It was a more-or-less satisfying position with a growing company. As with any business organization there were always office politics involved. I was attempting to keep my nose clean and stay away from the turf wars as much as possible. I would often stay late to work out scheduling conflicts in the coordination between manufacturing and the business office.

After the regular office hours it got quiet in my cubical and I could focus on the problems I was having in the system. The only thing that would interrupt me was the phone. I have never much cared for phones. Sometimes I could ignore them, but they were

　　　　　Don McGehe

an annoying interruption to the thought process. One night that phone rang and I ignored it the first set of rings. One minute later it rang again and I picked it up.

My greeting was, "Melco Labs, how can I help you?"

A female voice asked, "Is Bob Frye there?" Bob was the Human Services Manager.

"I'll transfer you to his line, just a moment please." The transfer was completed.

It was quiet for several minutes than the phone rang again. I let it go through six or seven rings and finally picked it up.

The same female voice asked, "He doesn't answer his line. Is he still there?"

I responded, "If he didn't answer he must be gone for the day. You could try calling him tomorrow during business hours."

She was persistent and then said, "Can you walk over to his office and check to see if he is still there?"

I was getting frustrated and responded, "I'm sorry ma'am. It's not my week to watch him."

Even though I had no idea who was on the line at the time, this was a totally inappropriate thing to say to Mrs. Bob Frye. I heard about it next day when Frye called me into his office. He was not mad. He could have even been feeling guilty for failure to communicate with his wife. He could have been involved in an affair, for all I know, and was trying to keep it from her. At any rate I got a mild scolding and promised not to do it again. But that was the beginning of my future personnel problems at Melco Labs.

In the spring of 1978 my smoking habit was up to three packs a day. I'd start off each day with a violent coughing episode over the bathroom sink after brushing my teeth. From there it was back to the bedroom to light up the first cigarette of the day. One day I asked a friend of mine, Anne Rossiter, what she thought of me. Her response was, "Whenever I think of you Don, I picture you with a cigarette in your mouth." I thought about that for a day.

Within two days I had built up my resolve to quit. I had tried years ago in Portland but now I was finally, totally, and completely ready to make it work. I threw out what packs and cartons I had at the condo and never picked up another cigarette again. I had known this was coming for months. That violent coughing spell, each and every morning, was the harbinger that no longer allowed me to ignore the smoking problem. Finally I'd fixed my will to act and change that habit.

Smoking cigarettes was the second of three habits that I tackled cold-turkey, and quit. Alcohol was successful. Cigarette smoking was now added to that quit list. I still had the weed. I credit the availability of marijuana with allowing me to quit the two, both totally legal drugs, that could and would eventually have killed me. (Once again, last year, there were no reported deaths from the consumption of marijuana.)

With alcohol and cigarettes, it seemed to be a choice. Death or life. I'd chosen life. When I was in Junior High School I had watched my father quit smoking, cold-turkey. I now felt that I was following his lead in life.

In the 1970s I was still looking for who I was, and who I wanted to be. One crazy idea I had in 1979 was to curl my hair. One of the Seattle sports idols at that time was Jack Sikma, the 6'11" center of the Seattle Supersonics. When Sikma graduated from Illinois Wesleyan University he had straight hair. While he played for the Sonics he had curly hair. Somewhere in there he found a stylist.

We humans are fickle. We always want what we don't have. Just ask anyone with curly hair. They want it straight. I had straight hair. I wanted it curly. So I got it curled. It was so much easier to take care of when it was curly. Except when it was beginning to grow back out.

One of the managers at Melco Labs, who seldom saw me in the office, once said to me, "McGehe, whenever I see you, you look different." I just smiled and said, "Thank you, I guess." He would eventually be the manager who I was reporting to when I was

   DON MCGEHE

fired by Melco. Evidently, he was not overly impressed. This hair experiment lasted for over a year. Finally it became too expensive to curl it, and it wasn't fooling anyone anyway. I finally cut it very short and let it grow out naturally straight. I guess that wasn't who I really wanted to be after all.

The early 1980s were unsettling years for me. I was nearly 40 and still searching. For what? I was not quite sure. I had a true friendship with Julie Rock to fall back on. We had a lot of fun together. We could rely on one another for both companionship and for personal sharing. Both Julie and I were holding back giving our all to this relationship. It was solid but never blossomed. Maybe that is why it was so strong. There was always a question mark at the end of every sentence.

I had formed a friendship with a lady named Sarah Clendenen who was in the purchasing department at Melco. I was still mindful of my cautions about romantic relations with workmates so this remained a friendship. Sarah was of medium tall stature and slim with shoulder length brown hair. She had a very quick mind. Working in purchasing she had a very good phone rapport with vendors and sales people. Her mind was usually two moves ahead of the mind on the other end of the phone. I always admired that. Sarah always had a big smile and a sharp sense of humor. Her son, Stevie, was a very good tennis player and she worked hard to keep him equipped with the latest Stan Smith tennis sneakers which he wore through at the pace of about a pair a month.

Many employees at Melco Labs brought their own lunch to work. This was a practice for both myself and for Sarah. The office was in Redmond, Washington. No surprise here. It rained a lot. When it didn't rain, and we experienced a nice warm sunny day, we would often drive to Bellevue in Sarah's maroon Monte Carlo and take a picnic lunch to Bellefield Park near the Mercer Slough.

We would park and roll out a blanket on the lawn. Sometimes our first luncheon course was a pre-rolled doobie passed back and forth to whet the appetite. No questions asked. The sandwiches always tasted better later. There were very few heads in this Melco work force. You had to be quite careful in your associations. Afternoons went a bit smoother with a lit up lunch. The executives at Melco had a standing four-martini tradition at lunch every day, so even if we were a bit late returning we were seldom missed.

In early 1982 there was handwriting on the walls at Melco. I was not quite ready to read it yet. The first piece of script that I saw was the hire of an independent contractor who was to come in and evaluate the manufacturing production procedures for transition to the installation of a computer. That's what I thought my job was. By this time I did not have the ear of the senior management team, however.

This new guy was real busy. He was a fast talker and loved to write long involved procedure manuals. That is not a bad trait but I did not have the confidence he knew what he was doing. The first thing that he did was to discourage the idea that an IBM System 3 computer would do the job for Melco Labs. He thought it was too small. He had some friends with the local Wang Computer distributer who he was coordinating with to do a practical demonstration for senior management.

He set up this demo and everyone went to downtown Seattle to watch it. I was there as well. The consultant then went to work writing up extensive procedures for implementation. These procedures had no flowcharts, nor did they have anyone from the production floor involved in planning the execution. I could see large holes in the process he was proposing. Management dismissed the proposal for the IBM System 3 computer and put the Wang on order. Wang was to offer only hardware advice and leave all the software work to the independent consultant who, as far as I knew, had never done either the systems work nor installed a Wang before.

I had intended to hire software work from IBM Systems Engineers to do the systems work of putting in a computer. The consultant convinced senior management to save all that money and let him do all the systems work. The Wang computer arrived

     DON MCGEHE

immediately and was installed in the office. We were able to install a pre-canned general ledger system on the new computer but all the other accounting tasks were still being handled by the old manual system that had been operating for years. This large piece of hardware in the office did not have much to do.

I was assigned to write an evaluation of the progress of the installation. I worked on this evaluation for two weeks and handed it to the president's secretary to be proofed and typed. I checked on the progress of the typing for the next eight business days. It was not completed and each day I was offered a new excuse as to why it was not yet done. On that eighth day there was a meeting of the "computer evaluation committee" to discuss the progress of the installation. I was not invited to the meeting. This was the next-to-last piece of handwriting I saw on the wall.

At this meeting there was a vote taken to fire me and to move the consultant into my position. While the meeting was in progress the secretary finally brought me the typed final report that was now eight days late. At the meeting the staff members were told that I had failed to do the report on time. I'd been set up to fail by the president. That was the last piece of script; the wall was now finished.

After the meeting I was called into the president's office and fired. I'd been sabotaged by a consultant and the president. I was fed up with the management of Melco anyway, but as yet had no good ideas as to how I was going to move ahead in my life. To the unemployment office once again. This was getting tiring.

At 10:00 am on the morning following my firing, I received a phone call at home from one of the administrators at the Melco office. The question in this call was if I would be willing to share with them the master password to get into the Wang system and turn it on. They had fired me without covering even the most basic information necessary to continue system operations in my absence. I then asked if Melco had any intentions to deny or challenge unemployment benefits with the Washington State Employment Security Department in my dismissal. I was put on hold for ten minutes while this question could be researched. The caller came back on the line and indicated that there was no intention to delay or challenge the claim. With this assurance, I gave them the password.

At this point in time I had been employed steadily for over five years. I immediately filed with the unemployment office for benefits. There was a two-week waiting period at the outset where no benefits were to be paid, but establishing the claim on a timely basis was key. Now I had to find another job.

I was exhausted with corporate life. Being fired does not look good on your resume. I knew that resumes are just a collection of believable lies anyway, but I still had this aversion to lies. In my mind I was working on putting that new resume together. I was wracking my brain about what I could do, where to go from here, and how to show that on a sheet of resume paper. The near future looked bleak.

One idea that I had, as a stop-gap measure, was to get the maintenance/clean-up job at the Ventura Condominiums where I lived. My next-door neighbor was president of the Condo Association and I made him an offer that he was able to get a quick vote of the board to approve. That was a start but it didn't offer much pay. My next-door neighbor on the other side, Michael LaGris, subscribed to the Seattle Times and he would give me the Sunday Want Ads section as a resource for free. This was back before want ads had moved over to the Internet. Reading that section was discouraging; it seemed that most jobs were asking for something that I didn't already have: a job.

PART 5

THE DOCTOR

July 1972–June 1989

CHAPTER 18

The next week I went over to see Mel at the house he was renting out in Duvall, Washington, 20 miles northeast of Redmond. I hadn't seen him in a long time and wanted to catch up with his life. I told him what was going on. He then asked me if I had ever considered going into business for myself. I told him that I would love to do that if I could figure out what to do, because I would then be my own boss. Independence. No more corporate politics. He asked if I had any money set aside. The answer to that was that I did have some, but not a lot. He said, "I have an idea. Let me show you what I've been doing lately."

He then took me downstairs to the basement and opened the door to a room that was slightly hidden down the hall. Suddenly I was hit with a light blast from two 1,000-watt metal halogen bulbs. These were the same bulbs that illuminated the interior of the Kingdome indoor sport stadium in Seattle, Washington. This structure was built in 1976 and was the initial home of the Seattle Mariners Baseball Club and the Seattle Seahawks NFL Football franchise. These bulbs were used to light up these indoor sports facilities because they lit up the indoor arenas like the sun did outdoors. We walked into the room and experienced the sudden rise in heat and humidity from a grow room with four large plastic hydroponic tanks supporting eight gorgeous marijuana plants. The next comment from Mel was, "You could do this too."

This was nothing like Julie and I were doing in her bedroom closet. This was sophisticated. He explained that there was an indoor growing cycle in cannabis that, when done effectively, calls for an eight-week growth period (with the lights on 18 hours a day) and an eight-week blooming cycle (when the lights are on only 12 hours a day). Once the plants receive the message that the light is now gone for six hours a day, they immediately think that it is autumn and transition into forming flowers which create the THC trichomes that produce the resin heads which are the source of all the psycho-activity. Granted, there was some very tiny amount of psycho-activity in those leaves Julie and I were roasting in her oven down on Lake Sammamish, but damn little.

I thought about that for just one minute, then admitted, "Yes I could."

That suddenly seemed to be the answer. Self-employment. No more corporate timekeeping. Independence. Finally using my degree from the Kansas State University of Agriculture and Applied Sciences. But no longer in the Applied Sciences. Now in Agriculture. Freedom. A different kind of freedom. A freedom found in the underground economy.

Under an arrangement we agreed to, I would need to buy all the necessary equipment and set up a grow room in my condo. I had two bedrooms. I only needed one to sleep in. We agreed that I would be provided with all the tutoring, guidance, and the know-how to grow that first crop. And I would be given the "starts" (baby cannabis plants) for crop number one. All this in exchange for 50% of the first crop. Sounded like a fair deal to me. Apprenticeship. It had worked for centuries, since the Middle Ages in Europe. Why not try it once again?

The first thing to be done was to re-wire the condo for the correct electrical power. I invited one of my wiring friends from Melco to come quietly over to the condo and re-do the circuitry. That accomplished, I laid down silver wall board over the carpet in the bedroom and taped it down with silver duct tape. We sealed off the window in the room with more wall board to keep any stray light from bleeding through. In order to conserve the light rays, I papered the interior walls with reflective Mylar to bounce all that energy back to the plants.

A major investment was made in the ballasts (transformers), hanging fixtures, two four-square-foot hood covers for the lights, and two 1,000 watt bulbs for the illumination. In order to run hydroponics it was also necessary to purchase four Water Works plastic hydro tanks, four Little Giant water pumps and electric timers, as well as rubber tubing and hoses to connect everything.

To create the needed hydroponic growing environment, double-hulled, rotational-molded white plastic tanks are used which are about 66" long, 30" wide, and 24" high. The top hull is the deeper of the two hulls and contains about two hundred pounds of clean pea gravel. The cannabis starts are placed in this gravel with two starts in each tank. The bottom hull of each tank contains the water and nutrient solution which is pumped up and into the top tank to irrigate the plant roots for fifteen minutes, either three times a day (in the grow phase), or twice a day (in the bloom phase), after which the pump is automatically turned off by a timer. Following the shut off of the irrigation cycle, the nutrient solution drains back into the bottom hull of the tank through small drain holes in the bottom of the upper hull, and as it drains out, oxygen (air) is drawn down into the gravel to aerate the roots of the plants, thus providing the necessary oxygenation for proper root growth. This cycle repeats every six hours during daylight hours.

Once a week the water is pumped out of the bottom of the tanks and new water is brought in through a hose connected to the sink fixture in an adjoining bathroom. New fresh nutrient solution is then added to the tank water and will be used for the following week's irrigation. During the grow phase the nutrient solution is heavy with nitrogen, and during the bloom phase potash replaces the nitrogen to stimulate flowering.

It took some planning and execution to establish these procedures, but once established, each crop follows a very similar pattern. On an outdoor farm, if you are lucky, and growing in the tropics, you might get two crops a year. Outdoor growth in Washington State is strictly a one-crop yearly cycle. Indoor you may get over four crops. It is important to be able to turn summer on and off, at will (without early frost, hail, drought, cyclones, hurricanes, locusts, etc.). You'll notice that I did not mention the bane of the indoor gardener…the dreaded spider mite. Mom never promised that life was going to be easy.

The real beauty of indoor growing is that the gardener has the option to let horticulture take over and simply keep a daily eye on the results. Nature will perform the work of growing the plants. The earth has fostered this natural process for over a billion years. Things can and sometimes do go wrong. If you keep an observant eye on the progress of the operation any errors can be quickly and easily corrected.

Most of the work in indoor gardening is performed automatically and naturally. This is done by providing light, water, and nutrients to proven genetic plant material and allowing the plants to respond to the environment you are growing them in. The plants do most of the work. It's in their genes. You provide the proper growing environment. You plant the best 'starts' available. Then you let them grow for eight weeks.

After the eight weeks of growth, and just before changing the lights from 18 hours a day down to 12 hours a day (to begin the flowering cycle), I took cuttings from the plants. It is important to do this while the plants are still in their initial growth stage. I simply nipped off about a 3 to 4 inch cutting from the end of a good-looking bract anywhere on the lower portions of the plant, dipped the base end into liquid vitamin B-12 and then into RootTone powder and planted it in pre-moistened vermiculite material. The purpose of this procedure is to make enough cuttings to populate the next crop of plants. It is important to continue these starts in the 18-hour light cycle that they have been used to in the growth stage.

I set up a florescent grow-light tube in a closet, with a timer set to 18-hour daylight and six-hour darkness, in order to provide the home environment for these starts. It is wise to take at least 150% of the cuttings that will be necessary to provide ample plants for

DON McGEHE

the next crop, because some of them may not grow roots. If you have more than you need when you are ready to plant again you can simply choose the best and healthiest starts to populate that next crop. If you have only one grow room—which I did—it is necessary to rely on friends to swap cuttings with.

Taking cuttings and trying to nurse them through a 9-week wait before replanting them for the next crop is impractical. I knew this problem could be solved by setting up a two-room growing operation, where one room is in grow mode and the other is in flowering mode. In that situation you simply swap the grow/bloom functions in the two rooms every eight weeks. If you control the timing of the lights and the supply of proper nutrients, you can play god.

Once brought indoors, the growing environment takes advantage of two of what Yuval Noah Harari referred to as "Revolutions" in his 2015 book "Sapiens, A Brief History of Humankind." The first was the Agricultural Revolution about 12,000 years ago. The second was the Industrial Revolution which started about 200 years ago. The Industrial Revolution introduced mechanization to the practice of farming.

Now indoors, with "near sunlight" artificial illumination, state-of-the-art fertilizer, complete control of the day/night light cycle, and protection from weather, the grower is, in fact, playing god to the cannabis plants. Harari points out "…the Industrial Revolution was above all else the Second Agricultural Revolution." Once you move the growing area indoors, with complete control of the day/night (grow/bloom) cycle, it can legitimately be called a Third Agricultural Revolution. As 18th-century English poet William Cowper wrote, "God moves in a mysterious way, His wonders to perform."

One of the hard-and-fast rules that I adapted when I set up the grow operation was to never have fire arms or any other weapon on the premises. The police establishment in America has the macho conviction that they should be the only "armed" force in the civilian population. Anyone else with guns is a threat to their dominance. If they find that you have committed a crime, they will charge you with that crime. If they find a gun anywhere near you and you commit the same crime you are charged with a "violent" criminal offense. The penalties for "violent" offenses are generally twice the prison time of those awarded for non-violent offenses. The only difference is the presence of a gun. Second Amendment rights apply to only the law-abiding citizen. Period. End of case.

At the time that this first crop of cuttings were being taken, the Alex Haley series of *Roots* had played on ABC-TV several years before. Mel and I were conscious of the necessity of roots for our cuttings to begin their all-important life cycle. We even jokingly inquired, when wondering if our starts had sprouted any roots, "Have you seen Kunta Kinte's yet?"

When the cuttings were taken and sequestered in their closet, I changed the timing on the lights to signal that autumn had arrived. This was a reduction from an 18-hour day down to a 12-hour day. Then I watched lovingly as the cannabis flowers formed. Through-out both the growth cycle and the flowering cycle a significant amount of leaf trimming must be done. At the end of the flowering cycle the time-consuming work began. Harvest.

In that initial harvest I cut my first plant out of the hydro tank with a pair of garden bypass loppers right at the gravel level and hung the entire plant upside down from a hook in the middle of the kitchen ceiling. The diameter of a healthy plant stalk, at its base, can be, and often is, above two inches in thickness. I then began at the (inverted) bottom of the plant to nip off stems and to trim the ends of the leaves from the buds. Each stem may have a number of buds growing from it. Each bud needs to be trimmed.

This is a time-consuming project. It is a good idea to leave a hook on the base of each of these bracts with which to hang them from a string in the drying room to cure. When harvested, the plant may contain up to 70% water by weight. When properly cured (dried), that percentage of water weight goes down to low single digits.

I would often spend a full 7-day week harvesting a crop. The time spent trimming buds during that week would normally be 17 or 18 hours each day. Only one plant would be cut at a time and the remainder of the crop remained in the flowering cycle in the bloom room. As the trimming on each bract would be finished, that bract would be taken into a curing closet and hung upside down on a string to dry out. The closet was eight feet wide.

Each level of strings might contain six separate strands. With three string levels, the available volume would be 144 feet of string. Because this closet was in the same bloom room that the remaining uncut plants were, the twelve hours of bulb illumination provided heat for the curing process. A curing would normally take a full week from the hanging of the last bract. After that the final step was to trim the dry buds from the bract stems, weigh them, and package them in seal-a-meal plastic bags.

With a cycle now complete, clean-up was next. The direction of flow in the rubber tubing in the tank was reversed. The Little Giant Pumps now flushed the last of the bloom fertilizer out and down the bathroom drain. The gravel was taken from the tanks, a bucket-full at a time, scooped into plastic bags, and taken for disposal. There were two heavy tangles of root ball that needed to be separated from the gravel, in this process, and disposed of separately. Once the gravel was bagged up and disposed of, the tank could be cleaned and dried for the next crop.

In the first two years of this grow operation I was working with only a single room. I had two bedrooms in the condo. One was significantly larger. That larger room was the room I was sleeping in. After that first crop I switched rooms and began growing in the larger of the two rooms and sleeping in the smaller. This allowed me to double the size of the grow room. I went from four hydro tanks to eight, and from only two lights up to four. Economies of scale.

I found out early in this single room growing experience that the starts for the next crop were in the vermiculite pots far too long. They were getting too spindly and wilting over before being planted into gravel. I soon made arrangements with other growers to get cuttings on a more timely basis. The only way to solve this cuttings continuity problem was to have two grow rooms on alternating cycles of growth/bloom. That solution would have to wait until later.

Those early years were fraught with money and cash-flow problems. I created a life with only a limited number of social outlets. That alone saved a lot of money. With the exception of a very few friends who knew of my cannabis cultures, I could invite no one over to the condo. I read a lot and went through many of James Michener's historical novels. I found that I was attracted to historical fiction as a category and Michener's historical research was superior to most in this genre. My father was also an avid reader of Michener and I shared much literary back-and-forth with Dad about his books, in both written and phone conversations, during this period.

I'd been gone from Sixty-01 Apartments for years now. One day I ran into Dianne Grossman who was formerly the activities manager at Sixty-01. Dianne had now created a business of her own selling bagels from a street stand in front of the Seattle City Hall on Fourth Avenue at James Street in Seattle. She explained to me that she wished to expand her business and add another street cart at a second location in the downtown area. She asked if I wanted a job at this second cart. It did sound interesting. I mentioned that I was interested in working only four days a week but also needed to take a week off every three months. I asked, "Could this be just part-time?" "Sure," she said.

She set up that second cart on Fourth Avenue at Pike Street on the sidewalk beside Rivkin's Jewelers. Herb Rivkin was known to both Dianne and me through his brother who was a resident at Sixty-01 while we were both still there. I started off working Monday thru Thursday and Dianne had others who would work the cart on Friday and Saturday. This was an experience, being out in the street in whatever weather Puget Sound would blow up Pike Street and through those downtown canyons. It could be ideal or it could be nasty. There was a rain canopy on the cart. That helped.

     DON McGEHE

I'd ride the city bus into the downtown area each Monday through Thursday morning, pick up my bagels from Dianne at her cart at City Hall, and then bus down Fourth Avenue to roll out the second cart from its underground storage location. I'd then pull it up Pike Street two blocks, and open it up about 10:00 am. I didn't make a lot of money selling bagels. I did make enough to make it worthwhile. And it was a lot of fun. I had a fairly regular clientele and made a number of friends over the two years I worked the cart that I would see daily.

The bagel business was always slow at the mid-morning opening hour of ten o'clock. After I set up the cart each morning, I would padlock the cash drawer and duck down the alley to the Monorail Espresso stand to see my friends there and get a cup of decaf espresso. This stand was a landmark at their spot beneath the Fifth Avenue Monorail at this time. In the afternoons I could take a break across Pike Street and buy a cookie at the Ms. Field's Cookie shop. If I needed a restroom I'd duck into the Nordstrom Store just across the alley up Pike Street.

There was occasional excitement when we might experience a speedy shop-lifter being hotly pursued by a store detective running up Pike Street. It was a fairly orderly corner, however—most of the time, anyway. But there were street people who would and could do nearly anything at any time. I remember one day watching a lady of the street squat, drop her drawers, and urinate right on the street corner while the light was red and then walk across the street very calmly once it had turned green. Much of this nefarious activity was covered from view by her loosely billowing skirt. It. Does. Take. All. Kinds. To make a world.

North on Fourth, half a block from the cart, was a gym called Washington Athletic Club. I dropped in there one afternoon after work and inquired about membership. Turns out they had two locations: this one on Fourth Avenue and another in Redmond, Washington. That rang the clear bell of convenience. I'd just turned 40 and thought it was time to start working out regularly for the first time in my life. The monthly dues were not that much, so I joined.

I would now leave on an earlier bus, go to the gym, and then go to work on my Monday-Thursday schedule. Friday, Saturday, and Sunday I could just drive to the Redmond location. After I had established some regularity on this schedule I discovered they also had a lifetime membership plan. For a $749.00, one-time contribution, I'd never have to pay dues again. That was the very first of a total of three "life-time memberships" I was to have in three separate gyms in my lifetime.

What I didn't realize, at the time, was that it was either my lifetime or the solvency of the gym that dictated the definition of what a "lifetime" meant. As Yoda might have said, "Live long and *learn.*" These "lifetime" offerings are nearly impossible to find anymore. Gym owners found that they needed the cash flow on a more consistent basis to maintain solvency.

CHAPTER 19

By the late spring of 1984 the bagel cart work was beginning to wear on me. I had a high school reunion that I wanted to attend back in Manhattan, Kansas in early July of that summer. It would be the 25th reunion since graduation in 1959. It occurred to me that it would be best to hold onto this job until after the trip to meet my classmates. The very first question asked by anyone at a reunion is "What are you doing now?" The bagel cart work would be a plausible, if not an altogether convincing, response to that question.

I had several photographs taken of myself standing in front of the cart, for show-and-tell purposes, to prove the point to any skeptics. At the reunion, my classmate Sue Kesner was not easily fooled, and laughingly threatened to come to Seattle and confront me on Fourth and Pike. I smiled and welcomed her to make that visit. I knew, full well, that the very travel expense alone would discourage her from proving that point. Nonetheless, I kept up my job at the cart until after the reunion.

A major life change came on the 14th of June, 1984. I got that call from See asking if I would like to meet her that evening down at Marina Park in Kirkland, Washington. I would. I did. The next five years of my life would be drastically altered as a result of that meeting.

See and I had known each other for more than five years from my visits to her office. She had always had a radiant smile and a glint in her eyes that could grab hold of your own eyeballs fast, and command attention. When I had first gone into the office five years previously, See was married, and as I saw her, from a seated position behind her desk, she appeared rather overweight. Over the years things changed. Over the years See changed.

In an appointment with Dr. Berthelote in early 1984, I'd not seen her when I arrived for the appointment. She'd been on break. The doctor now introduced her again. I was astounded.

She had lost over 90 pounds and her physical shape had been totally altered. I told her that she looked damn good. The Doctor dismissed her and she left the exam room. Doctor Berthelote then told me that she had been on a near-daily running program for close to two years. I realized that my brushing/flossing regimen had been so good for those two years I had not been in the office for an appointment. It was as if I had been trying to break Berthelote's rice bowl with my careful brushing.

I next heard from See on that fateful day of June 14th, 1984. Her invitation to meet in Marina Park that evening was perfect. The day had been sunny and warm. I could think of nothing I would enjoy more than meeting at the park. It was nearly the summer solstice and the days were already quite long at our Kirkland latitude of nearly 48 degrees north. We found each other at a park bench by the Pavilion. The wind was calm and the waves of Lake Washington were softly lapping upon the sandy beach of the lakeshore. See was wearing a pair of stylish, calf high, boots that accentuated her runner's leg muscles to perfection. I found her stunning.

The conversation that evening was smooth and insightful. We both knew how to listen. And we did listen to each other. We also related some intimate personal thoughts and feelings. It felt safe to share. It was comfortable to be together. Time flew by. By 9:30 the sun had set and the sky was darkening. I tested my blood sugar level, and we retreated up to Lake Street and into Hector's Restaurant for coffee, a snack, and more animated conversation.

As we walked to her car, See mentioned that she was on vacation from the dental office for three weeks to use up accumulated vacation time before leaving her job. She mentioned that she was

     DON McGEHE

planning to fly to California on Sunday to visit some of her friends. I asked if she would like a ride to the airport and she said, "Yes, thank you."

"May I see you tomorrow?" I asked.

She responded, "Would you like to come up to my Mountlake Terrace house tomorrow for dinner?"

I inquired, "Where's your husband?" Her answer was, "He's already in Southern California, but we're taking separate vacations this year." We then agreed to make a day of it tomorrow up in Mountlake.

"How about one pm?"

"Yes, one would be fine."

It seemed so smooth. We gently touched in a loose hug while maintaining dreamy eye contact. With her two-inch boot heals, we were at equal eye level. That felt perfect. The soft kiss was an expression of thanks for a remarkable evening of sharing. "See you tomorrow."

One of the loves we had shared on Friday evening was a lifelong worship of the sun. On Saturday I packed a swim suit, Dopp kit, half a dozen doobies, and a change of clothes. It was a rare two-day stretch of sunny Seattle weather which greeted us that weekend. Continuing magic. See and I threw a blanket out on the lawn in Mountlake Terrace and enjoyed that sun for two hours in the early afternoon.

Later, See suggested visiting the Edmonds, Washington Arts & Crafts Fair. It was one city over towards the Sound; a short Saturday drive to the west. We wandered around the fair for several hours, seeing and being seen. We were grinning and holding hands. Really having fun. We laughed at everything.

Before that Friday, I wasn't used to the use of plural pronouns. "We," "us," and "our" had been rarely heard in my conversations recently. I was secretly eager to change that English language usage. It was surprising how easily those plural pronouns slipped into the verbal and psychological parlance. Once again…it just felt right.

On the way back to Mountlake we stopped by the Puget Consumers Co-op Food Market to grab something for the evening meal. Hardly dinner, though. It was just grab-and-go stuff. She was leaving for Cali next day and leftovers were not wanted. I don't even remember what we bought. I do remember that the paired shopping experience was also fun.

We kept changing our minds about what sounded good, grinning, and swapping goods between shelf and grocery cart until we made it to the check out. We were lucky we hadn't had a doobie yet. It's not wise to go grocery shopping when stoned. You're always famished. It gets way too expensive. At the time I didn't even know if See was into cannabis. The subject hadn't come up yet.

When we got back to her house we set the groceries on the table and sat down in the kitchen. Where else? It's always the kitchen. Friendliest room in the house. Why not? Everybody eats. I pulled out a doobie and inquired with my eyes. There was a nod of acceptance. I lit it up and passed it over.

No smokers lived in that house so we found a saucer to use for the ashes. Details. The way we had selected the menu at PCC, there was no preparation necessary. We just opened up packages, spread it out, and enjoyed the tastes. Trust was already so established in my evaluation of our relationship that I copped to being the grower when she asked where the weed came from. I'll admit it. I was rightfully proud of the product. I couldn't and shouldn't have said that to nearly anyone. But in my gut, I trusted this lady. Time would confirm that trust. Our second evening together was memorable for the sharing and the giving on both of our parts. The return of human touch.

I dropped See off at Sea/Tac International Airport for her flight to California, Sunday noon. I had an address for her in California. We exchanged a promise to write. I offered to pick her up from her return flight. At that time she did not have a firm return schedule. She said she would let me know when she had scheduled that flight home.

 Don McGehe

As I drove north, up I-405 towards Redmond, I was once again alone. No longer lonely. Just alone. Back to singular pronouns for a while. I didn't have anyone I was yet willing to talk to about all that plural "we, us, and our" anyway. It was still too sudden. Too fresh. I just kept those memories of the beauty and tenderness of human touching to myself. Yet…I smiled all the way home.

The following several weeks were busy with the harvesting of an eight-tank crop of sixteen plants. This had to get finished before the trip to the 25th reunion in Manhattan. The cutting of the buds went smoothly and I was able to introduce the new starts to their fresh gravel beds to begin the next hydroponic cycle. Harvest is a very time-consuming cycle of sixteen-to-eighteen-hour days punctuated with entertainment from KUOW-FM radio. KUOW is the University of Washington PBS talk and news station broadcast from a portable radio on the cutting table.

The beauty of radio in this particular theatre is that it is pure audio. Your eyes and both hands are solely focused on the bud-cutting project. During this activity I preferred sitting on a Balans chair. This is a Norwegian-designed kneeling chair where you are sitting on a cushion which is at a slight angle of 60 or 70 degrees from vertical with the knees/shins supporting some of the body weight while resting on a padded knee rest in front of, and below, the buttocks cushion. This chair can relieve lower back pain caused by the many continuous hours of sitting in the same position. The big growers hire 21-year-olds to do this work. Once you've done it you will understand why. But…it is a labor of love.

After harvest, I wrote to See in California to express that I missed the new miss in my life. I thanked her for human touch and expressed my hope that it would continue when she returned. Then I packed my Dopp kit again for Kansas.

The reunion trip was a fairly relaxed affair. By the 25th reunion you're in your mid-forties and no longer competing for every scrap that falls from the conference table at the office. You've usually mellowed in your professional life and are not quite as critical of your classmates as you were at the 10th. Some of your classmates are sporting their second spouses, but who's counting? Most of the alums were still alive. I was happy. I was smiling. It was comfortable to be the bagel man and see all the old, middle-aged, grads. I had a photograph of myself, taken in front of the bagel cart, where I was posing in my work clothing with an apron. I showed this to everyone who was curious as to what I was doing for "work."

Nearly everyone just smiled and went on to another topic of conversation. Everyone, that is, except my aforementioned class-mate Sue Kesner. When Sue saw the photograph she just smiled and asked again, "No, Don, what do you really do?" It was difficult to convince Sue that I was peddling bagels on the corner of 4th Avenue and Pike Street in Seattle. She kept pressing it. The smiles never left her face. Finally I invited her to come out to the West Coast and offered her a free bagel lunch when she did come to see for herself. Sue acknowledged that offer without volunteering any firm travel plans.

My folks were also glad to see me. I was fortunate to be able to stay at home with them while I was in Manhattan. That made it a double reunion. I wasn't able to invite them to visit me in Redmond at the moment for fairly obvious reasons. They had been out to Seattle several years ago, before I broke gravel for the farm. Just one of the problems of a life in the underground economy. It does put a serious damper on your social exposure.

When I got home to Redmond, there was an anticipated and welcomed letter from See. She had a flight number, an arrival date, and a gate number about a week out. I was lucky that she traveled light. There wasn't that much luggage space in a Porsche 914. See was kind enough to phone me the day before the flight to confirm our arrangements.

I met See at the airport with a big hug and a "Welcome home." She looked refreshed. Her big smile appeared genuine. We walked through the concourse and toward the parking area. I stowed her luggage in the 914 bonnet and we exited the garage for I-405 head-

     DON McGEHE

ing to Southcenter. As we entered the freeway I inquired, "Great to have you home. Which home would you like me to head for, Mountlake Terrace or Redmond?" "Redmond," she said.

When we had last spoken, more than three weeks before, she had told me she was not happy in her 17-year, childless, marriage. She wanted to end it. She wanted out. Evidently she had made a hard decision while in California. I had not expected a decision this fast. I did feel honored. I also felt a bit scared. The ramifications of this choice would be major. At that moment, however, my joy overcame any worries about tomorrow's problems. Rather than going north to Mountlake on I-5 we drove straight through Tukwila and toward the Eastside on I-405 to Redmond.

While driving up I-405 I was feeling a bit lightheaded. When we reached the I-405 and SR 520 freeway intersection, she asked if we could stop at the old dental office. Sure. We pulled into the parking lot and See bounded into the office. I was right behind. She was having a joyous reunion with her former workmates and I was pulling out my blood-sugar test kit. I poked my finger and applied the blood to the test strip. It read like 38. Normal would have been 80 – 120. Damn, I was low.

I'd been at this dentist often enough for them to know I was a type-1 diabetic, so they always had pineapple juice on hand to boost a low blood sugar reading. One of the technicians cracked two cans and shoved them in my hands. I inhaled them both, placed my hands on the counter, and steadied myself. It took about five minutes to bring the reading back up to 80. Then I knew I was OK. This type of thing had happened to me before. I'd always been lucky and caught it in time when I'd been driving. With insulin reactions in the home that was not the case. I had hurt myself and wrecked furniture in my home before. And I would again. Stay tuned. But, up to this current writing, I've been lucky in the car.

From the dental office we drove home to the Redmond condo, toted bags upstairs and did what we could at the time to move See in. All she had at that time were her traveling clothes.

Next morning See asked if we could go up to the Mountlake house to pick up more clothes and her car. Her husband Wayne was still in California and was not expected home for more than a week. I drove her up to Mountlake Terrace and loaded up her car with clothing and personal effects that she wanted to keep with her. We then drove over to one of her girlfriend's homes and grabbed some stuff that was stashed there. She also took some time to brief this friend about what was going on currently in her life. That accomplished, we backtracked to the Redmond condo and filled up a closet or two.

The next day I wanted to wash my car. See wanted to help. We got out the bucket, hose, soap, and sponges and went to work. I was being pig-headily stupid out there on the wash pad and pointed out to See that what she was doing was definitely not the way to wash the car. Ice-cream cone to forehead…smash! Our first disagreement. And it's only day # 3 already. They should have an all-male training course for this couple-type etiquette. I, evidently, did not have that class on my schedule. How could I be so stupid? Well, McGehe, it starts when you open your mouth. The next step is the insertion of the foot, therein. Boy! You talk about a cold wind blowing across that pavement. I was getting frost-bite in July. We immediately switched to washing her car. That was the last time she ever assisted in washing my car. Singular pronouns again. That wound would take a long time to heal.

A month into the Redmond residency, See was having trouble with her car, a late model Mazda. She had a garage in Redmond which had been servicing this vehicle for several years and she took it in to that facility to have it tuned and serviced. I followed her down to the garage and drove her back because they wanted the car all day. They called to say it was ready the next day. I reversed that trip and we went to pick up the car.

Several weeks after she moved in, I asked See what she had told her husband about the separation. She said she had talked to him but was fairly vague about the details. I thought that it was totally

     Don McGehe

her business and I did not push the point. She had spent the first week back looking for a job to keep her busy and provide income. As it happened, she had made contact with a friend named John Hanscom who was setting up a new company to write software. This whole thing was being done on a shoe-string. See didn't have any software experience but she was willing to be a gal-Friday and handle phone and communications for the new firm. John was a quiet and introverted engineering type and needed an extrovert like See to be the public face of their organization.

They managed to get a small office in Bellevue, Washington near the interchange of I-405 and 130th Street. I doubted that they were paying her much but it did give her daily activity and a feeling of being a part of the business community again. I had personally met John; he was an excellent support person for her in this current situation. He listened well. Personal support of See was a long suit that John possessed, and provided freely and with a smile.

One hot week-day morning in late July there was a heavy knock on the condo door. See was at work and I was alone at the condo. The lights in the grow room had gone off for the night cycle and the grow room door was closed. Almost without thinking I opened the door. Why I opened that door, I do not know. Of course. You never ask that question until after you've already opened the door.

The man on the porch said, "My name is Wayne and I'm looking for my wife. Is she here?"

My response was, "No she's not here right now. She is at her office."

"Look, as I was coming down the stairs a second ago, I looked in the window and saw her suitcase sitting on that dresser that she took from the house before I got back."

I then said, "I'm sorry Wayne, she's not here. Can you call her at her work number?" I'm sure he was still angry but he turned around and walked back up the stairs to the upper parking lot. Her car was not here so he must have believed that she wasn't here either, even though he did see the suitcase through the window. But he obviously knew he was knocking on the correct door.

I called See at her office to tell her what happened. After I rendered the story of the surprise visit, I added, "Please call him and tell him what's up so he doesn't come back here." She indicated that she would. After See had talked to Wayne she told me that he had called the Mazda shop and asked if the car had been in there recently. They said yes it had. He then drove down there and looked at their records and got the condo address from her paperwork.

She said that she had given an explanation to Wayne, and that she didn't think he would be back. Once again I figured that that ball was now in her court and I dropped the subject. She was right. He didn't come back. They started working through the separation and filed for a divorce. It was some time in coming. These legal marital affairs are never easy. Nor are they speedy.

CHAPTER 20

THAT SUMMER OF 1984 WAS A SUMMER OF FIRSTS. IT WAS ALSO populated by a previously-unused plural possessive-pronoun. "Our" suddenly came into fashion. Our first trip to the strawberry fields in Carnation, Washington to pick strawberries at Remlinger Farms. Ten in the bucket. One in the mouth. Ten more in the bucket. One more in the mouth. At that time in my life I had not yet faced the pesticide saturation that prevailed in the strawberry industry.

In mid-July it was our first trip to the blueberry patches in Woodinville, Washington. I even created a new recipe for blueberry jam that summer, using stevia sweetener to avoid the added sugar. Street Fairs were often our weekend attraction. A favorite of See's was the University Street Fair. It was the first time she had been to the University Fair in years. It was always held on the same weekend that the Washington State Dental Convention was scheduled. While she worked in the dental office, the dental convention had taken precedence for those previous four or five years.

Our last fair to wrap up the summer was the October Salmon Festival in Issaquah, Washington. Hundreds of booths to shop at, and absolutely no extra room in the condo to put anything, so we mostly just looked a lot. The rare exception to this guideline was to find something we could eat or wear. I had a camera with me so if we found an outrageous hat I would put it on See's head, she'd smile, I'd photograph her, and replace it back on the hat stand. That's like having your cake and…well, you know the rest. Photo memory recorded. No money spent.

The fall of 1984-1985 blew in with a vengeance and dumped nearly a foot of snow in Redmond for Thanksgiving. It was one of those storms where you don't even bother to move the car for a week. The Redmond condo was right downtown. We could walk to the grocery, library, post office, and gym without use of the car. So we did. There was half a chord of dry wood in the carport. We built a fire on the hearth and made lemon tea. It was cozy. One of the advantages of having a grow room in the condo was that the 1,000 watt lights were on eighteen hours a day and kept the place quite toasty. See had been looking diligently for a new job but this storm put temporary brakes on that search.

Toward the tail end of fall in 1984, See did find another position as an office manager with a large dental firm in downtown Seattle. This was a big step up for her in her dental field. This managership did require a longer commute to the city but the Evergreen Point Floating Bridge was a direct shot into Seattle and, at the time, not a toll bridge. The big advantage in this job was the money. For the first time we were both earning good incomes. There was a societal term for this. We were now considered DINKs. Dual Income - No Kids. Earnings now exceeded expenses. Just barely.

I do not recall exactly when See's divorce became final. It was, however, sometime in 1985. We progressed through that first quarter of '85 looking forward to spring as any resident of a latitude 47-degree north climate would. Where is that first crocus blossom?

For several years in the early '80s the first outing of spring was a bicycle ride around Bainbridge Island, Washington, sponsored by the Cascade Bicycle Club. This ride was known as the Chilly Hilly. The ride was always scheduled for last weekend of February. Typically, somewhere in late February, you got one of those magic weekends with sunshine and temperatures in the low 60's. If the Chilly Hilly weekend coincided that first good weather weekend, it was a veritable stroke of luck.

Peter McRae and I would enlist all interested parties we could find, and get down to Pier 52 in Seattle early on Sunday morning to catch the Bainbridge Island Ferry. The Ferry ride would deposit us on the island in Winslow, Washington and we would cycle around the "shoreline" of Bainbridge Island. You'd think that if you followed the shoreline it would be a flat ride all the way around. You would be wrong. They didn't call it the Chilly Hilly for nothing. Being the first trip out for the season, it could be grueling. You never knew what weather you would get. Sunny, windy, rainy, and chilly were all distinct possibilities—or any possible combination of the above. In 1984 it was sunny. See stayed home. She didn't have a bike yet. She soon would.

That early spring of 1985 was the perfect time to find See a bicycle of her own. She selected and purchased one just before the tulips bloomed in the Skagit Valley near Mount Vernon, Washington. Peter McRae and I had been frequenting the Tulip Ride for years. We found that the only way to get around the Skagit Valley on weekends, when the tulips were in bloom (yearly around April 1st), was to drive to Mount Vernon and then mount our bicycles to tour the fields on two wheels. By so doing, we could zip by all the standing traffic and avoid the automobile jams in favor of strawberry jams on our scones at the roadside stands. See had not been riding long and this was a perfect introductory ride for her. The Skagit Valley ride is very nearly flat, that's why they officially call it the Skagit Flats. We had sunny, brisk weather and a good time was had by all. No injuries were reported.

The summer of 1985 was a season of decision for both See and me. We were fairly cramped in a 950 sq. ft. condo, the largest bedroom of which was being used as the indoor farm. We had one covered and one uncovered parking space for our two cars. See and I both wanted to entertain more and invite friends into our surroundings. The only people we could invite over were the absolutely trustworthy. Those were few and dear. No family members were included.

We both had solid income now. We could afford to explore the market. Buying another place would, in fact, be beneficial for the growing business. It would allow for the two-room grow operation I had originally envisioned and it would increase the plant capacity from 12 to 20, a 40% increase in volume.

We had attended the 1984 and 1985 Seattle Street of Dreams showings of new homes and learned that we might have to set our sights a bit lower than what we saw there. Those type of shows really do whet the appetite. In expensive ways. The cities we considered were Kirkland and Redmond. Even in 1985 Kirkland seemed expensive. That brought the search back to Redmond.

In late summer we went to an open house for a rambler in the English Hill subdivision of Redmond. We both liked this home better than any we had seen in our search. I scraped together enough cash for a down payment and we looked for a loan. Some, what I will call creative verification, affirmed that I was a "software engineer" with the firm run by John Hanscom, See's boss and partner from the first job she had after leaving the Redmond Dental office. I had given up the bagel business months before and that "job" would never have qualified for a home mortgage loan anyway. See and I did get the loan and moved into that home in late 1985.

This three-bedroom, two-bath, English Hill house had an open-to-the-sky hot tub on a deck off the master bedroom. This was the first time I had ever had a hot tub and we used it extensively for the first year or so that we made our home there. Later the novelty wore off, and it was expensive to heat the hot tub in the winter. This deck was completely closed off from street view so hot-tubbing or sunbathing sans suits was at the sole digression of the participant. Great house. We loved it.

The See & me combination did a lot of car camping. We spent many days in the national parks of Washington State. Mount Rainier was our favorite. Nearly all of our camping was car camping. We never got serious about back packing. Wherever we went we always stopped by rock shops and were collectors of minerals and unique stones. We did a bit of stoning as well. Product testing was an important aspect of quality control on "the farm."

 Don McGehe

We reveled in the back roads of the state and always stopped at roadside fruit stands and u-pick orchards and farms. After we had been together for a year, See bought a Subaru hatchback which rapidly became our camping vehicle of choice. The Stonehenge Monument near Goldendale, Washington became a refuge for contemplation and meditation often visited at the summer solstice. See was quite photogenic. It was a privilege to have a willing model to grace any scene I wished to photograph.

I'd never been to a world's fair. One soon came along with Expo '86 in Vancouver, B.C., Canada. See and I made reservations on a September trip and boarded a tour bus to Canada for the Expo '86 experience. It was a gorgeous weekend for weather and an outstanding presentation by our Canadian neighbors. We brought home the usual trinkets and memorabilia clothing to prove we'd been there and done that.

We were so excited about Canada, and B.C. in particular, that we went back on three more outings in the next several years. I still wear a Cowichan (First-Nation-made) wool sweater that I purchased on a trip to Nanaimo on Vancouver Island on our second trip up. The sweater is now over thirty years old and still warm and stylish—too warm, in fact, for any but the coldest of winters. The First Nation weavers left the lanolin in the wool when they were knitted and the sweaters are therefore water repellent and toasty warm.

The city of Vancouver, on mainland British Columbia, is a very cosmopolitan city, but I found rural B.C. to be like rural America back in the 1950s when I was ten years old with the enthusiasm to run everywhere and see everything before it changed or rusted away on you. The farms look like they were sprouted in Missouri and blown northwest into B.C. intact. The Case and John Deere tractors in the yards have that repainted look of yesteryear's models. The red Maple Leaf flags flying from their covered porches, around the first of July, are the only giveaways that would contradict the "Made in USA 50 years ago" feeling.

One of the qualities that I experienced in my relationship with See was her keen and perceptive sense in the giving of gifts. If I mentioned something that I needed or wanted when I was with her, that item would appear at the next gift giving occasion. When these gifts appeared, they were invariably the finest of quality in that item category available. These gifts seemed to always have long term staying power. Several of them are still with me, in active daily use, thirty-three years after they were received. I did not understand how she did it, at the time, but one of her talents was that she was an active and very careful listener. She knew what I was wishing for and remembered. I was impressed by this quality.

Christmas of 1985 was a memorable holiday for See and me. We were both working at the time. The couple finances were good. We left town to spend the weekend at her folks' empty vacation home on the Olympic Peninsula in Sequim, Washington. At the time I had a friend and customer who was in the jewelry business. This friend had connections in the wholesale diamond business in downtown Seattle.

I wanted to get a pair of diamond stud ear-rings for See for Christmas and this connection was able to sell me two 1/2 carat stones which my friend John Profit had mounted for this gift. When See opened that package on Christmas morning I experienced the most profound and surprising emotional expression from her that I had ever witnessed from any gift giving experience. The emotion went from her eyes on the studs, up through her brain, down into the heart touching some soul fibers on the way back up through the cerebral cortex and when her eyes finally met mine, seconds later, her jaw dropped perceptively in astonishment and she was speechless for just a moment. The astonishment soon dissolved into an amazing smile of thanks and gratitude. I don't recall any words; only that facial expression of thanks and joy. I suddenly felt that I had found the secret to gift-giving. Maybe they really are, as the advertising campaign would lead you to believe, a girl's best friend. Or, perhaps, they can be a symbol signifying movement toward a stronger or more lasting relationship. They are only a symbol, though. Not the real thing.

 Don McGehe

It wasn't until 20 years after this memorable Christmas that I finally understood the connections between See and gifts. In a Half Price Books store, one day in 2005, I came across the Dr. Gary Chapman book "The Five Languages of Love." Chapman separates love expressions into five separate "languages" or categories. They are 1) Words of Affirmation, 2) Quality Time, 3) Receiving Gifts, 4) Acts of Service, and 5) Physical Touch. For See, love was all about giving and receiving gifts. Finally I understood this.

I then took the test presented in the book myself. For me the aspects that signified love were a toss-up between quality time and acts of service. If you are in a couple-bond, and have any questions, at all, about where your partners love priorities might lie, I would highly recommend becoming familiar with Chapman's book and the five languages he describes. It could save your relationship. If not save the relationship, it might show you where you just screwed it up. Hind-sight can also be an effective learning experience.

One of the reasons I enjoyed traveling and getting away with See was that when we were away from town the constant paranoia that I often felt surrounding me in the city would ease up, and we could laugh and have fun. Play with each other. Smile and romp. Granted, all that paranoia was self-inflicted, nonetheless, I still felt it. It was there. You never knew if, when, or where the law might want to fight you. They are everywhere. But, on the road, you can usually disappear into that stream of vacation traffic. Don't break the speed limit or run the light and you are usually OK.

I could always walk away from the farm, especially in mid-week, for three or four days without problems. Agriculture has a way of continuing to grow while you're gone. But not for extensive periods of time. While See was employed, our getting away was dependent on her work schedule. It was tough to travel when she had the office manager position in the Seattle dental office.

Weekends were not free either. Each Saturday or Sunday I would need to change the water in the tanks at the farm and refill the nutrient solution reservoir with fresh fertilizer. If we wanted to be gone for the weekend, I could cheat and schedule this task for Friday or Monday. It was about a three-or-four-hour job.

On a weekend getaway that year at her folks' vacation home in Sequim, Washington, See told me of a dream she'd just had. She'd often used the dream state to get a conception of what her future held. In this particular dream she told me that she got the image that our relationship was only a temporary one. She saw that the friendship might always be a strong and accepting one, but the togetherness had a more limited timing. I listened. I didn't want to believe this vision she was expressing. That was not how I felt at the time. When she related it, I simply put it out of my mind and hoped that she would soon see that it was only a dream and not a living reality. I had never had strong direct-life correlations with my dreams. In that respect we were quite different.

It took a decent amount of money each month to keep us above board. I had two mortgages, maintenance fees on the condo, and utilities on both properties to pay, plus insurance. The cash flow ebbed, and often stopped, so it was necessary to space out capital spending to occur only after harvest. I recall making a two-pound delivery to Portland one time and having to drive down there on literally bald tires on the Porsche. I couldn't afford to buy the new tires until after the sale. I drove down and back in the far right hand lane of I-5, at 55 MPH, with the 18-wheelers, all the way. At 55 I wouldn't be stopped for speeding. I could have handled one flat tire. Two would have been disaster. The trip was completed with no flats. I bought new Pirellis for all four wheels the next day.

In the underground economy few records are kept. In the 1980s the one necessary list was your address book with phone numbers. The address book was the first thing the cops grabbed in a bust. Now it is the cell phone. It was difficult to do without the address book. With the passage of time any grower gets to know many fellow entrepreneurs and usually refers to them by nick-names or some kind of descriptive moniker. I came to be known as "The Doctor."

 DON MCGEHE

I had several close friends with whom I would do business directly. I attempted to keep very few of these. I was, after all, a grower/producer and wanted to keep out of the distribution chain as much as possible. It was safer that way. The fewer folks who knew my name, the better. I did develop two major distributer/wholesalers who would buy by the pound and cut the product into smaller packages (ounce, ½ ounce, ¼ ounce) for further distribution.

The down-market consumer would often ask what the source of the product was, so as to be clear in their own mind the quality of the product they were purchasing. My major distributor would always say that the product came from "The Doctor," indicating that it was an Rx prescription of very high quality. Once he mentioned that source, no more questions were usually asked. So, as a reference source, "The Doctor" stuck.

CHAPTER 21

After See and I moved to the English Hill rambler, it was rare that anyone would come to the condo on business. And I could count on one hand the folks who dropped by the English Hill house. Less traffic kept neighbors from asking questions about activity on the block. That was the "how" part of the business question. The why was a much longer story.

My history of the war on drugs, waged in the United States of America in the past century, was gleaned from the research written in the 2015 book "Chasing the Scream – The First and Last Days of the War On Drugs" by Johann Hari. The war on drugs started in 1930 when Harry Jacob Anslinger was appointed the founding Commissioner of the U.S. Treasury's Federal Bureau of Narcotics which he ran until 1962. When Prohibition ended in the United States, with the passage of the 21st Amendment to the Constitution in 1933, the government suddenly found itself with about 90 alcohol revenue agents who were out of work. Anslinger purloined most of these agents and reemployed them as narcotic agents in the new war on drugs he was creating. Throughout his 32-year career as the first narcotic drug czar his primary purpose was to categorize, demonize, and propagandize black, brown, and white-skinned Americans who were finding relief from pain and the pressures of life through the use of drugs, into a persecuted class of pseudo-citizens upon which he could blame all the supposed ills of killer weed and cocaine use.

From a Wikipedia posting on Harry Anslinger, I quote the following. "Appointed by (Treasury) department Secretary Andrew W.

Don McGehe

Mellon, his wife's uncle, Anslinger was given a budget of $100,000 and turned loose. Prior to the end of alcohol prohibition, Anslinger had claimed that cannabis was not a problem, did not harm people, and "there is no more absurd fallacy" than the idea it makes people violent. His critics argue he shifted, not due to objective evidence, but self-interest due to the obsolescence of the Department of Prohibition he headed when alcohol prohibition ceased - campaigning for a new Prohibition against its use. Anslinger collected dubious anecdotes of marijuana causing crime and violence, and ignored contrary evidence such as doctor Walter Bromberg, who pointed out that substance abuse and crime are heavily confounded and that none of a group of 2,216 criminal convictions he examined were clearly done under marijuana's influence, or a discussion forwarded to him by the American Medical Association in which 29 of 30 pharmacists & drug industry representatives objected to his proposals to ban marijuana. One such statement claimed that the proposal was "Absolute rot. It is not necessary. I have never known of its misuse.", although only the single dissenter (who noted he had once encountered a doctor who had been addicted to marijuana) was preserved in Bureau files."

Continuing from Wikipedia, "Anslinger sought and ultimately received, as head of the Federal Bureau of Narcotics, an increase of reports about smoking of marijuana in 1936 that continued to spread at an accelerated pace in 1937. Before, smoking of marijuana had been relatively slight and confined to the Southwest, particularly along the Mexican border.

The Bureau first prepared a legislative plan to seek from Congress a new law that would place marijuana and its distribution directly under federal control. Second, Anslinger ran a campaign against marijuana on radio and at major forums. His view was clear, ideological and judgmental:

By the tons it is coming into this country — the deadly, dreadful poison that racks and tears not only the body, but the very heart and soul of every human being who once becomes a slave to it in any of its cruel and devastating forms…. Marihuana is a short cut to the insane asylum. Smoke marihuana cigarettes for a month and what was once your brain will be nothing but a storehouse of horrid specters. Hasheesh makes a murderer who kills for the love of killing out of the mildest mannered man who ever laughed at the idea that any habit could ever get him…"

Continuing from Wikipedia, "In the 1930s Anslinger's articles often contained racial themes in his anti-marijuana campaign: Colored students at the Univ. of Minn. partying with (white) female students, smoking [marijuana] and getting their sympathy with stories of racial persecution. [Result: pregnancy.] Two Negros took a girl fourteen years old and kept her for two days under the influence of hemp. Upon recovery she was found to be suffering from syphilis. Reefer makes darkies think they're as good as white men."

Again from Wikipedia: "When Anslinger was interviewed in 1954 about drug abuse, however, he mentioned nothing about race or sex. In his book "The Protectors" (1964), Anslinger has a chapter called "Jazz and Junk Don't Mix" about black jazz musicians Billie Holiday (who he had handcuffed on her death bed due to suspicion of drug use and possession) and Charlie Parker, who both died after years of illegal heroin and alcohol abuse:

Jazz entertainers are neither fish nor fowl. They do not get the million-dollar protection Hollywood and Broadway can afford for their stars who have become addicted – and there are many more than will ever be revealed. Perhaps this is because jazz, once considered a decadent kind of music, has only token respectability. Jazz grew up next door to crime, so to speak. Clubs of dubious reputation were, for a long time, the only places where it could be heard. But the times bring changes, and as Billie Holiday was a victim of time and change, so too was Charlie Parker, a man whose music, like Billie's, is still widely imitated. Most musicians credit Parker among others as spearheading what is called modern jazz."

Anslinger hoped to orchestrate a nationwide dragnet of jazz musicians and kept a file called "Marijuana and Musicians."

  Don McGehe

Continuing from Wikipedia, "Critics of Anslinger believe the campaign against marijuana had a hidden agenda. For example, the E. I. DuPont De Nemours And Company industrial firm, petrochemical interests, and William Randolph Hearst conspired together to create the highly sensational anti-marijuana campaign to eliminate hemp as an industrial competitor to synthetic materials. However, the DuPont Company and industrial historians have disputed this link between development of nylon and changes in the laws for hemp (marijuana); the success for nylon was huge from start. It was not until 1934, and the fourth year in office, that Anslinger considered marijuana to be a serious threat to American society (Wallace Carothers first synthesized nylon on February 28, 1935). The League of Nations had already implemented restrictions for marijuana in the beginning of the 1930s and restrictions started in many states in the U.S years before Anslinger was appointed. Both president Franklin D. Roosevelt and his attorney general publicly supported this development in 1935. Anslinger was part of a larger movement aimed at alarming the public as part of the government's broader push to outlaw all recreational drugs.

The La Guardia Committee, promoted in 1939 by New York Mayor Fiorello La Guardia, was the first in-depth study into the effects of smoking marijuana. It systematically contradicted claims made by the U.S. Treasury Department that smoking marijuana resulted in insanity, and determined that '"the practice of smoking marihuana does not lead to addiction in the medical sense of the word." Released in 1944, the report infuriated Anslinger, who was campaigning against marijuana, and he condemned it as unscientific."

With his propaganda Anslinger poisoned the politicians and perverted the law books of the American Nation from the 1930s through 2012. Those of us who experienced the 60s knew this "killer weed" myth was lies and bullshit. Yet, through the 20th century, the politicians continued to use Anslinger's lies to drive race and age divisions into the electorate in the name of "Law and Order," where marijuana was concerned. We live in a nation where, if 30% of the registered voters participate in any election, it is considered a fantastic turnout. Also, the older citizens were more likely to be the ones who voted. That being the reality, it was obvious that many years needed to flow into the future while the tainted generations who still believed Anslinger's lies were passing through the mortuaries of America.

Finally the children of the 60s and beyond, figured out it was important to go to the polls and vote. The pro-marijuana dominos began to fall first in Colorado in 2012. Washington State followed in the next election cycle. The band wagon then rolled on through Oregon, Nevada, Washington D.C., Alaska, California, Massachusetts, and Maine for legal recreational use. Sixteen other states were passing laws permitting medical use of cannabis in the meantime.

The Baby Boom generation—the children of the 60s—were now going to the polls to voice their choice. The message was heard. Cannabis is not, and should no longer be considered, a schedule 1 drug in the United States of America. By the end of the summer in 2018 Canada's provinces and territories had all legalized marijuana. Could the politicians in our nation's capitol be the next to get this message? How long will that take?

When I started farming in the 80s I could not envision the sea change in American opinion on cannabis that was to explode in 2012. Change, in America, occurs from the bottom up, not the top down. The successful politicians in the USA are those who can strategically sense a change in the public's attitude, alter their political tactics to incorporate that change, and manage to cut in line in front of the parade, then lead their constituents with a smile. We…make it happen. It is exactly as they are wont to say in Chicago. Vote early. Vote often.

In the 80s weed was illegal. So…why in the hell pursue it? Satirically speaking, I liked to say it was for the same reasons you raise kids: fun and profit. But it was more than that. The business was a sole proprietorship. I loved working by, and for, myself. I had the freedom to succeed, or to fail, on my own. That is entrepreneurship. The only Board-of-Directors I had to report to was my own wallet. I was no longer stifled by the corporation. I was the corporation.

But the biggest reason I enjoyed it was that I had finally found something that I could do by myself that I was really good at. My distributors called me "The Doctor" because the product was of absolute premium quality and it was in demand. There were no dissatisfied customers. I have had a lot of jobs in my lifetime. If someone were to ask me what job I enjoyed most, the answer would be farming.

Whatever business you're in, it always runs on supply and demand. Cannabis is no different. The demand was constant. Since there was no legal supply, the supply side of the business equation was filled by entrepreneurial effort. Wherever a demand for product occurs, that demand will find a supply. That is the fundamental law of business.

In 1984 the wholesale price (in quantity) for a pound of top quality cannabis in Seattle was $3,000.00. We often called it gold. We often compared it to gold. In order to make the comparison between the prices of gold and weed it is necessary to understand that there is a difference in the weight standards involved in this comparison. Gold is weighed in Troy ounces @ 31.1 grams per ounce. That is the Troy ounce weight. All other commodities, like cannabis and sugar (except silver and gems), are weighed @ 28.35 grams per ounce for what is referred to as the "avoirdupois" ounce.

In 1984, the high price for gold was $12,653.00 per 16-ounce pound, and the low was $9,431.00. The pound of gold weighed 497.6 grams. A pound of weed would have weighed only 453.6 grams. This is due to the difference in weight standards. Ignoring the confusion with the weight standards, the pound of weed was worth approximately one quarter the price of gold at its high and one third the price of gold at its lowest value for the year. As a grower, it almost made you feel like Rumpelstiltskin.

In the winter of 1986-87, See became concerned about what she called anger which she said was showing up in my personality. I would often demonstrate this by slamming cupboard doors in the kitchen. She would ask me why I was angry and I would deny any anger. To this day I can still not identify the source or cause of the anger. I have never hit See. I never would. She wasn't worried about that.

I have not hit a woman since junior high school when I swatted at the posterior of Diette Fair while she was walking up the aisle on the band bus. I don't know why I did that. Miss Fair countered with a wicked right, full hand slap, to my cheek. I was stunned. I was also educated that day. As a result of that learning experience, I have never hit another woman in my lifetime.

Since I had no idea what the source of this anger was, See suggested that I see a psychiatrist. My old school learning, from growing up in the midwest, told me that if I saw a psychiatrist that must mean that I was crazy. I knew I wasn't crazy. Yet, the anger was still there. The cupboard doors still kept slamming. But I never slammed the cupboard doors when I was alone. Ergo, it must have been done for the effect that the slam would have on others.

In the spring of 1987 I finally gave in and agreed to see a shrink. I asked my friend Peter McRae if he knew of one. He gave me a referral to an office in Bellevue. I called the shrink and made an appointment for two months out. He was a busy guy.

The day of the appointment I shoved a wad of cash in my Levi's and drove to Bellevue. After filling out what seemed like reams of paperwork he finally saw me. He asked if I had insurance. I said no. The next question was how I intended to pay for the services? I told him I preferred to pay in cash because I was employed in the underground economy.

I figured that if I was to get anything out of this experience I needed to be honest with my psychiatrist. He found this employment information highly offensive and asked me to leave his office. He was unwilling to treat me. So much for being honest with your

     DON McGEHE

psychiatrist. Based on experience, that evidently didn't work. I paid him $85.00 for his time and left. Yes…it was in cash. He did accept it.

I then let a month or two go by while finding another shrink. By this time it was summer. I found a female psychiatrist this next time and went to an initial interview at her Bellevue office. (It seemed that all the shrinks had offices in Bellevue. If you have ever lived there you might understand why.) This time I put some cash into my checking account and wrote her a check. In the "Employed by _______" space I just wrote "self." We had a comfortable initial conversation and I thought we might end up having a rewarding relationship.

The next Saturday afternoon, out on the deck at the English Hill rambler, I was replanting a jade that was getting root-bound when See came out and sat down for a talk. She indicated that she was not having much fun at her job managing the Seattle dental office and asked if I minded if she quit working for them. She'd been working in this job for nearly two years. I picked up my jaw off the deck, thought a minute, and asked what alternative she had in mind for work? She said she did not have any firm plans but that she wanted to take some time off.

We had been doing rather well in our financial life with two incomes. I quickly saw that with one less income things were going to be very tight. She seemed to have her mind made up, however, and I felt that if we tightened up that we could make it. The problem was that in the underground economy the cash came in at unpredictable times and wasn't steady like a pay check from an employer.

The first thing to go was the psychiatrist. That was a load off my mind. I was never that enthusiastic about seeing the shrink in the first place. See understood and said nothing. We simply wouldn't have the money for counseling. That old midwest logic about only the crazy people seeing the psychiatrists was reinforced in my mind.

Sometime in 1985 See's divorce became final. In the settlement she took over ownership of one of the properties split off from that dissolution. This was a home in the Finn Hill section of King County which eventually became incorporated into Kirkland, Washington. I do not recall at this time if there was a mortgage on the home or not. It seems that there must have been one, but I left the running of that asset completely up to See. She rented the house out to three friends of hers who were part of a Native American conscientiousness group she had become associated with. These folks were not the most regular rent payers she could have found. Her friendship with them disinclined her to press too hard for the rent regularity either. She was not a particularly diligent landlord.

In the fall of 1987 See's finances took a serious turn south. I discovered that she was paying significant interest on balances on three separate credit cards. She had been hiding these debts by paying interest only on past due balances for months. She'd been feeding her gift-giving-for-love impulses for years by putting all the gifts on credit cards. Maybe Paul McCartney had it right when he sang "Can't buy me love." Those interest penalties were eating her alive. I offered to pay off the credit cards to eliminate the interest penalties and See accepted that offer. We paid off nearly ten grand and froze the cards. She said she'd pay me back.

In the spring of '88 See sold her car to get rid of even more debt, and the car payment. We'd now sold the vehicle we used for our road trips. That did work out, however. We had no cash to spend for road trips anyway. See was fortunate to have a friend in Edmonds who could provide her with four days of work each month. I'd drive her to the Totem Lake Park-'N-Ride on those days to catch the bus, and pick her up in the evening when she returned. Sometimes we were so broke we couldn't even afford to pay attention. But somehow we made it work.

The winter of 1988-1989 was a cold challenge for See and me. Our finances were so tight that winter that we closed off half the house with plastic sheeting to avoid heating the entire place. The half we closed off included—wouldn't you guess—the fire place. Go figure. If we'd had one of the weed grow rooms in the English

     DON MCGEHE

Hill house that year we could have heated the whole house with it. Come spring the crop cycle was good enough to bail us out of most of the cash flow problems.

One day that spring I met with my prime distributor and his wife at the condo. I was expecting them and saw them drive up and park in my reserved parking spot opposite the sliding glass doors overlooking the parking lot. As he got out of the car he made an arm gesture like he was smelling something strong and he had a big smile on his face. When he got inside he said that there was a very strong odor like skunk marijuana in bloom wafting out of the condo and down to the parking lot. There was a crop in the large room that was just about ready to harvest. That was the smell.

I'd always left the sliding glass door open about 18 inches (this was on the second floor balcony) to allow cool air from outside to flow into the condo and replace the hot air that was convecting out off the crop. There wasn't much I could do about it. The place could not be closed up. It would just get too hot in there. I just hoped that no one knew what they were smelling and would ignore it. Good luck, McGehe.

In January of 1989 See decided to sell her Finn Hill house and she put it on the market. It had not been a very successful rental and she wanted to be rid of it. She needed the proceeds from that sale as well. She'd been out of work for nearly two years. The real estate market wasn't great but it was acceptable. It took over a month but she finally got an offer that she was willing to accept. The closing was of short duration and after that she gave me a check for the money we'd used to pay off her credit cards.

The three friends who were the original renters of See's Finn Hill house after the divorce, had since moved over to Vashon Island, Washington. They'd purchased a resale home on this island in Puget Sound. With the financial proceeds of the Finn Hill house, See decided that she would like to move to Vashon Island, get a job there, and live on her own. Even though we had used her employment income to qualify for the mortgage on the English Hill house, See had contributed almost nothing towards the financial support of that mortgage.

Her desire to move to Vashon wasn't good news for me. It meant separation. That was the first step in making the dream that she had had that night in Sequim a reality. She did leave everything except necessary spring clothing at English Hill. She wasn't totally gone. You can't take body and soul and walk out of a relationship, while leaving only your material possessions there, however, and not change the relationship by 180 degrees.

My camp site was now in Redmond. I wasn't ready to pull up the tent pegs and move. I did endeavor to acknowledge her need for independence. I'd walked out on relationships before. Several times. I understood the need to feel free from financial and emotional entrapment. It wasn't pretty. Life often isn't. This was life.

With understanding, rather than anger, I was able to accept the transition and work to make it a success for both of us. And yes…I did hurt. When the handwriting is already on the wall you don't need to test for fingerprints. Yankee and I would now be the sole residents of our English Hill home. Metamorphosis. Again.

In April See's journey to Vashon Island was complete. See tried several job opportunities before she connected with the owner of a second-hand store in Vashon Center. This proprietor was able to offer not only a job but also boarding in the proprietor's own home on the east shore of the island. See was set.

May was a good month for Yankee and me. The weather was unusually fair for a May in Redmond. One Monday in late May my morning route took me on my normal, once-a-fortnight, trip to the "air" store where I swapped out my two empty CO_2 cylinders for new full ones. The next stop was to the condo to check the farm. On the way into the parking lot I noticed a gray panel van parked in the auxiliary parking space of my neighbor Mike LaGris.

That looked odd. I did not recognize it as really belonging there. I opened the boot of the 914 and pulled the two aluminum CO_2 canisters out, shut the boot lid, and carried the canisters up one floor to the condo. Everything at the farm looked good. I then jumped back into the Porsche and drove to the gym for a workout.

　　Don McGehe

That grey van would later come back to haunt me. I found out that it was a video equipped, Redmond Police narcotics undercover van filming evidence on me.

Storm clouds were now gathering over an ominous gray horizon for June 1989 (that 1989 to 1998 time span is covered in Part 1 of this Memoir).

NEW MILLENNIUM

September 1998–January 2008

CHAPTER 22

The year 1998 marked my transition from Aero Rent-A-Car to Safeco Mutual Funds. I was forced to surrender my previously-accustomed 72-hour work week for a much calmer 37 ½ hour on-the-job schedule. Safeco also paid the health insurance premium for their work force. Aero had not. My commute to the office was also reduced to a twenty-block drive, across the flats, to the far hill that buttressed my Sammamish Valley on the west.

Safeco hired me as a 57-year-old Mutual Fund Customer Service Representative. I was later told that I didn't look that old. They did not require you to reveal your age until you were already on the payroll. All three interviews were with female managers. Safeco was a very stable, old line, Seattle company. It appeared that I could be with this organization until retirement.

I was now in the very exciting field of mutual fund investing. I was to become a telephone representative taking calls from Safeco customers who were interested in buying, selling, and trading mutual fund securities to enhance their personal stock portfolios. The NYSE stock market, with which these funds dealt, was a dynamically fluid animal whose daily gyrations captivated American investors and created a constantly stimulating work environment.

It gave me a real charge to just get into work each morning. You never knew what market news would be coming down across the wire on any given day. The stock market is driven by change. Change is the essence of life. How you handle that change dictates your future. I was ready. I was excited.

Training for this job involved two months of classroom instruction and one-on-one training with successful phone reps. The culmination of the training was the passing of the tests that resulted in the awarding of the Series 6 Securities License from the FINRA (Financial Industry Regulatory Authority) and the Series 63 License from NASAA (North American Securities Administrators Association).

One of the requirements for the Series 6 License was to appear at the Redmond Police Department to be finger printed so that the prints could be submitted to the NASD (National Association of Securities Dealers) in their check for previous criminal records. I knew where the place was. I'd been there twice before. The first time was to be booked for felony manufacturing of a controlled substance (to wit marijuana). The second time was to buy back my Porsche from the Narc Squad who had purloined it three years earlier to use in busting other growers and users of the nefarious weed.

While at the RPD, I kept my eyes open for the two officers who had portrayed the coveted rolls of "good cop" and "bad cop" in my 1989 bust production. Neither were on duty that morning. Fortunately. And, true to his word, Judge Wesley had expunged the record. No felony entries were found.

I had earned the privilege to have the felony vacated by 100 percent completion of my sentence requirements, paying off all monetary obligations to the courts, having no criminal violations for five years, and a $200.00 check to my lawyer. Those five years were essential. The indispensable key in my societal rehabilitation was that first job. Without the benevolent co-operation of the Hollenbeck family at Aero Rent-A-Car, I would have been on the streets.

To live in American society requires money. To have money, and live lawfully, it takes a job. That's why that first job was so vital. The problem in the American justice system is that it is focused on punishment, not on justice and rehabilitation. Ours is a class society. Who wants to hire a felon? Few do. That first job gave me an opportunity to clean up my record and move on without the felony bulls-eye painted on my back. Many are not so lucky. This stigma against hiring felons is softening. Very, very slowly.

1998 was a propitious time to begin work with the Safeco Corporation. Safeco spent multi-millions of dollars to secure the naming rights to the new ball park that would display the Seattle Mariners MLB talents (or lack thereof) for the next 20 years. Safeco Field opened to the world on July 15th, 1999. Company employees had several pre-opening opportunities to scout out the confines of this new park. Every season offered us a "Safeco Day" at the ball park where free tickets were given to corporate employees. I could take three friends along on these outings. Few people refused these offers.

In 2001 I even won in a lottery drawing, among employees, and Peter McRae and I (with 20 others) were guests of the company president in the Safeco Box down in the Sodo district for a Red Sox game. Sodo stood for "south of the Dome" (Settle's King Dome covered stadium which was demolished March 26, 2000, for the erection of the new Seattle Seahawk CenturyLink Field). The Red Sox won one that day. We were still treated like royalty in the Safeco box.

Nineteen Hundred Ninety-Nine was an inter-wrist-ing year. Especially so for my left wrist. I managed to break that same wrist twice in the same year. The first time was on a Saturday morning in February. I had crawled out of bed with high blood sugar, taken a strong shot of insulin (including extra Humilog, fast acting insulin, to knock down the high blood sugar reading), and then loaded a batch of dirty clothes into the clothes washer. I'd then tried to straighten up the kitchen and clean the counter tops. Next the washer was finished and the clothes needed to be taken out and dumped into the drier. By the time I got around to poaching my three eggs for breakfast, I could feel the insulin taking effect and I suddenly recognized that there was a freight-train of Humilog insulin charging up my blood stream through my heart and toward my brain. I had waited far too long to eat. I was sweating profusely and doing my best to down those eggs.

At this point I should have reached for the orange juice. The insulin, however, had already attacked my brain. It was blocking those brain logic circuits which should have instinctively led me to grab the OJ first. I managed to get the eggs down but there are few quick calories in eggs. They are mostly protein. Protein doesn't slow down freight-trains a bit. Fructose does.

I was now in panic mode. When the Humilog begins to attack the brain it always goes for the circuits that control the motor neurons that fire the muscles in the arms, wrists, and legs. I become a spastic being, incapable of controlling the motions of those arms and legs. I ran into furniture, flailed at walls, fell down and writhed on the floor in uncontrollable spastic fits. During this period of time I totally lost consciousness.

When I regained my awareness, I noticed that two hours had passed. I was in a rumpled mess in the front hallway of the condo. In trying to get up I noticed that my left wrist and hand were sticking out at an odd angle toward the wall. I didn't feel any pain because I was still in shock.

Even though there was no bone poking through the skin I knew the wrist was broken. I managed to make it out on the balcony to get some fresh air. There I saw my next door neighbor Mike who was out near his car with his two children. I asked Mike if he could drive me to the emergency clinic at Virginia Mason East. He said he could but it would be a half hour before he could get to that. Fine. I was still in shock. I could wait. I would be in Mike's care now. On his schedule.

When I finally got to a care center, they x-rayed and straightened the wrist, wrapped it in a cloth wrap with ace bandages, gave me an Rx for some painkiller pills, and sent me home. Their instructions were to visit the downtown Seattle clinic the following week, after the swelling had gone down, to be fitted for a cast.

The cast went on a week later. They even gave me a choice of the color. I chose red. It's always been my favorite color. That cast was on for six weeks. During that time I had to go downtown and get X-rays taken to assure proper healing.

     DON MCGEHE

One day, as I was seated in the waiting room of the X-ray department for my wrist to be shot, I had the opportunity to sit next to a lady who had both wrists broken and was wearing two casts. After we chatted for a while I suddenly realized how lucky I had been with my own break. Not only was my wrist break on my "off" hand (I am right handed and the break was on the left wrist) but I had only the one break.

This lady sitting next to me told me that because she had broken both wrists, she required a constant care giver: her mother. She confided that she couldn't even go to the rest room without her care mother in attendance. Whether it was a number 1 visit or a number 2 visit, it made no difference. A care giver was still required to perform the wiping function. Heaven forbid a bit of diarrhea should introduce itself into the proceedings. I was suddenly humbled. Deeply humbled. I was also very appreciative of my own present condition.

The next November; same insulin reaction; same wrist. This second one wasn't so bad though. No clean break this time, only a crack. This time I got a shorty cast. Now I chose a different color. I liked purple too. You'd think I'd learn, wouldn't you?

Irrespective of the broken wrists, those first eighteen months on this new job went by very quickly. By the end of 1999 there was much concern in the world wide business community about the "millennium problem." This all revolved around the practice, for years in computer programming systems design, of using only a two-digit field for "year" in company records. With the approach of the new century, there was a question as to whether the computers could tell the difference between century 1900 dates and those in the 2000s. This precipitated a mad scramble to change all the computer code to update that date field to four digits (so that 1901 could be differentiated from 2001 and not be represented with just "01"—which would lead to chaos).

Having read the 1997 Stephen Jay Gould book "Questioning The Millennium," I was prepped for the intricacies of interpreting the Gregorian calendar. It's a mess. Always has been. The 60 years of inflexible computer coding conventions were just a small piece of the puzzle. We only change centuries every hundred years; human lifespans seldom last that long.

So…it is now a new ball game for over 6 billion people. Safeco was anticipating the possibilities of chaos on January 1st, 2000. The corporation felt that it had its programming in order. It wasn't sure everyone else did. The news outlets (both real and fake) were harbingers of ill will, spreading warnings of this chaos, in the fourth quarter of 1999, at every opportunity.

Safeco Mutual Funds was offering double-time-and-one-half pay for anyone who was willing to come into work on January 1st. I volunteered. For years I had been going to bed on New Year's Eve at 10:00 pm anyway. Since I was born in the Central Time Zone, my New Year started at midnight in Manhattan, Kansas. (Midnight in Manhattan. Sounds like a good title for a Woody Allan movie.) In the week leading up to the yearend I was amused to see otherwise-sane hordes of shoppers loading up roller-carts with case upon case of canned goods at Costco, and wheeling them out to their SUVs. Was this fear of the New Millennium?

On New Year's Day at 6:00 am, we volunteers were at our phones wearing our custom printed black "Team 01-01-00" t-shirts awaiting the calls. Very few calls came. The NYSE was closed. The NASDAQ was closed. The nation was hung over. It was more like an Easter Sunrise Service than chaos.

Now that the calendar had flipped there was hardly a whimper. Hallelujah. Praise the Lord. By 11:00 am, management announced that we would be paid for a full eight-hour shift, at double-time-and-one-half, and asked us to go home and enjoy the remainder of the day with our families. I'd volunteer to do that every day. Thank you.

Costco stores were closed on New Year's Day. On January second, I went to my local Costco to shop. I smiled once again at the long queues of customers lined up in front of the returns counter,

 DON MCGEHE

pushing their roller-carts full of case upon case of unused canned goods. I wished them all Happy New Fear.

Summers, and the two shoulder seasons of spring and fall, now offered me travel time with this new job schedule. I now had paid vacation. I was still attracted to my old haunts in the Owens Valley of California with Rick Ferens on a yearly basis. Another trip that I enjoyed was a back-packing triangle trip.

I left the mini-van at the north end of Ozette Lake, in the parking lot at the Olympic National Park Ranger Station. From there you can back pack the boardwalk down to Sand Point Beach to camp the first night. The second day is a walk up the Pacific Ocean beach in the National Wildlife Refuge to Cape Alava. This cape marks the western-most point of longitude in the lower 48 states.

The second night camp is in the tent sites at Cape Alava with its abundant assortment of raccoons and the occasional bear. From Cape Alava there is another boardwalk back to the starting point of the triangle at the Lake Ozette Ranger Station. This is a "carry your own water" excursion. The photography is spectacular.

At night you can hear the barking of the sea lions who live on the outer rock islands in the protected Wildlife Refuge. Campers are urged to keep all foodstuffs run up in elevated bear boxes in the trees to make sure you have something to eat next morning. If you leave it on the ground, the bears and raccoons get fed. It is, after all, their home. They do get hungry.

Just north of Cape Alava is the Ozette Indian Reservation. This is an archaeological and antiquity historical site. The Ozette village, at this site, was destroyed by a tsunami, and buried in layers of mud in the year 1700. The inundation was so sudden and complete that the entire village was preserved in situ by the mud and has been excavated with artifacts preserved in the Makah Tribal Museum three miles north (as the raven flies) in Neah Bay, Washington. The date for the tsunami was only discovered by looking up the records for the tidal wave, created by the tsunami, that traveled the north Pacific and struck Japan. The Japanese kept records.

Some minor excitement occurred in our Safeco office on the morning of February 28, 2001. We were taking calls, which was typical at about 10:54 any morning, when the building suddenly started to shake violently. I had been in Southern California and Washington long enough to recognize an earthquake when I felt one. This was one. A major one. An associate and I had been speaking by phone with a mutual funds client at the time.

We were wearing headsets connected to the phone by a hard wire. We both immediately dropped to our knees, pushed back our chairs, and collapsed under the desk of the cubicle. The shaking continued for a little less than a minute. Because we were on headsets, we were able to continue the conversation with the client. We apologized to the caller and explained that we were having an earthquake.

When you are talking to someone from across a continent that kind of information is important to share. We had call records on the top of the desk and knew the caller's return phone number so we asked permission to call them back the following day. The caller understood and wished us luck.

When the shaking halted we emerged from under our desk and looked around. Everyone had that "Wow…did you feel that" look on their faces. Eyes were wide and mouths agape. No one we could see was hurt. Everyone expressed surprise.

There were several cracks in one wall but no major damage to the building. This building had been built only four years earlier. It was fairly new construction. There was a public address system announcement that we should "Please exit the building. Assemble in the parking area. Maintain a physical distance of at least 25 feet away from the structure." We were eager to follow those instructions and left with all due haste.

The first thing that I saw in the parking lot was that everyone who had a cell phone yanked it out of their pocket and made that obligatory call to their "significant other." "Are you OK?" "Yeah, I'm OK." There's just something about a natural catastrophe that encourages us to share it. I had no cell phone. I had no significant other to call anyway.

 Don McGehe

I don't smoke so I didn't light up a cigarette. I just stood there in the pale February sunshine and appreciated the fact that I was out in the open, away from any falling gargoyles. We were out there for half an hour. Finally the address system called us back in to retrieve our personal effects and go home. The building was fine. Next morning we were back to work and taking calls again.

We had survived the Nisqually earthquake. The quake had originated from a fault that was deep beneath the Nisqually River Delta, fifty miles south of Seattle between Olympia and Tacoma, Washington. It registered a magnitude 6.8 on the Richter scale—a significant quake, the largest in Puget Sound since a 6.7 quake in April of 1965. There was an estimated 1–4 billion dollars in damage inflicted. Most of that was in the older sections of the city like Pioneer Square where the gargoyles really did fall.

Somewhere in the summer of 2002 there was a significant stock market decline and a corporate decision was made to reduce the Mutual Funds customer service force by 25%. I was called into my manager's office and informed that I was to be included in the cut. I was chagrined to once again be destined for a layoff. In the layoff meeting we were told that we would be on the payroll for four more weeks and were encouraged to use the office facilities to update our resumes and wrap up our affairs at Safeco.

I went home that night and had a come-to-God meeting between my soul and my brain. Ninety percent of those who were cut left immediately. I made the decision to make the best of this transition opportunity, continue reporting to the office, and be positive about my future. So that's what I did.

During that next week I finished updating my resume and used the office copy machine to produce enough resumes to last a while. I brought a cardboard box into my cube, separated out my personal gear and stowed it in that box under my cubicle desk. I also kept my eye on the phone queue whenever I was in the office. When the call volumes spiked up, and the wait times increased, I would jump on the line and take phone calls until the wait-queue leveled out.

Why not? I was still on the payroll. They had been gracious with me. I owed Safeco that loyalty. This willingness to assist was also noticed by my management team. I was emailed a "Thank you for your efforts" message. That was all part of being positive.

One of my close associates, who had been retained in his position, was named Tom Sweeney. Tom was 55 years old. Two weeks after the lay-offs were announced, Tom weighed his retirement options and decided to resign from Safeco and apply to the State of Washington to get another job where he would qualify for full retirement after ten years of service. That was a better offer than Safeco had available.

So Tom quit. Well, golly gee-whiz folks, here I was, Mr. loyal and dependable, in the next cube ready to fill that spot on the phone team. I was put back on the payroll without a hiccup. Thanks to the positive attitude, born out of that come-to-God meeting, I'd kept my job. One of life's small lessons learned. A positive win. Once again.

Several months after the lay-offs, Safeco Mutual Funds made the decision to give up the offices on Willows Road in Redmond and move the staff down to the larger Safeco Corporate Campus on 51st Street in Redmond. This was an understandable consolidation. We had been the only company branch in that Willows Road facility. My drive to work was just a bit longer, by two miles. The 51st Street building also offered covered parking and a company dining facility for excellent hot lunches. The pluses won here.

The next company shake-up came with the September 30, 2003, announcement of the sale of the Mutual Funds Division to Pioneer Financial Management. Safeco elected to get out of the financial management business, sell the Life Insurance part of Safeco to Symetra and specialize in property and casualty only. The Mutual Funds representatives were offered an opportunity to go into the P&C area with Safeco, or transition into customer service with the Life Insurance Division who were split off as a new corporation known as Symetra.

     DON MCGEHE

I was now 62 years old. Life Insurance was not nearly as exciting as Mutual Funds but it was a job in phone customer service that I was trained for and it would be a perfect fit to keep me busy for the next 18 months until I turned 63 ½ years old. I hoped to retire at 63 ½. If I could last it out with the Life Insurance Division of Symetra, until 63 ½, I would qualify for 18 months of personally paid Cobra Health Insurance coverage until Medicare took over at age 65. So this was my plan.

In order to qualify for any retirement benefits from the Safeco/Symetra plan I would need to have put in at least 10 years of service. And with only ten years the benefits were not much. By that time I would be 67 years old. I was really ready to quit when Mutual Funds was sold in 2003. But I needed that health insurance arrangement with Cobra/Medicare to kick in so I elected to put in the eighteen months with Life Insurance instead of retiring at that time.

I had been renting out the English Hill house ever since 1989. It was in 2003 that I realized that I would need to live in that home for two of the five years prior to selling it in order to avoid paying capital gains tax on the sale proceeds. The condo mortgage had been paid off before I had left Aero Rent-A-Car so the only mortgage left was on the English Hill house. In order to fulfill the two-year residency rule I moved back up to English Hill in 2003 and left the condo vacant.

CHAPTER 23

My health and the diabetes had been stable for years up until 2003. So good, in fact, that I had a record of four and one-half years of perfect attendance at the Safeco office. The only reward for that was an "atta-boy button" every month and attendance with all the other perfect attendees at an afternoon movie (in the office confines) with treats and a break from phone duty for three hours. Not much reward. It was also one less headache for management if you showed up every day. That perfect attendance was broken in 2003.

At that time I was taking two types of insulin daily. One type was a 24-hour insulin named Lantus. I was shooting 14 units of Lantus in one shot daily at dinner time. Lantus was considered a basal type insulin which was slow acting and did, in fact, last for 24 hours. The other insulin was the very fast-acting Humilog, that I mentioned earlier, which lasted for four hours.

The Humilog could be very dangerous. When you shot it, you had about twenty minutes, then it was surging through your veins like a runaway freight train. You had to eat immediately after the shot. The Lantus was so slow you could feel it coming on and be aware enough to quickly get something to eat to stave off an insulin reaction and hypoglycemia. The Humilog was not slow. It hit you smack in the face if you didn't get food in you to cover its affects immediately. I could normally cover a very large dinner meal with only five units of Humilog.

One Monday night that fall I got home to the English Hill house and went into the bathroom to take my long-acting Lantus shot.

Instead of reaching for the Lantus vile, I accidentally picked up the Humilog vile and administered the 14 unit shot of the *Humilog* not the Lantus. I went into the kitchen to fix something for dinner and almost immediately began to sweat profusely. Heavy sweating was a sure sign of an oncoming insulin reaction. I started to eat everything in sight. I wasn't aware enough to grab fruit juice which would have delivered fast acting liquid fruit sugar to the blood system. I was trying to chew. Anything I could find. You can't chew fast enough to catch that Humilog freight-train.

I was in panic mode. There was no way I could stay ahead of that train. When Humilog eats up all the sugar in your blood stream it starts to attack the brain and destroy brain cells to find more sugar. The reason that I was not able to reason out the need to reach for the fruit juice, rather than the chew food, was that the Humilog had already attacked the part of my brain (the pre-frontal cortex, I think) that controlled the reasoning function and temporarily crippled it. I was left with only the fight-or-flight response brought on by the sympathetic nervous system and the adrenal-cortical system to deal with this crisis. I ate everything I could find. Then I'd go test and still be low. Back to the kitchen again.

Later that night I was drifting in and out of consciousness. I'd come to for a while and manage another test, eat some more, then pass out again. I slept very fitfully that night. I recalled that I needed the sleep to repair the damage to the mind and the body that I had inflicted the previous evening. When I awoke in the morning I called my manager and told her I was too sick to even drive. I do not recall what my insulin regimen was reduced to that Tuesday. I do recall going very lightly on the insulin. I also ate very little.

I'd eaten almost everything in the house on Monday night. For the next two days, Tuesday and Wednesday, I mostly slept and allowed the rest to repair the damaged body and mind. Finally on Thursday morning I got up, showered, dressed and managed to drive to the office on time. When I got there I had just sat down at my computer screen and I'd forgotten how to log in to the system. I'd even forgotten how to power up the system.

I had thrown that on/off switch every day for five years. Today I could not remember how. My associate in the next cube managed to log me in. That was useless though. I couldn't remember the canned greeting words to answer the phone either. My manager finally came over and said that she would drive me up to see my doctor in Totem Lake. I accepted that offer.

Dr. Kim Pittenger at Virginia Mason Clinic, Kirkland told me to get down to the downtown Seattle Virginia Mason Hospital to be re-hydrated. I had so little fluid in my body I was trembling. The manager drove me down and dropped me off at the 9th & Spring Street ER. I spent the next five hours in ER with a needle in my arm to get the fluids back into my system. My manager then sent over one of my friends on our work team to drive me back to the east side. By Thursday evening I felt far better. I was still alive. Surprise!

In order to avoid that heavy dose of Humilog, rather than the Lantus, from ever occurring again I now split that once-a-day dose of Lantus into two separate shots. In the morning I would take eight units and in the evening I would take only six. By splitting the 14-unit single shot into two smaller (eight unit and six unit) shots I would avoid a possible 14-unit accidental fiasco altogether. Even if I got the wrong bottle next time, by splitting the shots, I would only have to compensate for a maximum rush of an eight-unit freight train, not a 14-unit one. That I could handle. Please pardon the expression but, I could live with that.

In March of 2005 I had completed my two years of occupancy of the English Hill house and could now sell it. Puget Sound real estate was in bull market performance so I decided to list the home. I hired a painter, took a week of vacation from work, and together we repainted the house both inside and outside. I had moved all my furniture to the downtown Redmond condo in order to have a vacant house for painting. After the paint had dried, I moved selected pieces back into English Hill and staged the home for sale.

I listed the home in late April and gave my notice of resignation to the Life Insurance management at Symetra. My resignation was

 DON MCGEHE

to be effective from May 31, 2005. I had some accumulated vacation time which I took in those last three weeks of May. For my last day on May 31, I returned to the office to check out and they had a brief going-away party for me. It was rather typical. They served an iced sheet cake from Costco.

That was a touching calorie bomb of a treat, to reward a sugar diabetic for eight years of near-perfect attendance. I managed to down a one-inch cube of the cake (without icing). I then offered them a big smile, and a sincere thank you. I already had a gold watch. It had come from IBM years ago. Symetra was not offering a watch. I tried not to let the door slam me in the butt on the way out.

For a retirement trip, after Symetra, I had been dreaming for many years about a four-corners tour around the United States. I had considered buying a Class B motor home for this trip. I'd looked at a Pleasure Ways model for about $54,000.00 (2005 dollars). That price seemed a bit high for me. A question also arose as to what to do with a Class B after the trip was over. The Class B didn't look like an every-day driver for the years to come. My goal was to buy something that I could sleep in to save money on the road. I was also familiar with the Chrysler Town & Country Mini Van, which I could sleep in, at half the cost of the Class B. The Chrysler mini-van was my final decision.

I purchased the Chrysler Town & Country in April of 2005, and drove it up to the Opaw Photography Conference in Kelowna, BC, Canada from August 5th to August 7th. I'd planned to take this trip with my friend David Fitzgerald from the Kirkland Photo Club. The van drove well, offered driver comfort, had cruise-control, and got good gas mileage on the road (25 mpg highway). I loved it. It performed very well on that Canada trip. That was the vehicle for my trip around the country.

The trip planning began with calls to the electric company, phone company, and condo association. I had estimated my potential usage until the end of the year and sent each entity a check for money to cover their bills.

My departure date from Redmond, Washington was Monday August 29, 2005. I headed east through Idaho and into Montana. On the way out of Redmond, the first reports of Hurricane Katrina slamming into the Gulf coast and New Orleans were coming from my local NPR station on the car radio. I would be in New Orleans in December. I was glad I wasn't there today.

I spent a day or two in Glacier National Park and in Canada's extension of Glacier NP which is called Waterton Lakes National Park. The road from Banff, Alberta north to Jasper, along the Ice Field Parkway, presented the most beautiful photographic panoramas of the trip. The air was crystal clear and crisp. The lakes were a robin's-egg blue from their glacial melt water. The Canadian people were friendly, generous, and hospitable. It was a fortuitous beginning for my trip of a lifetime.

Heading south, I re-entered the States at Sweetgrass, Montana. A kindly US border agent said, "Welcome home, Mr. McGehe." Driving through Montana I came upon a sign for Manhattan, Montana. I stopped and talked to a lady in the visitor's center there. I'd been born in Manhattan, Kansas. I was to visit Manhattan, New York and Manhattan Beach, California on this trip. With those three coming up, this was the first Manhattan I'd seen in the trip. Suddenly I changed the name of the journey. It was now going to be the "Four Manhattans Tour."

After another jog to the south I arrived at Yellowstone NP. This was my first experience in an active caldera. I was fascinated by the geologic nearness, and the power, of the eruptive volcano I was now standing in. It was September. The summer crowds were gone. The air was crisp, and smelled sage-sweet in my nostrils. On September 10th there was a six-inch snow covering in Yellowstone and the time had come to return to a lower altitude at Grand Teton National Park between Yellowstone and Jackson, Wy.

From the Tetons my path headed east and south towards the Denver, Colorado area. In Aurora, Colorado I got together with three classmates from my Manhattan High School Class of 1959,

     DON MCGEHE

Howard McGlothlin, Earl Keintz, and Steve Sargent. After meeting these three I motored east again to Manhattan, Kansas the second of my four Manhattans on the tour. There I saw old Manhattan friends Monty and Karen Williamson, and Barbara Pritzer on my return to my old home town.

From Manhattan it was just a short jaunt to Platt City, Missouri (Kansas City area) for a reunion with my nephew Jason McGehe, his wife Piper, and daughters Sage and Bryn. On the way to KC, I dropped by Holton, Kansas to visit my Aunt Edith Cox (age 99 years), her son—my cousin, Richard Cox and his wife Dorothy. After Kansas City I saw another aunt and two cousins Florence Parker (age 102), Frank Parker, Jr., and Robert Parker in Cameron, Missouri.

Crossing the border into Iowa, I visited my younger brother, Bruce and his wife Betty Gail. This was a well-earned rest stop for several days of relaxation. While in Norwalk, Iowa (Des Moines area), the first thing that Betty Gail asked me was if I was keeping a trip journal. I responded that I wasn't, but I would like to do so.

BG went to her desk drawer, pulled out a spiral-bound note book, handed it to me and said, "Start writing," with a big smile. At this point, I had been on the road for only 23 days. The details of those three-plus weeks were still very fresh in my mind.

I sat down with paper and pencil in BG's home, and wrote up the trip so far. In several days of great conversation and frequent journaling, I was up to date in the note-taking. One gift that Betty Gail bequeathed me for the trip, was a Grundig G5 portable radio that I used for entertainment wherever I went on the tour, and it has continued to be part of my life for these past 13 years, to the present day. Finally I was ready to head on east to see my other brother John David and his wife Lily in Rhinebeck, New York.

Sunday September 25th was a grand slog east. In 15 hours of straight motoring, in a driving rain storm, I trudged through Iowa, Illinois, Indiana, Ohio, Pennsylvania, and into New York. Six states; one day. That rest area in Fredonia, New York was well earned.

Monday continued the push on east through the Catskill Mountains, across the Hudson, and north to Rhinebeck, New York. I had a rewarding four-day visit with Dave and Lily. We had a fantastic gourmet dinner one night at the CIA (Culinary Institute of America) in Hyde Park. Another day we took off for the city and shopped in Manhattan, New York, my third Manhattan on the Four Manhattans Tour. We also slipped across the East River to Sahadi's Middle Eastern Grocery in Brooklyn and got snacks, which I stashed in the van for the upcoming month in New England. October 1st was my target date to attack the wilds of Vermont and the vaunted New England fall color.

I arrived in St Johnsbury, Vermont that first day of October, without any rain. That would not last long. The washout of mild hurricanes coming up from the gulf meeting with the colder air blowing down out of Canada over the next three weeks, created steady, consistent New England rain. This precipitated a severe dampening of the fall colors in 2005. Generally, warm days with cool nights are temperatures that produce the best colors.

With rain for days on end, the warmth was not there. The rain also moderated those hoped-for highs and lows, into a static consistent daily temperature. It was frustrating. But, what you get is what you've got. Like it or leave it. Although the primary reason that I was in New England was my desire to photograph fall color, I also wanted to see these native Yankees and how they lived.

I saw that at least 25% of the private homes in rural Vermont, fly the Stars and Stripes every day from their porches. The Yankee blood runs deep in their veins. It was not at all uncommon, on days without rain, to see laundry hanging outside on clothes lines to dry; sheets billowing loftily in the breeze. Monday seemed to be the big choice for best wash day.

You cannot see this from the interstate. You must drive the "blue highways" in rural New England to experience how the real people live. I loved stopping for a cup of coffee (de-caff was not always available) just to hear the lilt of these north-easterner vocal patterns. How they chew their "r's," and then spit them out, with a smile on their faces. To the Mainers the vowel "a" is pronounced "Aah." This bears a very close resemblance to the sound of their "r." However, you roll the "Aah" on the tongue longer for the "r" (unless the "r" is silent, as in the word "car").

The New England map makers have an easy-peasy time of it. They just use the same name for many small towns. Each of these often has a separate governmental structure and town council. They are only divided by the direction on the map from each other.

Case in point – Fryeburg, Maine, on US 302. Within an easy 9-mile distance of Fryeburg are the following, Fryeburg Center, North Fryeburg, West Fryeburg, and East Fryeburg. All separate cities. Each with its own identity crisis. This naming tradition happens all over New England. I imagine Google Earth has a ball up there.

Whenever I needed evening entertainment in New England I could find it on the Grundig G5 portable radio Betty Gail had given me. This was the first time I have been thankful for the extended Major League Baseball playoff brackets, since they were first introduced in 1994. For a month, in the northeast, there was at least a game every night, and sometimes two games. And, this was live stuff. With such a dense population in one geographic area, there was always a station in listening distance.

In Woodstock, Vermont, I had the Woodstock Inn & Resort which had a free-for-all viewing area in its basement lounge. Here I could sit inside, out of the rain, and enjoy widescreen games. On Saturday October 8, in Woodstock it rained 2½ inches in 12 hours. I did get some good photographs in Vermont and New Hampshire but the rain kept falling and on Tuesday October 11, I left for Ellsworth, Maine.

I spent several days in Acadia National Park and then began my trip down the eastern coast shooting lighthouses wherever possible. On my way into a fishing village named Stonington, Maine, I drove past a restaurant featuring a sign that read, "Lousy

Food & Warm Beer." More tonnage of fish and lobsters have been run through Stonington than any other town in Maine. I had a fantastic 1¾-pound lobster dinner that night at the "Fisherman's Friend" restaurant. The market price for dinner was $25.00. The wait-person even let me choose my own lobster.

I struck south, out of Maine at Portsmouth, skirted Boston, and counter-clockwised around Cape Cod into Provincetown, Massachusetts. Provincetown has a substantial fishing/boating community and also has a significant LBGT population, both thriving on a very small spit of land at the tip of the Cape. There were two lighthouses on Cape Cod. I was able to shoot both. I wandered the streets of Provincetown shooting street photographs all evening. Towards midnight the rain returned, and the next morning I departed for the drive through Connecticut and on into New York State again toward the home of my 1959 MHS classmate Bill LaShell in Wayne, New Jersey.

On the west coast the big box stores each have a separate location. In Wayne, New Jersey all the big box stores are in a Big Box Mall. More people. More congestion. More opportunities to buy. I stopped at the Wayne Costco just for the thrilling experience of it all.

Had a lovely dinner on Sunday night, October 23 with Bill and Lorraine LaShell, and her mom and dad Frank and Madeline Giacopino. Some of Bill's kids stopped by in the evening to see this strange creature from the West Coast that claimed to know their father from the hood in the fairytale land of Manhattan, Kansas. Bill told me that I was the only one from the old hood that had ever visited them in Wayne. Damn, I felt honored. So honored, I stayed for two days. Thank you, Lorraine. You run a great B&B.

On Tuesday I drove to Baltimore and reveled in my second "regional" dinner of crab cakes in the Inner Harbor. By Wednesday I was in Washington D.C., where I was able to get lost at least seven or eight times in two days. I was impressed by two sites near the National Mall. The Holocaust Museum reminded me of both

  Don McGehe

Anne Frank's "Diary of a Young Girl," and my experiences at Manzanar, California's Japanese-American WW II Internment Camp in the desert of the Owen's Valley. Same war. Same incarcerations. Different outcomes.

The Vietnam Memorial represented my generation's youth-killing battlefield. To what end? I'd seen two traveling displays of the "Wall," in the Northwest, before I got to DC. When I saw it out there in the hinterlands, those who visited were those who had lost a husband, brother, father, son, or daughter in the war. They were extremely reverent in their approach to the "Wall." Today they just seemed like tourists who were viewing it because it was on their list of sites in D.C. that you should see. Sad; in more ways than one.

Next stop was Colonial Williamsburg, Virginia. Difficult photography here. It was cramped and dark indoors (they had, after all, no electricity) so interior shots were of very high contrast. Outdoors the work went slowly. Long, two-man hand saws were used. No power tools. It paid to be on an hourly wage in the seventeenth century.

Lighthouses had provided a welcome stop, all the way down the Atlantic Coast. As soon as I could, I crossed over onto the Outer Banks highway, North Carolina Rt. #12. Lighthouses paled in comparison to my next stop. Kill Devil Hills. I tracked east about 400 yards to enter the National Historical Site where Orville and Wilbur Wright flew their first four flights on December 17, 1903.

How far we've come, in air travel, in just over 101 years. From 120 feet at Kitty Hawk, to the Sea of Tranquility on the moon. Wow! My Aunt Florence Parker was born three months before that first flight and we have just celebrated her 102nd birthday. A lady of the space age.

I then shot the Bodie Lighthouse on Bodie Island, the Cape Hatteras Light on Cape Hatteras, and jumped on the ferry over to Ocracoke Island. It was now time to set my clocks back to standard time and watch the sun set into the pile of cotton-ball clouds that cushioned the horizon over Pamlico Sound. On Sunday morning

October 30, I shot the Ocracoke Lighthouse from Silver Lake with pelicans roosting peacefully atop the mooring posts in the lake. I got in line at the Ocracoke Ferry dock for the 9:30 am boat to the mainland. In a phone call to Virginia Neff in Naples I got some ideas on sites in Florida to shoot before seeing her at her home on November 11.

On the ferry I met a 35-year-old banker from Woodstock, (Atlanta area) Georgia. His aim in life at that time was to get to, and photograph, every lighthouse in the USA. Mitch then told me that most of them are on the Great Lakes in Michigan and Minnesota. I would not have guessed that. I was glad to see that I was not the only crazy tourist who was shooting up all the lighthouses. Have camera, will travel.

I slipped into South Carolina on Monday, October 31. At the "Welcome to South Carolina" border station I stopped to view a display garden plot of blooming cotton. I'd been wearing cotton T-shirts all my life but had never seen a field of cotton blooming. I was amazed at how sharp the spikes at the base of the cotton balls were. Ouch! Picking that can't be easy.

South Carolina has some unique features. Every mile or so along US 17 there is a miniature golf course layout. When I say layout, they are elaborate. Some features on these courses are four stories tall or higher. This was the first occurrence of palm trees on my trip. They were everywhere. It must be the warmer climate.

Amusement parks are all over the coastal area. There must be a real need to entertain the children while dad and mom are playing at the shore. Every couple of miles there was a permanent fireworks business. It must be legal there to sell them all year long. Either that or the fireworks manufacturers are sleeping with the governor.

I saw an interesting item on a 75-degree day. Several birds were gathered in the shade underneath an SUV drinking the condensation water that was dripping off the air conditioning unit. Birds are smart. I arrived in Charleston, South Carolina late Tuesday night November 1 and drove to South Charleston and around the bottom of Folly Island to shoot the lighthouse next morning.

Wednesday November 2. Got up at 6:10. I walked out toward where the lighthouse should be. I still did not see it. A couple out walking their dog told me to keep on going. Where the road ended and the sand began, there it was. It was offshore another half mile on a tiny island called Morris Island. The set up for the shot was beautiful. I composed it so there was a footprint path in the sand, leading into the shot in the foreground. Bulrushes framed the footprint path on either side, and just beyond it the waves were breaking onto the shore at the water's edge.

Across the bay was the lighthouse, starkly exposed in the morning sun. I shot 21 exposures, both with and without polarizing filter. It was all over at 7:00 am, so I shot a stop sign with "Bush" written underneath the "STOP," making a brief political statement on my way back to the city. My only question now was, "George W., Jeb, or the whole famn damily?"

I entered the State of Georgia on Friday, November 4. Stopping at an information center for the City of Savannah, I got directions to the Bonaventure Cemetery. I knew of it from the John Berendt best-selling book "Midnight in the Garden of Good and Evil." Bonaventure is a remarkable place with low-walled family plots interspersed between the moss-draped live oak trees. You'll know you are parked under a live oak when you hear the clunk, clunk, clunk of the oak nuts (acorns) banging onto the roof of your car. They are noticeable.

Other than the live oak nuts, there are few other sounds in the cemetery, save the birds. The grounds are just alive with vegetation. The warm, moist climate keeps everything, except the planted residents, growing. I looked for the Bird Girl sculpture that had graced the 1994 book cover. A docent told me later that it had been moved to a Savannah museum in 1997.

The foot traffic the statue had caused had marred the peace and quiet of the cemetery. I could understand that. It was a deathly peaceful feeling. Johnny Mercer was buried here. I was able to find and photograph his stone marker. I left Savannah that afternoon for Florida, specifically St. Augustine.

I pulled into the first rest stop in Florida. I expected to see Jeb Bush here with a red carpet, a big smile, and several rigged voting machines. But, alas, no governor did I find. Nonetheless, I did relieve myself before motoring on.

St. Augustine, Florida is centered around the old fort which was built in 1576. This ancient fort is surrounded by a business area called Old Town. Most of the shops here are small, and cater to tourists. After leaving Old Town I was able to find the St. Augustine Lighthouse and was quite impressed. There wasn't much room to shoot, with all the overhanging trees, but with a 35 mm lens I managed the shot.

I took off south again toward A1A and decided that I wanted to drive nearer to the beach. I jogged left onto the next street toward the ocean. This street did not stop at the beach, it continued right out onto the beach itself. I discovered that in St. Augustine you can actually drive on the beach. There is a 10 mph speed limit, but who cares, you're there. I parked right up on the hard sand, pulled out my beach chair, took off my shirt, and caught 90 minutes of good rays.

On Sunday, November 6, I once again headed for the beach, grabbed a Sunday paper, then read and sunned until noon. After noon I found a Super Cuts shop to get a haircut, and heard from the barbers that there was a function of special gastronomic interest in St. Augustine that day. It was booked as "The Great Chowder Debate." All the top restaurants brought their best chowder recipes together and had a "Taste of St. Augustine" day. For a 50 cent ticket you were entitled to about a two-tablespoon cup of clam chowder, or shrimp bisque from the booth of any of the restaurants. All the food was donated by the various establishments and the proceeds from ticket sales went to Shriners Children's Charities.

I bought a $10 packet of 20 tickets. I sampled recipes from twenty separate booths, and thoroughly enjoyed myself for several hours at this cook-off near the St. Augustine Lighthouse. The Floridians were dressed up in their sexiest, sunniest, sporting outfits and were having a great time. The chowder was varied and delicious. I drove back to the Super Cuts with giveaway necklaces from Harry's Seafood Bar & Grill for the two gals at the shop who were cutting hair. These two weren't able to get away to go to the "Great Debate." They appreciated the visit, along with my tales of the tasty chowders.

The next day I drove back to the beach near Ponce Inlet and spent several hours there before high tide had taken all my sand back by noon. Heading south I shot the Ponce De Leon Lighthouse then continued on down Hwy. A1A. I attempted to get into the NASA base at Cape Kennedy but was turned back and refused entry. Continuing south I saw Melbourne Beach before heading west to Lake Okeechobee.

Okeechobee is a huge fresh-water lake with a high berm or dike around it. It is used for irrigation, leading out of the lake in all directions. I returned to the Atlantic seaboard to connect with US 1 at Palm Beach and on through Ft. Lauderdale. I then switched over to I-95 with the intention of skirting around Miami. I was heading for Homestead, Florida with the intention of driving down US 1 to Key West the following day. After two stretches of toll road on the Florida Turnpike the road fed into US1 at Florida City. I then left the freeway and found a Holiday Inn Motel parking lot and parked the car.

I had shot insulin on the freeway, after the second toll booth, and I had some residual Humilog already in my system from a late afternoon shot. After shooting to a 103 blood sugar, I ate a quarter pound of Swiss cheese and a ½ pound tub of chopped chicken liver pate that I had picked up at Publix Market in Lauderdale, while sitting in the parking lot. It must not have been enough. Before the end of the liver pate the insulin hit me, once again, like a freight train.

I went absolutely spastic with the insulin causing electric brain impulses to the muscles which drove those non-voluntary spastic muscle responses. I pretty much trashed the inside of the front seat in the van and launched myself outside into the parking lot of the Holiday Inn running wild. The desk clerk later said that he noticed the insane actions, in the lot, and (he later said) asked "can I help you?" (This is all hearsay evidence, because I do not remember any of this.) He said I responded with "Help me! Help me!" At this point he called 911 and the Miami-Dade County Fire EMT response team was sent.

When consciousness returned I was on my back, on the black top of the parking lot, with my broken Omega watch in my hand wondering what the hell had happened. I had that sense that said, "Oh God. No. I hope this isn't what I think it is." It was. When the EMT took the blood sugar it was on its way back *UP* and was still only at 26 (normal should be 80-120). When I say "on its way back up" I mean, I was aware of what had happened and that awareness never occurs until after the liver has released some sugar back into the blood stream and brings back consciousness.

When asked the usual questions by the EMT's (Who are you? Where do you live? What day is this? Who is the President?), I was forthcoming and responsive to each question and absolutely accurate in my answers. They shot some glucose in my vein and hooked up an IV. When I got up, my right knee was in pain and very weak. My forearms were bloody and bruised from lacerations, so they wrapped them with gauze and asked me where any medications were because they wanted to take them along to the ER. I looked for my blood test kit but couldn't find it. When I was loaded into the van I asked one of the techs to use my car key and bring the two grocery bags full of food, medicine and vitamins from the passenger seat. We locked the van where it stood and they took me to Homestead Baptist Hospital in Homestead, Florida.

On the intake at the hospital they judged me to be "not critical" so I sat in a wheelchair in the ER while others were treated. This was before 9 pm. The outfit I was wearing was a tank top and gym shorts, both of which were sweated out from the insulin reaction. As I sat there the body cooled rapidly and since the ER was air conditioned, I began to get cold. They had done intake triage on me, when I first came in, and had a blood sugar reading of 107. (Once again, normal is 80-120.)

     DON MCGEHE

Next I went to X-ray where it was 20 degrees colder than the ward and I began to shiver uncontrollably. I was offered a blanket and took a pee while the X-ray tech was reviewing the knee shots he had just taken. He came back asking for three more, so we did it again. I peed again while we waited for those better results and was wheeled back to ER to sit in my wheelchair until about 11 pm. I pulled out my cell phone and called Dave and Lily in New York to report the incident. At this point I still had no results.

I continued huddling beneath my blanket with my one grocery bag by my side. I had consolidated everything into one bag and threw away unnecessary stuff in the X-ray room. Dr. Sule (pronounced Sue Lay) finally saw me at 1:00 am. He discovered that I had some muscle soreness in my left chest. Back to X-ray for the chest. After this they were about to take me for a cat scan but I put my foot down and said, not only no, but hell no. They honored my request to opt out of their little $800.00 exercise, since there was nothing wrong with my head. Hospitals!

Back in the ER at 2:00 am they found me a vacant bed, by the nursing station, so I got out of that damn wheelchair. X-ray had put the chills back in me so I got two more blankets and finally felt comfortable after five hours. Two o'clock blood sugar was 250 so I got 4 units of regular insulin. At about 3:00 am Dr. Sule told me I had a cracked fifth rib on the left side and the patella was broken in the right knee, but the knee was not wrenched. This was fairly good news, all things considered.

It was now Wednesday November 9. We all played with blood sugar during the morning and never got it below 137, but they were willing to err only on the high side. I was released at 8:00 am Wednesday and got a ride back to the Holiday Inn with a van that had a lift gate like a Metro bus. When I got to the car I found my test kit on the floor of the driver side wedged between the seat and the door. This relieved much worry about having to replace a meter and four hundred dollars worth of insulin. A Holiday Inn employee named Steve helped unload most of my gear intending to put it in a room at the Holiday Inn.

When I hobbled in to the counter, I found out they were full up with FEMA employees surveying the Hurricane Wilma damage. I had seen a lot of blow-down debris throughout the day on Tuesday but it was mainly in big piles, awaiting pick up. The innkeeper found me a room across the street at the Travelodge and Steve reloaded the car, drove me to the Travelodge, and helped me register and unload again. He was a great help.

I left the van open most of the afternoon, parked in front of my room, helping to dry it out from the half gallon of water that was on the floor from a destroyed jug. I settled into the room and made phone calls to Dave for an update, Aetna for coordinating the healthcare, and Dr. Kim Pittenger's office. I took a spit bath with a washcloth and felt better. I went to bed about midnight.

On Thursday, 10 November, I awoke at 9:30 am. It was late because I was making up for a near-sleepless night in the ER. My blood sugar was still high, so I spent the day indoors after calling Aetna for an orthopedic surgeon. Aetna faxed a list of approved providers to me on the Travelodge fax number. I watched Titanic in the afternoon on HBO, then at 4:30 I tried to get into the car. I succeeded, and then drove to a Mobil station to fill with gas. I would be able to drive the next day! I decided to call Peter to let him know I could drive, then Virginia Neff to get directions to Naples, Florida.

I got organized and departed Homestead for Naples at 10:45 am, on Friday November 11. While driving, I was wearing a 40"-long Velcro sleeve on my right leg to keep the patella stationary. That right leg was stretched out all cattywampus into the well in front of the passenger seat. I was using the left foot for the gas pedal and brake. I could not have done this with a stick-shift car.

Most of the route from Miami to Naples is on the I-75 freeway. With its limited access, I was able to use cruise control most of my way to Naples. It was a very smooth two-plus hour trip. I spent the afternoon on a hobble-around tour of Virginia's home and property and catching up on our lives lately. Virginia let me know that she had been able to make an appointment with an orthopedic surgeon

     DON MCGEHE

for Monday at 10:00 am in Naples.

On Saturday we took my watch to a jeweler for repair, and we both went to lunch at The Green Flash. In the afternoon I asked Virginia to drive the van, with me in the back seat, and both of the sliding doors open. My right leg was stuck between the front seats in the pass-through hole. With both sliders open, and my seat belt fastened, I was able to shoot pictures out both sides of the van as she drove me slowly through the Ding Darling National Wildlife Refuge.

It was a privilege to shoot without having to get in and out of the van. At one point we had to wait ten minutes, at one intersection, while an eight-foot alligator crawled across the road. The bird I was most fascinated with in the refuge was the anhinga. Because they swim with their bodies underwater and their necks and heads above the surface, they look like snakes in the water getting ready to strike. Therefore, they are also called snakebirds. The anhinga also lose body heat quite easily and are often seen, whenever ashore, with their wings spread wide to absorb solar heat.

On Monday I met with the orthopedic doctor. He said that everything looked good but still recommended a full five weeks in the brace before continuing the journey. In discussion with Virginia, I decided to get a one-month rental in Naples to let the patella heal, and then continue the last half of the trip after that.

By Thursday November 17, I had rented an efficiency condo two blocks from the sand on Vanderbilt Beach Road in Naples. I was all set. Thanksgiving came and I was invited to Virginia's home. I enjoyed the dinner with her family, most of whom had flown down from Kansas City to get away from the cold.

On Monday November 28, I had another major low blood sugar crisis at the condo. I had been talking to Barb Pritzer in the evening, by phone to Manhattan, Kansas and she sensed that I was in trouble. By the time I knew it, I was waking up on the floor of the kitchen with the EMT squad banging on the door. She had called the Naples Sheriff's Office at least 100 minutes earlier. The Sheriff had dispatched the EMTs to the condo.

The EMTs took me to another ER. This seemed to be getting old. Except for the low blood sugar, no damage had been done to either the rib or patella. I did, however, succeed in pretty much trashing the condo. Barb flew down to Naples on Tuesday November 29, and stayed for three days. She was a very supportive source of help after one more crisis.

After the first week in the condo I would go down to the beach daily and relax in the sun with a portable radio where I could listen to the weather report from Seattle and smile. I was feeling stronger each day. By Wednesday 14 December, I had a going-away lunch with Virginia at The Lighthouse in Naples to thank her for her kindness and concern over the last six weeks. On Saturday 17 December, I checked out of the condo and hit the road north in the wickedest rain cell I had seen all trip from Tampa on up through the Florida Panhandle. It was raining so hard on I-75 that all the cars were using their emergency flashers just to be seen. I made it into Alabama to a rest area by 8:30 pm to spend the night.

On Sunday I drove through Alabama and Mississippi and was into New Orleans by noon. My God it was desolate. Debris was everywhere and there was massive building destruction as well. The devastation I had heard about on NPR, on the day that I left Seattle (August 29, 2005), was now before my eyes. It had been four long months, and the destruction was still here. The only thing that had changed was that the wind was gone. The storm had blown through. The wreckage remained.

My blood sugar got real low driving through the Big Easy and I was weaving between lanes until a kind, fellow motorist, honked me into grabbing several apples and a kiwi to revive myself. While in New Orleans I never got off I-10. Even with low blood sugar, I did not want to. The freeway was still a wreck. Sign posts and traffic signs were still all a-kilter and it looked like it was an emergency bypass. Because it was. So I just kept driving, with just a couple of gas stops, and a piss stop or two, to walk off my sore knee.

Finally I got into Texas where I stopped at the first rest area that looked good about two and a half hours west of San Antonio at 9:30 pm. It had been a long day. When you drive from Miami to LA, by this southern route, you spend one-third of your trip in Texas. It's that wide.

On Monday I made it out of El Paso by noon and veered north to White Sands to photograph the desert and cacti. From White Sands it was just a short jaunt to Bosque del Apache National Wildlife Refuge. Here there were far more birds than I had seen at Ding Darling. Bosque was smack dab in the center of the migratory bird North American flyway, and many of the same birds I had seen in Eastern Washington in the summer, were there now on their way to South America. I spent several days there before heading west to Phoenix to check in with Jason Edwards.

Jason was a friend from Kirkland who had decided, several years earlier, that he was tired of the western Washington rain and had fled to the Southwest desert. We had a day or two about 21 December to bring each other up to date with our various wanderings over the past several years. Then we said goodbye, with a hug.

I departed Phoenix on December 23 to get to I-8 and west to the California border. I was border-checked just inside the California line. Sniffer dogs and all. They couldn't tell I hadn't had a shower yet today. I think they were sniffing for weed. I drove directly to Dave Rehfeld's home in Carlsbad, California. Dave was my Delta Tau Delta pledge-father from K-State whom I had known since 1960. Dave and his lovely wife Nancy were warm and gracious for my one-day visit. I'd really missed these two.

After breakfast with Dave at the Poseidon Restaurant at Del Mar Beach I got on I-5 on Christmas Eve and drove north to Manhattan Beach, California. This was my fourth Manhattan on the Four Manhattans Tour. It had been 36 years, from 1969, since I had lived here. Everyone I'd known then was gone and everything had changed except the bank I'd used and the Manhattan Grocery. I did walk around the whole downtown area looking for someone or something

I recognized. I asked several bartenders for information but nothing came up. I then looked down the Manhattan Beach Pier and out on the Pacific Ocean and realized "You can't go home again."

I left Manhattan Beach at 5:00 pm and drove up to the San Fernando Valley to get as far north as possible to start off on Christmas Day for the trip up I-5. I slept on a side street behind a motor home. Not a stable; lonely; Christmas Eve. Not a feeling that I hadn't had before. Oh well…Merry Christmas!

Christmas Day, such as it was. I left the San Fernando Valley at 4:15 am and began to run into fog north of Bakersfield. There was not much traffic on the freeway that day. The further north I drove the more rain I ran into. The fog kept up all the way through the state. I spent the morning with the NPR Sunday Morning News show and stopped every two hours to check blood sugar, and for relief. I drove all the way into Oregon and stopped in Medford for gas and, being Christmas, I took a room at the inn (Motel 6) for the night. I asked myself, "What (else) would Jesus have done?"

I awoke, on Boxing Day, December 26, to leaden skies and Oregon drizzle. I killed the morning at the motel and left for the coast at noon. My destination was Lakeside, Oregon and the home of my friend Mel. When I turned right, off US 101, for Ten Mile Lake my blood sugar was low. I got up the road about three miles and pulled off into a turnout. I just sat there for God only knows how long. I knew I couldn't manage to drive, but I couldn't figure out why not? That California fog set in again, between my ears.

Finally, Mel drove down the road, from his double-wide, and saw my van sitting beside the road. He pulled off the road next to the van, somehow knowing what was going on with me, and asked me to get in their car with his lady Mary. Mary then drove me to their house while Mel drove the van. Saved again. I spent two days with Mel at Lakeside. Their double-wide was warm and comfortable, with a wood stove being used for heat. Mel had forty acres of land that he had devoted, among other projects, to raising Christmas trees. Their sales season had just ended before the year-end holidays.

On Thursday morning, December 29, I drove across Willamette Pass over to Bend, Oregon to visit Marge and Keith Yokum. The Yokums were my friends of longest duration in Oregon. We all met back in 1969 up on Mt. Hood where they were living at the time. We'd been the closest of friends ever since. I spent two wonderful days in Bend with them, as the last visit on my around–the-nation journey.

I left Bend at 5:00 am on the final day of the year, and toured north through Madras, Hood River, and over to Portland to connect with I-5 north to Seattle. I made good time on this New Year's Eve and arrived at my own Costco store in Kirkland, Washington at 2:00 pm to stock in some food for the weekend. When I got to the condo in Redmond and opened the front door it all looked familiar. I was finally home again. The rib and patella had healed. It felt good to be home safe with all the fenders on the mini-van still un-bent.

My trip totals:
Elapsed time: four months plus two days
32 States (66% of the lower 48)
U.S. District of Columbia
Two Canadian provinces
17,543 miles driven

CHAPTER 24

JANUARY OF 2006 WAS A MONTH DEVOTED TO VIEWING AND organizing the slides from the Four Manhattans Tour. There were well over 1,600 of them. But now, no one seemed to want to look at slides. Slides had suddenly become out of phase with technology. My good friend, and fellow photographer, David Fitzgerald had volunteered to scan some of my best slides from the trip and convert them to digital images.

In a switch to digital I would need a computer. The first choice was the Apple versus PC coin-toss. David and most of my other friends had PCs. That seemed like a logical choice. My financial advisor, Peter McRae, had just invested in computers for his office. He had a source for hardware that was far less expensive than the Apple price. I bought a PC with Peter's help.

My usual source for photo gear was B&H Photo-Video. All of my old Nikon lenses were full frame. The new digital camera I ordered from B&H was a cropped-sensor camera but my full-frame lenses would work even with this new model. I ordered Photoshop CS3 along with the computer. Now that I had the gear, the learning curve was the next obstacle. Learning curves take far longer to accomplish than gear purchases.

The first time that I used the new digital camera was in the Owen's Valley of California in October. I met Rick Ferens in Bishop on October 7. We were shooting the fall color down there until October 20.

I had joined the Kirkland Photo Club in 1991. This group was an asset in climbing the digital learning curve. But, just like Sargent

Schultz on Hogan's Hero's, I felt that "I know Nothing! Nothing!"
I enrolled in every training course that came to town. Especially
those taught by Scott Kelby of Photoshop User magazine. By the
end of 2006 I finally felt fundamentally competent. "Experienced"
was a goal that was many years ahead. Mom never said this was
going to be easy.

A strategic core-group closed out the 2006 camping season,
with a memorable "Men's Camp Out" at Deception Pass State
Park, Washington on December 30–January 1. We bought the
best filet mignon steaks available at Costco, baked potatoes,
green beans from South America sautéed in olive oil and garlic,
with braised mushrooms to mix in with the green beans. This
was all served with foil wrapped and fire-heated, garlic buttered,
French bread. The erstwhile participants in this epicurean
adventure were, Rick Ferens, Don McGehe, David Fitzgerald,
Ron Wingerson, and Jeff Bossart.

The potatoes went in foil, then in the coals for forty minutes.
Each man grilled his own steak, and Rick Ferens cooked up the
finest plate of green beans, in my memory, in a large frying pan over
a gas stove. After dinner, we all drew up our camp chairs around
the fire pit, with adult beverage of choice, and relaxed. Jeff Bossart
had his feet up on the stones surrounding the fire pit.

Jeff was just nodding off, when we noticed that the soles on his
sneakers were very close to being on-fire, with steaming smoke
wafting into the cool night air. Jeff was immediately up, on his hot
feet, and jumping around the fire, with a surprised look on his face.
Hoppy New Year, Jeff! Before we went to bed some kids started
throwing lit sticks of dynamite off the Deception Pass Bridge to
celebrate the New Year or some revolution that they were cooking
up on their own. The repercussions were deafening.

In January of 2007 I began a relationship with a new lady. For
the sake of preserving some sense of anonymity, I'll refer to her
as AJ. I'd known AJ from years before, while she was still with her
husband. AJ was actually estranged in this marital affiliation. She

and her husband retained their married-but-living-separately relationship in order to keep him covered under her corporate health
insurance plan. AJ was now retired. The insurance coverage came
from the business entity where she was drawing her pension. He
was now living out of state. They were on friendly terms, however,
even though they seldom saw each other.

Our first outing was to attend the Mochi Tsuski ("mochi
making" – mochi is a sticky rice dish eaten to celebrate the New
Year) Festival on Bainbridge Island, Washington. AJ was of Japanese
American heritage and was part of the Yonsei generation which
was the fourth USA-born generation of descent from original Issei
immigrants. This Mochi Tsuski Festival was fascinating to me as
an American of European decent.

In the Japanese tradition they would pound the sticky rice paste
in a large wooden crock with long mallets. The pounded dough
would then be surrendered to the bakers to make sticky buns for
the festival participants. Following the mochi-making there was
a performance of Japanese Taiko drums with their resonant and
exuberant pounding and chanting from an adjacent stage.

Our second outing was to drive AJ's mini-motor home up to
Marblemount, Washington on the Skagit River to photograph Bald
Eagles. The motor home's name was "Dolly." The eagles are here
in late January to feed on the salmon running up the Skagit River.
Those magnificent birds were a joy to experience.

We had a great opportunity, there alone on the river, to listen
to, and to learn from one another. AJ and I were able to "play" with
one another too, like kids do, and have fun while we were together.
It was a joy to be with her. She was bright and extremely witty. We
both kidded each other and smiled a lot. AJ didn't much care to be
photographed, though, or so she always said. I'd sometimes catch
her with a long lens, but not often. She would "shy" away when I
had a camera in hand. Of course, this shyness only tempted my
desire to photograph her more.

 DON MCGEHE

At this point in my life (age 67), I was having an on-again, off-again concern about erectile dysfunction. Early, after getting together with AJ, I'd asked my primary care physician about a Cialis prescription. I was surprised at how expensive that Rx was. Even with health insurance.

For years I'd been using the threefold expression about sex, that went, "The enjoyment is only temporary. The positions are ridiculous. And the cost is prohibitive." And, I would say this with a smile. But, say what you wish about sex, you never see a romantic-comedy movie that doesn't begin with, or end with, a fantastic bang-bang sex scene. This scene usually culminates with both of the partners expressing that dreamy, ethereal look on their faces that says "God, I've never had it this good before. Where have you been all my life?" That is the Hollywood rom-com myth. Incarnate!

There was a minor exception to this in the movie "When Harry Met Sally." In that flick, Meg Ryan created that unbelievably climactic scene, in the restaurant, which was pure acting. If Meg's performance was just acting, could that also happen in real life? Could couples fake it with good "acting" performances? Sure they could. And they do. Which leads to the open question, "what do men with ED do?" If you're not hard, you're charred. It's obvious to your partner. Some things you can only fake in the movies. Yet…"I (still) think I'll have what she's having."

This question led me, in 2016, to write a poem that I labeled my "December poem."

I first delivered it to a poetry group meeting in December of that year at Parkplace Books in Kirkland, Washington. I had always been fascinated by the poetry of Ogden Nash. I was amazed by the brevity of his poems. His shortest was one called Fleas: "Adam, Had 'em." I attempted to emulate this brevity when I wrote the "December Poem."

Age of Ennui
by Don McGehe

Woe is me.
Retiree.
Past sixty.
Got E D.

Trick knee.
Bad Chi.
Can't see.
Gotta pee.

Must
be
low
T.

IN MARCH OF 2007, I ORDERED A KILT OF MY OWN CLAN MCKAY sporting blue tartan. The kilt wool fabric was shipped from Scotland and a Ballard shop sewed the kilt together for me. The kilt was ready in April and I was able to match it with a sport jacket, in the Scottish style, which was sewn together for me by the Seven Taylor's shop in Kirkland.

Visits to several other Scottish shops in the Seattle area allowed me to put together my complete clan outfit. I first wore it to the Scottish Highland Games in Enumclaw, Washington in July. I have been proud of this clan attire, kilt, sporran, ghillie brogues and all. I have worn it on even formal occasions, ever since.

In February, AJ and I were talking about repeating a "once-in-a-lifetime" (OK, maybe twice) trip through the entire 240-mile stretch of the Grand Canyon on the Colorado River by raft. I had taken this trip in 2000 and was eager to repeat it. AJ liked the idea. We also interested Peter McRae in the journey and he recruited his 27 YO daughter Ashley to join us. We all flew separately to Las Vegas on May 19, 2007.

We were booked into a Vegas hotel that night and boarded a bus the next morning for Lee's Ferry, Arizona. Vegas to Lee's Ferry

DON MCGEHE

is a six-hour trip. On May 20, we boarded the rafts at Lee's Ferry and swung into the Colorado. We were on the river.

Camping was in furnished tents, sleeping bags, with dry bags for clothing and gear. We were virtually alone on the river for eight days and 240 miles. No cell phone. No radio. No 7-11 stores. No nothing. Just us and the Grand Canyon National Park wilderness.

Six million people visit GCNP each year. Only 25,000 raft the river. I knew my friends David & Susan Fitzgerald and Don Halgren were also on the river with another raft operator. When we saw their rafts tied up at the river edge on the third day, we motored back and waved and yelled at them from the river. Then we took their pictures for posterity. We were in 14-person motorized rafts and their boats were oar boats. We were more maneuverable. As a result of the outboard motor power, we were able to do the 240 miles in eight days. Their journey was longer at 13 days.

Each day we would take two off-river hikes, up tributary streams which flowed into the Colorado, to see side canyons and spectacu-lar, sky-blue waterfalls. These were the really striking and memo-rable experiences of the trip. We tied up in Lake Mead on May 27 and boarded a bus back to Las Vegas to pick up our off-river gear and catch flights back to Seattle.

Much of the time, on the river, I had felt estranged in my rela-tionship with AJ. As I look back now, I had been so focused on maintaining stable blood sugar levels that it was running my mind ragged. We were on rafts in the wilderness. No day was predictable. Consistent blood sugar levels sometimes rely on predictability and sameness from day to day. Due to being out of my element, I was running scared on the river.

One night after dinner a storm blew down through the canyon. As it approached, it did provide some spectacular photographic images across the river as the clouds provided stark selective light-ing on the cliffs across the Colorado. Some of the best shots of the trip were taken that evening. When the clouds closed in, it rained all night. Some tents, pitched on the slick rock, took on water and were soaked. I was lucky. Mine didn't. Next morning we ate break-fast beneath an erected tarp cover in a steady drizzle. We packed wet gear in our dry bags and wore our full rain gear into the rafts. I was cold, wet, and shivering all day.

I'd just returned to Seattle again when it was time for a seafood run down to Ilwaco, Washington at the mouth of the Columbia River, southeast of Long Beach. We were in a group put together by David Fitzgerald. We played at the beach and camped at the KOA Campground in Ilwaco. On Saturday night, June 15, we all piled in the van and drove to Jessie's Seafood shack down by the river. Jesse had everything in his seafood case.

We bought some of everything he had. We barbecued king salmon and halibut, steamed a bucket of clams and mussels, boiled shrimp and prawns, nibbled on salmon jerky while everything was cooking, and licked butter off our fingers for hours into the night. David Fitzgerald built one of his classic beach bonfires and we erected our camp chairs and told stories until everyone nodded off near midnight. Dinners like that are the pure delight of our hedo-nistic culture. It was good to be home again in Washington State.

On the way back to Redmond and home, I had planned a "git-down" visit to see AJ at her home. The afternoon I got there we took a short trip in her motor boat up the inlet and retrieved a piece of garden driftwood from a spot where she had stashed it several days before. It was more than three feet in height and took both of our efforts to bring it aboard. After snacking on some dinner, AJ asked me to sit down on the couch. She said she had something she wanted to talk about.

That sounded strange, and rather menacing. It sounded like one of those invitations to lunch, on a Friday, from your boss at the office. (Pink-slip time again?) She was direct, but also very tactful. It had been six months for us, together. She said that she was fine with the friendship we shared, but she wasn't getting any fulfillment from the intimate part of the relationship and wanted to end that.

I'd secretly known this. I knew it, but I had refused to admit it to myself. She was right. I'd been running so scared, about losing my potency to ED, that I had totally ignored her need to be slowly and tenderly stroked, nurtured, and honestly appreciated as a partner in an intimate relationship.

I'd had a previous ED conversation in the 1980s with my friend Bob Price. His father and mother were both physicians. Bob was also a type #1 juvenile diabetic. He'd told me that over time we diabetics lose a lot of blood flow when our capillaries, the very smallest of the blood vessels, close down with age and plaque build-up. There is no place you need blood more critically, or immediately, than in an erection.

Bob mentioned, at that time, that he was considering a penis implant with a small, hand operated, pump near the scrotum to achieve erection. That sounded like way too much, for me, at the time. I was still in my 40s. Twenty five years later, that fear was now a reality. The price of diabetes. Bob had died in Kailua after the amputation of a leg, due to gangrene, which was an end result of his diabetes.

AJ had asked me, several times over the months, if I was happy with the intimate parts of the relationship? I had lied to her, in response, and said, "Sure! Fine, yeah just great." I was so fearful of admitting that I might be totally losing it, sexually, that I'd put on a bravado which in the depth of my soul, I never really felt, and which I knew to be a lie. Now I was hurt. I was ashamed. I was mute. I was angry with myself. I didn't know quite how to handle this so I just refused to look her in the eye and said nothing of consequence.

Looking back in hind sight (God! Here he goes again!) if I'd only been honest, when she had first asked, that might have helped a great deal. I thought about quietly getting in my van, turning over the key, and stealing away in the night. Right then. Now, I'm glad I didn't do that. That was the chicken's way out. I stayed until the next day. I was still ashamed, but I was now feeling stronger within myself. I was also thankful that a friendship could be salvaged out of this mess that I had precipitated. I believe today that the friendship has been preserved.

Recalling Dr. Gary Chapman's book "The Five Love Languages," in the coming months, as the relationship continued to evolve, I began to rely on "acts of service" to express love toward AJ. Of course, I didn't mention the word love. I'd used that word months ago. It was not received well then. It wouldn't be now.

AJ had evidently been around that block several more times in her life than I had. I later helped her paint some rooms and to trim brush in a new home she had purchased on Hood Canal. I voted with my feet and made my presence felt. We got along well, yet quietly. She may even have appreciated it. We yet communicate very amicably even ten years later.

In the fall I shot an image I had sought for years. It was of Mt. Shuksan in the North Cascades National Park just east of Mt. Baker. I was still a member of the Mountaineers Photo Club in Seattle and could use their lodge at Mt. Baker that fall to get this shot. There is an old dock in the park that extends out into Baker Lake, which is the platform for this image.

Snow-clad Mt. Shuksan rises above the far end of the lake. Surrounding the lake there are great stands of wild mountain blueberries. These blueberry stands take on a deep crimson hew each fall in September. With the red of the blueberries accenting the white of the glacier and the blue sky behind the mountain you have the color elements for a classic "Kodachrome" image. Three o'clock in the afternoon is the time for this shot, just before the sun dips below the western mountain ridge. Got it!

Rick Ferens and I then headed for the Pendleton Round-Up on September 14. AJ was kind enough to let us borrow Dolly to house us in the grade school parking lot space we had reserved in Pendleton. We had both been going to the Round-Up for so many years that we got complementary photographers passes into the stands each day. I always told them I was shooting for a small town newspaper east of Redmond called the Duvall Daily Disappointment.

I also volunteered to shoot the children's rodeo each year and donated those images to their support committee to use for advertising. The children's rodeo was for mentally challenged kids in the Pendleton area and was just a kick to shoot. The regular rodeo cowboys all assisted, and were paired up with the children to do barrel racing (with the kids riding stick horses), bull riding (cow heads on teetering saw horses), and each child got to ride a real pony with the rodeo cowboys assisting.

Just like the Special Olympics, it is a tremendously rewarding experience to see the kids achieve at a sport and each get a trophy. Not only did we shoot the rodeo itself but also did street photography with the throngs of rodeo fans and Native Americans who were in Pendleton for the week. On the way back up towards Seattle a strong wind on the freeway blew the hatch on "Dolly" askew and sprung the latch that held her top on. Rick wired it shut. When I got back to Kirkland we had a friend of David Fitzgerald's repair the latch mechanism professionally before returning Dolly to AJ. No harm. No fowl. AJ's really quite a lady.

In October I asked my good friend David Huls to be my buyer's agent to find a new home in Kirkland. I'd been living in the Redmond condo for two years now, since the sale of the English Hill rambler. I was now, once again, qualified to use the two-year tax rule and sell without incurring a tax penalty. David showed me a number of homes. I nearly bought a condo right downtown but couldn't get the price that I wanted so dropped it. I was lucky that I did.

I found another condo that was perfect while out looking on my own. It was a 1,550 Sq. Ft., three-bed, three-bath, at 6226 Lakeview Drive. They wanted a bunch of money for this place. This was just before the 2008 market downturn. In order to get it, I accepted a $180,000.00 mortgage. That ended up being a real drag eight years later but I thought I could afford it at the time. Times changed.

I sold my condo to the daughter of my friend Susie Sather. I finally had the perfect condo. I really liked this new place. There were only six condos in the building. Each condo had its own separate address and it had a west facing balcony with an unobstructed

Lake Washington view. I had a house-warming party on my birthday, November 3, with all my Kirkland friends and AJ there. I wore
my kilt that night but drank no scotch. It was a blast.

With an increase in square footage from 950 to 1,550 I now
had a lot of space to fill. I immediately began scouring the con-
signment shops looking for unique items of furniture. If you have
ever moved into a larger home, you will understand this mad-
house purchasing opportunity.

At the end of the year I was invited over to AJ's new home on
Hood Canal for her New Year's Eve celebration. A number of AJ's
friends where there, many of whom I had already met and loved to
be around. It was a very rewarding wrap up to a fine year of change.

PART 7

OREGON TRAIL

2008–2018

CHAPTER 25

IN THE NEW YEAR OF 2008, I CAME FACE-TO-FACE WITH THE truth of my new condo purchase. At the condo I sold in Redmond, the mortgage had been paid off for eight years before I moved. Accepting the new mortgage on the Kirkland condo required a sizable monthly transfer from my brokerage account to the checking account to pay the mortgage, and to keep butter on the bread, and bacon in the skillet. Now I was retired without an income source, other than Social Security. I now realized that this was not the wisest of decisions, but I just loved this new abode and figured that I could make it work out. I anticipated being in this new condo forever.

With a new computer, the Internet was now part of my life. I used it for PhotoShop, Yahoo Personals and also came across a quote on Peter Baskerville's web site that I just loved; "This too, shall pass." Baskerville pointed out: "The legend of the quote finds its roots in the court of a powerful eastern Persian ruler who called his sages (wise men) to him, including the Sufi poet Attar of Nishapur, and asked them for one quote that would be accurate at all times and in all situations. The wise men consulted with one another, and threw themselves into deep contemplation, and finally came up with the answer…*this too, shall pass.*" The ruler was so impressed by the quote that he had it inscribed in a ring." This story confirmed, to me, that change is the one constant in the universe.

I was so enamored with this quote, rolling around in the back of my brain, that I found Karthia Jewelers at a street fair that spring. From Karthia, I ordered a slider ring, which I had engraved with that very citation on the slider-band. I now wear it as an enduring reminder that change is ever-present. It would take eight years for the first big change to come. The ring would then bear its truth.

In the late summer I purchased a full-frame digital camera, a Nikon D-700. I had the money. I figured, "what the hell, spend it." So I did. I had excellent results with this new camera. I was once again enthusiastic about the art of photography. I first used it at the Fremont Solstice Parade on June 21st. This is an annual parade in the Fremont district of Seattle where the parade participants ride their bicycles (and other conveyances) through the streets in the nude. Well, not totally nude, they can wear shoes and body paint. They paint their bodies with regalia, slogans, sparkles, and jabs at the current Washington State and Washington DC political she-nanigans. Anything is fair game.

This is a riotous gathering. The sidewalks are packed sar-dine-deep with revelers, cameras in hand, for this open flaunting of societal norms and Presbyterian prudence in the free society of Fremont. There is no constitutional amendment which permits public nudity. But, for this one day each year, they just do it. The cops are there, for traffic direction, but with smiles on their faces, that's about all they enforce.

Before and after the noon parade, visitors amuse themselves at the Fremont Street Fair. I often find my best photographs in the parade staging area before the noon event occurs. You can get the participants to pose for you in this pre-parade queue. Here you need not be rushed by the throngs of spectators which line the streets ten deep. In addition to the bikers, there are some fifty floats which line up and parade past the Statue of Lenin which towers over N 36th Street on the parade route.

Years ago David Fitzgerald and I developed a fascination for hot-air ballooning. We've attended festivals in Walla Walla, Wash-ington but our favorite, each year, is the Winthrop, Washington Balloon Meet. This is scheduled on the first weekend in March, each spring. I say spring, but the first weekend of March is always winter-cold in Winthrop. The town of 396 residents is in the foothills of the Cascade Mountain range at 1,768 feet of altitude. There is always snow on the ground at Balloon Festival time.

We've seen few things in photography as striking as the colorful balloons rising in the still, cold air of Winthrop, silhouetted in front of stark white, snow-covered hills on both sides of the Methow River Valley. The hot-air lift is phenomenal for the ballooners in this frozen, still environment. This is not a crowded event. You can walk right up to the ballooners, shake hands, talk to them, and even get a selfie. The intimacy available with these sportspeople, at this first event of their season, is direct and personal.

They've been cooped up in the city all winter long, just as we have. When they get out in this cold sunshine in March they're all smiles and ready to share stories about lighter-than-air experiences in balloons. If you are lucky you may even get a ride aloft. After the ballooning, the go-to spot is the Wolf Creek Bar at Sun Mountain Lodge in the snowy hills above Winthrop. Good place to warm up your body, soul, and esophagus with friends at hand.

Following the 2008 Pendleton Round-Up trip I returned to the Owen's Valley in California for the near-annual Eastern Sierra shooting shindig with Rick Ferens. October in the Owen's Valley is fall-color time and the climate is of the Indian Summer variety. This year we shot the October full-moon rise over Mono Lake at the South Tufa State Reserve. This salt-water lake has a druid ghost-like quality with the full moon rising above those silent, statuesque Tufa formations.

We also shot at the Ancient Bristlecone Pine Forest in the White Mountains. The Sierras and the White Mountains form the two buttresses that enclose the Owen's Valley on either side. Some of the oldest trees in the US are located in this 11,000-foot-high forest. Many exceed 2,000 years in age. One, named the Methuselah Tree, in Schulman Grove, is dated at more than 4,773 years old. The forest service won't tell you where it is, to avoid destruction of the tree. We Americans, like all humans on Earth, are lousy stewards of nature. If we can't hunt it, kill it, and take it home with us to trophy-up, on our wall in the den, we seem to have no use for it. Rick and I try to take only photographs, and leave only footprints.

For more than thirty years, since the mid 1980s and before, there has been a group of coffee nuts who meet daily in one of the downtown Kirkland, Washington cafes to consume caffeine and to schmooze. This used to be before work for that early group. Later, most of them retired but the old habits are difficult to alter. This all began, for me, at the JJJ Cafe (named after the three owners whose first names all began with the letter J) in about 1998. I was still working at Safeco, at the time, but I would meet with the group on the weekends.

Since 1981 I have been doing gym workouts daily. After retiring in 2005 the coffee group was an everyday affair. I would join them after my daily work-out. Much of our social life, for many in the group, would touch-stone off contacts or plans made over coffee. It seemed to keep us all together and it was an enjoyable group to be with. Over the years the group would move from one cafe to another, when a favorite haunt closed, or a better one opened. The meeting grounds moved from the JJJ, to the Kahili, to the St. James, and in 2010, to its current favorite location, the Caffe Rococo.

One of the primary, and original members of this coffee group was Mr. David Fitzgerald. David was a very social person and he just loved to organize outings, field trips, and get-away vacations. For each of these occasions David would do meticulous research and then he would only offer a package, to the group, when he had the perfect venue and the rock bottom price for participation. It was like having a personal travel agent, and getting an email once a month, with a fantastic package at a price that was half of what a for-profit agent would charge. One of the trips that David loved to put together was called the "Cross Country Ski Weekend."

It was always scheduled in the second or third week of January. In the years before I was part of the group, they had gone by train to Yellowstone, and by car to Yosemite. After I began my participation, the weekends were closer to home in the Winthrop area of

         DON McGEHE

Central Washington. David always pointed out that "Cross Country Skiing" was "only a theme." I doubt that David had ever been cross country skiing. But, it was a great opportunity to get out of town in the middle of the rainy season in Seattle, and go play (and for some, to consume adult beverages) in the snow.

When we went to Winthrop we would rent an entire chalet that slept 14 to 16 folks, do all of our own cooking in group meals, and just play for four days. Our favorite refuge was the "Vista Grande" in Carlton, Washington. People took skis, snow shoes, sleds, huge inter-tubes for snow tubing, games, and those novels you had been meaning to read for months but never got around to. Everyone in the group seemed to have a cooking talent for a special dish they enjoyed making. David's wife, Susan Fitzgerald would schedule those who volunteered, to cook their special meal for the entire group. All you needed do was email Susan with your recipe and she would explode your recipe list to cover the number of people scheduled, do the shopping, and provide you with all the ingredients you had requested for your grand entree.

Breakfast omelets were always my favorite to cook. It was great for the second or third morning of the trip. They needed to be made one at a time. By that time in the trip, folks weren't just jumping out of bed at the crack of dawn, so the staggered wake-up times were to my advantage. Everyone got a custom-made omelet, with their choice of the many ingredients I had available, and served with an orange twist and a sprig of parsley.

After I moved to Kirkland in 2007 a new hobby came rocketing into my life. Rockhounding. See and I had always had an infatuation with rocks in the 1980s. We would stop in at any rock shop that we passed on our journeys around the Northwest. We bought lots of those rocks but used them only in tableau displays or as garden accents. We never cut or polished them ourselves. We didn't have the equipment. But the rock seeds were sown in those years.

What to do with rocks, all changed when I first met Myron Lewis. Myron is a retired architect but his lifelong enthusiasms were for fly fishing and geology. Myron and his wife Marlene Lewis had been beachcombers and mountain rockhounds all their married lives. He had polishers, buffers, and even a large oil-bath rock saw. All I had to do was to see his collection of rocks, in his home, and I was hooked. In the Kirkland condo, I had a perfect place to build a small rock workshop in a wing just off the attached garage. I started by buying a tumbler on Craigslist that could polish ten pounds of rocks.

Next thing I knew, in May of 2009, Myron and I were planning an auto trip to central Oregon to hunt for rocks. We started off in Ashwood, Oregon visiting the farm of John Marston who owned this crazy, spotted dog named Nuisance. Myron had purchased a slab of red jasper (chalcedony) from John's father, on this very ranch some thirty years before, and was so taken by that stone that we came back to see if there was any more of it left. John had inherited his love of rocks, the ranch, and Nuisance's mother, from his dad (who was now dead) but John said that none of that rock strain was any longer available.

We looked at what John had on hand, however, and ended up buying 55 pounds of rock from him anyway. He was kind enough to cut one large bolder of "picture" jasper into three pieces for us while we were there so we could each have several pieces of it. The next leg of the journey took us 32 miles southwest to Richardson's Rock Ranch outside Madras. Richardson's is the mother lode of rock in central Oregon.

Richardson's imports raw rock from all over the globe and dumps it in huge piles in their yard for sale to the public. Their ranch is also home to the Priday Thunderegg beds of world-renowned fame. We spent much of the next day, on the ranch, digging Priday eggs from the rhyolite soil of the "red" bed. I would use Richardson's many, many times in the next nine years to corral tons of rock to bring home and cut, tumble, polish and give away to friends and children who were the future lapidary lovers of America.

DON McGEHE

Myron Lewis wasn't much of a joiner. I was interested in a rock club to associate with. On the web I found the East King County Rock Club and also joined the Bellevue Rock Club. It was with the Bellevue club that I found my most ardent lapidary fans. As a result of joining this club I built up my collection of equipment with two 10-pound tumblers, a ten-inch rock saw, a Richardson's High Speed Dry Sander and a Richardson's Polisher. That equipment turned out a lot of rock over the next six years from that alcove off the garage.

All High Schools have Class Reunions. In 2009 I was privileged to share in the 50th reunion of my 1959 class at Manhattan High School. My parents had both died before this June reunion so the family home had long since been sold. This gave me an opportunity to share lodgings with my fellow classmates, within the confines of the classic Manhattan Holiday Inn.

The bones of this motel were nearly as old as the bones of us graduates. It had two stories of rooms, stacked one atop the other. The room doors all opened out into, and surrounded, a totally enclosed indoor pool, putt-putt golf course, and ping-pong table tableau. This enclosure allowed the cubic space to be air conditioned. That somewhat mitigated the humidity exuded from the pool. The place was dated. It was also rather familiar though. We had all been here many times before, ever since Junior High School.

Our class had an excellent turnout for this, our 50th. We weren't getting any younger. At least, not that any of us would admit. But, there is just some special thing about the kids you graduated from high school with. They are even closer than most of your own kin to you. Certainly closer than second cousins who grew up miles away from you in another community. These were your birth-year buddies. Over the years, I'd grown to love them all.

In November of 2009, I was honored to receive a visit from Bill and Lorraine LaShell from Wayne, New Jersey. Bill was a neighbor, one block away, in Manhattan while I was growing up. I had visited them at their home in Wayne when I drove around the country in 2005. While they visited, we dined on some spicy hot Mexican food at Mama's Mexican Restaurant in Seattle and some even hotter dishes at Dixie's BBQ in Bellevue, Washington. At Dixie's, Bill decided NOT to "Meet the Man" (an expression which described licking a tooth pick dipped into their classic hot sauce—only a toothpick mind you, and Bill still passed!). Hot stuff!

Another memorable summer outing, each year, was the Native American Canoe-In. This gathering of the West Coast Tribes was held each August. Each year the Canoe-In was awarded to a different tribe. All West Coast bands were invited to join in the celebration at the home reservation of the host tribe. Upwards of 40 canoes row in from as far away as Alaska and Southern California. In 2010 the invitation went out, from the Makah Nation, for all the tribes to Canoe-In, and gather at Neah Bay, Washington.

The Makah Reservation is at the upper left hand corner of Washington State, near Cape Flattery. Our group reserved a campsite just off the reservation and drove into Neah Bay every morning to join in the festivities. The opening of each Canoe-In celebration is marked by the presentation of each tribal canoe, that has journeyed to the site. Each canoe skipper then asks permission of the host nation to come ashore and participate in the festival. The canoes row into the reception cove one at a time to be recognized. Once the welcome is given, the next canoe paddles in with their request for recognition. These canoes are big ocean-going vessels, some up to 40 feet in length, and seating up to 18 paddlers. Most of these tribal canoes are manufactured by Clipper Canoes at Abbotsford BC, Canada. The price tag on these larger canoes ranges up to $14,000.00 (Canadian) for the Pacific Dancer model.

The celebration lasts for six days and features what are called "protocol" ceremonies throughout the day, where each tribe performs their own tribe's dances and songs for the other visiting tribes and spectators. Each protocol performance may last an hour. Then the tribe will present gifts to the host tribe in their appreciation, and for the honor of attending. The various tribes use an individual member's participation in the canoe crews as a character-building tool. When involved in any canoeing event, no drugs or alcohol are allowed. If a paddler breaks this rule it means his or her immediate exit from the team. When a team rows from a distant reservation, rigorous physical training of team members is involved long before departure.

In preparation for rowing to the Canoe-In, each team carefully plans their route for overnight stays ashore each night. Support units also shadow the crews, by car and truck, to provide encampment facilities for, and feeding of the crews. Tribal pride and loyalty are key results for the paddlers. Men and women are typically accepted equally on these crews. When the crew paddles into the host nation bay there is jubilation and celebration. Their crew's job is now accomplished. The canoes are typically mounted on trailers, and trucked back to the distant reservation after the event. As a paddler, all you need do is to get there.

One of the traditions that reflect personal and tribal pride is the work that goes into making each member's individual regalia for any ceremonial and dancing purpose. The primary materials used for regalia are woolen felt and cotton. Ever since the introduction of European goods into the Northwest native cultures in the seventeenth century, the button has been a very popularly used notion. The very early buttons were fashioned out of brass or cowrie shells. It was the cowrie shells that became the choice decoration after their early appearance.

Colorful wool robes, sewn in many shades of red, blue, black and white, are worn as outer garments, especially by females, but also by males. These were commonly called "button robes." These robes are extremely popular among the Canadian First Nation tribes. Their use has, of course, also been adapted by all other nations. For photographers, capturing hundreds of native dancers, wearing these colorful button robes, is the essence of "getting the shot" at a Canoe-In presentation or a pow-wow.

It was in the summer of 2011 that I finally sold the silver 1972 Porsche 914. I'd had a love affair with that automobile (and several love affairs in it) for 39 years. I'd been broken hearted in 1989 when the Redmond cops took it away from me for several years in the bust. But I had bought her back at auction. When I had first purchased this car, someone had told me that if I didn't total it within the first six months, I would drive it for years and love it. I think that reflects the tendency to push your first Porsche to the "breaking point" when you first get it. That is just to see how far you, and it can go. Once you find that point, you have learned your limits, and the cars as well, and you will drive it within your—and its—boundaries from then on.

I had first advertised the 914 for $7,000.00 on the Automobile Atlanta (914 specialists) web site and on Craigslist. It took some time. I talked to a lot of potential buyers. I didn't really need the money from the sale. This car was in excellent shape, with very little rust. I was just looking for someone who would love her as I had. I finally received a call from Mr. Mark Fulton of Kirkland. Mark's father had owned this same model when his dad was dating his mom. Now Mark wanted one to restore and drive around in, with a Porsche club he belonged to. I liked Mark. I let it go for 6K. Mark was the right guy to have the silver streak. He intended to keep the 914 in the garage at home to do the restoration, and park his wife's car on the drive way. The man had his priorities straight.

The year of 2012 was when I took out pre-paid cremation insurance with Forethought Insurance, re-financed the mortgage on 6226 Lakeview Dr. condo, and purchased a new Epson 3880 printer in order to upgrade the quality of the annual holiday cards I send out each year.

The choice of cremation insurance was part of my "end-game" to take any possible burden off my family in the future. The idea here was to pre-pay for the cremation, with a life insurance policy from Foremost Insurance Company of Grand Rapids, Michigan, and then let the closest funeral home to me know of the existence of this policy. In case of passing, that funeral home then performs the cremation and is reimbursed by the Foremost life policy payout.

 DON MCGEHE

Taking out a new mortgage at 6226 Lakeview Drive was a stop gap measure to take advantage of 3% rates and to postpone what I now imagined was the inevitable necessity to sell the property to get out from under the mortgage. I was living in a dream world. I couldn't afford this condo. This re-fi postponed that decision for another four years.

In October of 2012 there was a needed replacement in the computer room: a new Epson 3880 Printer. I had, for years, been sending out Holiday Cards at the December-January holidays to upwards of 90 recipients. Each card was individually written on the computer. This was a very serious undertaking for me. I planned all year for the design and production of this card. The new printer permitted me to use double-sided 86 lb. gloss stock for this card. The results were sharp and unique. I also used the printer to produce birthday cards for family, and for those friends that I had taken photographs of, in the past year. A card becomes special if you can include a personal photo.

CHAPTER 26

The year of 2013 became another acquisition year with the addition of a new computer, and physical therapy to straighten out my back. The computer came first. My old desktop PC finally failed in February. This time I went with an Apple. I marched down to the Apple Store in Bellevue Square and ordered a 27" screen iMac. That solved the computing problems. Not the financial ones. But wow, was it great.

In June I finally admitted to myself that my back was crooked and had been listing to the port side for the past three or four years. Having scoliosis, I just couldn't stand up straight. One of my friends at the gym, a male nurse, suggested that I see Dr. Bob Adams who was a sports medicine physician. Adams diagnosed that this was a "core" problem and sent me to physical therapy.

The doctor was correct. The therapist designed a daily 90-minute set of exercises for me which included planks, sit-ups, and a couple of dozen other routines. Over the course of the next year the back realigned itself and I could finally stand up straight. The problem was solved, as long as I kept up the core exercises. Core work takes time. Anything that adds improvement to life usually does.

Towards the end of the year Rick Ferens created a website for me to add bragging rights to my photography. It was a gorgeous site. I was very proud of it. Whenever anyone found out I was a photographer, the first question often asked was, "Where is your web site?" This gave me an answer to that question. The web host was seeking over $100.00 a year payment for the site, so after five years I gave it up. I was not getting a financial payback from the expenditure.

There is one photograph in the Seattle skyline that I had been enamored with for 25 years. That shot is the January full-moon rising over downtown Seattle, as shot from California Avenue in West Seattle. This is a tough shot to capture. The first concern is that the shot is only possible one night a year. There are 13 full moons a year. The moon moves from the south in the summer sky, to the north in the winter sky. It is only the January full moon that rises directly over the city's downtown core when seen from West Seattle.

The second concern is that only one Seattle day, out of every four, on average, is clear at sunset, in the month of January. And we are dealing only in averages, not predictable occurrences. You could easily go ten straight years without clear skies on that January full moon night. All you can do is show up on the right night at Hamilton Viewpoint Park, set up your camera tripod, and take your chances for a clear moon rise. All the stars were in my favor on January 15, 2014, at 6:07:57 pm. That night I got the shot I had been waiting for all those 25 years.

I used that image as the cover photograph on my 2014 Holiday Card. In April of 2015 I commissioned George Tuton to print the shot on a 40" x 60" canvas reproduction from one of his huge Epson Printers. That image has graced a wall in my home ever since with the caption "the lesser light to rule the night." This, a quotation from Genesis Chapter 1, verse 16, "And God made two great lights; the greater light to rule the day, and the lesser light to rule the night…" I took over 75 images that night. The one at 6:07:57 pm had just the right height for the moon. It also had the soft, warm, golden glow of the sun, which was just below the horizon at its civil twilight position, still reflecting off the faces of the high-rises in the city. Voila! The Wolf Moon rise. …

There is a loyal crew, who, each year, form the band of brothers and sisters who attend the Native American Canoe-In. We all got invitations in January of 2014; this year the gathering would be in Bella Bella, BC, Canada. This required some pre-planning. You needed a valid a US Passport. I renewed mine in April for another ten years. Bella Bella is on Campbell Island which is halfway up the Canadian coast between Vancouver and Alaska. The only way to get there is by Canadian Ferry. We all made those reservations immediately. Now we waited for the David Fitzgerald travel plans and for the departure date on July 5th.

My Manhattan High School Class of 1959 held their 55th Reunion in Manhattan, Kansas on May 1-5, 2014. I met with my older brother David at the Kansas City, Missouri airport and we rented a car to motor to Manhattan. Dave was not in my class, of course, but he had several classmates of his own from '57 who were married to classmates of mine. So we made it a brace of McGehes, and attended. This arrangement also lasted for several days after the reunion. We visited all our relatives in the Kansas City and Des Moines area who gathered at my nephew Jason McGehe's home. I also got to see my grand-nieces Sage (15) and Bryn (11), who are Jason and Piper McGehe's daughters, at their Platte City, Missouri home.

I'd missed so much of the growing up experience of Sage and Bryn. I was always so far away from their home. When we were together, there were usually ten or more relatives, who all needed attention paid to them as well. Unless you are around children at the growth stages when they really stretch, you miss all the 'firsts' that they accomplish in their lives. To me that was a sad fact of my life. If you do not have children, you are often left out of that chain of existence that emphasizes what family is all about.

Our Canadian adventure began on 5 July. Three cars left Kirkland and wound through North Cascades National Park and into Canada, via Osoyoos, BC, on Hwy. 97 toward Kamloops. The camp was on Okanagan Lake that first night and we went on to Williams Lake the second night. The third day we turned left onto BC RT. 20 and made it to Bella Coola by nightfall. The last two-mile stretch of road, off the high plateau and down to sea level, from Stuie towards Bella Coola, was nearly straight down. We put our automatic shift cars into first gear (low), and descended from clouds to surf over a vertical mile, in far less than two horizontal miles of pavement.

On the long drive across the British Columbia plateau, I discovered a CD in the Chrysler that I had purchased several years before, but which I had never played in the CD deck before. I resorted to this CD because there is no acceptable radio reception up there. The CD was the "Original Three Tenors Concert" first recorded in 1990. On this CD is a cut from the Puccini Opera *Turandot* titled "Nessun Dorma." I listened to this cut and suddenly discovered a three-minute aria that sent shivers up and down my spine and set off nervous energy surging through the base of my brain. Never before had I heard such orchestration behind the clear tenor voice of Lucianno Pavarotti. It immediately went into my top five vocals of all time. It's been there ever since.

Our group had reserved two nights of camping at Bella Coola. We then left two vehicles and a camp trailer at our campground and piled five of us into my van to drive on to the BC Ferry dock early on the next morning. The ferry we boarded was the smallest in the BC Ferry fleet. It housed five vehicles and the passengers. The trip to our destination town of Shearwater, on Denny Island, took a full eight hours on the ferry—all day. Shearwater, on Denny Island, was the closest lodging we could find to Bella Bella. From there it was only a 20-minute ferry ride over to Bella Bella on Campbell Island where the Canoe-In was being staged.

Those over the age of 55 got free ferry fares. We'd jump on the commuter ferry in the morning, spend all day in Bella Bella at the Canoe-In, and ride the ferry back at night. I had to pack carefully to get all my heavy lenses into the back pack.

The Heiltsuk First Nation, at Bella Bella, presented the most colorful opening ceremony of any Canoe-In that I have ever experienced. There were easily 1,000 First Nation members in button robes, colorful red and black regalia, and feather-banded headgear standing and chanting on multiple levels of the shoreline above the bay. Twenty drums were pounding out the beat, behind the chanters. The light was soft white that morning, with scattered cumulus clouds on the western horizon. Bald eagles were flying over the gathering and perching in the evergreens along the surf.

The First Nation peoples of the Canadian coastal region have a deep tradition for colorful and detailed regalia. Their raiment is all individually crafted and worn with pride and distinction. They are a very proud people.

We were all invited to a feast that first evening in the tribal hall. Each of the First Nations attending presented dishes of their own peoples' traditional recipes for feasting; the variety of seafood dishes seemed limitless. Often I did not ask what was in the particular dish I was served. I just tasted and enjoyed. We were truly honored guests. They have a tradition of honoring their elders. When you reach the age of 55 you become an elder. The elders have reserved tables in the tribal hall. It almost makes you long to become a Canadian.

It was with sad eyes that we climbed aboard the BC Ferry, six days later, and retraced our watery route back to Bella Coola. Returning to the original campground, we reclaimed our cars and gear after dark that evening. The next day we were up and moving early, driving east this time up onto the plateau and across BC toward home. There was a scheduled overnight for the others but I just pressed on and drove the entire way back to Kirkland on July 18—a long 16-hour driving day.

In 2015 brother Dave and I retraced our Kansas Reunion trip to attend a gathering of all the classes which had graduated from Manhattan High in all the 1950s. All ten classes were invited. We all got to see an entirely new group of townies which we hadn't seen in half a century. There were some surprising results. Neighbors we'd had when we were kids suddenly appeared again in the flesh. It was great to see everyone there.

After the 50s classes reunion, there was a gathering of the McGehe clan at Big Cedar Resort just south of Branson, Missouri in Arkansas. Both my younger brother Bruce and his oldest son Jason had time-share memberships there. One day we rented a boat to go out on the lake for a day in the sun. Sage and Bryn showed us a cliff on a peninsula of land jutting out into the lake. You could jump off the boat, swim to shore, climb the cliff, and leap 15 vertical feet back into the lake from the cliff ledge. Three generations made that leap. Sage and Bryn from the grandchildren, Ryan and Piper from the parents, and only my older brother Dave from the grandparent's generation. Dave was aged 75 that day. Good for him. I had to remain in the boat just to photograph the event. :) We ate well, shared a lot of laughs, and bonded as a family at Big Cedar.

There is a two-block stretch of pavement and brick walls in Seattle's Pioneer Square—Post Alley—that got steam cleaned on November 10, 2015. It was called the Gum Wall. It had been a twenty-year tradition to walk down that alley and deposit the gum, right out of your mouth, onto that wall. The city booked it as the second-germiest tourist attraction in the world. Officials claimed that the chemicals, sugar, and additives in the gum are starting to wear on the buildings brick exterior.

The City of Seattle used industrial steam machines to remove the approximately 1 million pieces of gum and deposited them into 5 gallon buckets at a cost of $4,000.00. The following week, local vandals began the process of re-depositing new gum on the walls. This colorful, smelly event made Time Magazine and was the lead photograph on my 2015 Holiday Card. For all the world to see and revel in. This was *NOT* fake news. You would have thought it was Wrigley Field in Chicago, or something.

The first week in December 2015, I received my monthly report from my financial advisor. It advised that my cash account was running quite low. I still had a lot of IRA money but the trading account was slim. The slogan on the ring had come true. "This Too *Had* Passed." It was time to sell the condo, get a less expensive home, and retrench. Two days before Christmas I had D. A. Burns come around and steam clean the carpets in preparation for a sale.

My friends Tom and Sally Neir, down at Rococo Caffe, suggested I talk to their friend Jeff Dilley, a realtor. Jeff and I spoke just after Christmas and we agreed to put the condo on the market just after the first of the year. So, at the year's end, change was once again the harbinger to welcome in the New Year of 2016. It was time…to change.

The years 2016 and 2017 represented a rather dark two-year period in my life. Even though I chose the condo that I moved into, I never really liked the place and definitely did not "own" it. To own a place is to unpack all your boxes, set up all your stuff, and love your new environs. This, I did not do.

My criteria for the new unit was to find a condo community with solid financial "reserve" funds, a price I could pay cash for (with money left over), and have it located in Kirkland. I found this place on Craigslist. Because I did the leg work to find it, the agent gave me a break on the commission on the sale on 6226 Lakeside Drive.

The new home bore the address: 10418 NE 115th Place, Kirkland, Washington. It was in the Springtree Condominium complex of some 80 units in the South Juanita neighborhood of Kirkland. There was no view and little privacy. The condo association was well-run and reliable. The place was affordable. I made an earnest money offer on 3 February, 2016. That same day I listed the Lakeview Condo.

6226 Lakeview Drive sold in nine days for the asking price. The agent had listed it for more than I thought it was worth. I was happy. The closing date we chose was March 11, 2016. There was a lifetime's worth of stuff to pack up in boxes in the next five weeks. I wasn't smart enough to sell, give away, or donate anything so it all went into cardboard crates purchased from U-Haul.

Two weeks before the move I already had most of the stuff in boxes. I was carrying a box up the stairs one day, and fell backwards down the stairs, wrenching my back. In frustration, I crawled into the car and drove to LA Fitness to ease myself into their hot tub. I was in there too long; my blood sugar got too low. I nearly passed out. Someone called 911 and they brought me back to awareness. They wanted to take me to ER. I refused. But they took my car keys and refused to let me drive.

Fortunately, my friends Darryl and Shirley Lytle were in the club at that same time. They took pity on my crumpled condition. Shirley offered me a ride home in her car, and Darryl volunteered to drive the mini-van back to the condo. The EMTs, and club management, agreed. Thank the Lord for friendships, in a crisis. That was one. I was in bed for the next three days straight.

My body was now destroyed for the next six weeks. I'd hired a truck and a team of four guys for the move. I could do nothing save supervise. Most of the packing had been done, except for the rocks and all the other stuff in the garage. Sadly, the movers had to box all that garage gear up. I say sadly, because without me doing it, I had no idea what was in any of them.

The new condo had a double car garage. Most of the boxes from the old garage were just stacked in the new garage. After the move on March 14, I was still unable to unpack much of anything for another four weeks due to the back wrenching. I was mentally beat. Everything just remained in those brown card-board boxes which were stacked everywhere. When you live alone, if you don't do it, it doesn't get done. Why do I choose this life style? That was a rhetorical question.

The new Springtree condo was on two floors. Living room, master bedroom, office, kitchen and a bath were upstairs. On the lower floor were the den, a bedroom, a bath, clothes washer/drier, and the double-car garage. Between these two floors was a flight of stone stairs seven steps deep, a landing, and another seven stone steps. The ingress and egress from the condo required negotiating these stairs both ways. When I first looked at the property I was in excellent health. Then came the fall. Now those stairs looked treacherous.

That treacherous chicken came home to roost on May 28, 2016. I was standing in the kitchen that morning after taking a very heavy insulin shot when I suddenly felt that Humilog insulin freight-training through my blood vessels and heading toward my brain. When I finally regained consciousness it was three hours later, I was lying on the landing, down seven stairs, with blood all over the tiles. This is what I call "being on the floor."

The insulin had eaten up all the blood sugar in the blood stream and begun to attack the brain to find more sugar. After a period of about three hours, on average, the liver kicks in and releases more blood sugar into the system to bring the awareness back and restore consciousness. It's not fun. It could be deadly. It happens about once every two years.

Being "on the floor" is dangerous. Falling down that stone staircase, and hitting my head could cause blunt-force trauma to the brain, and death. It was time to look for a one-floor condo. I now knew that this condo would not do for the long run. Suddenly it was my enemy, not my home. I made an effort to be careful around the house and use the banisters whenever I was on the stairs.

Two days after Christmas, in 2016, I had lunch at the home of my good friend Charlotte Renata Simpson in Kirkland. I mentioned to Renata, at table, that I had been wanting for years, to write my personal memoir. She urged me to do that. A strange dream came to me that night. Next day I awoke, placed my hands on the keyboard and the mouse, and the writing began.

The first four months of 2017 were full into the memoir writing. I was heavily involved in the word crafting and sentence slinging through April. The sun came out in May. I took a break. I took some sunshine too. My vitamin B3 was getting low. My friend from Oregon, Mel, called in June and asked if I had made plans for the total eclipse in August. I told him I wanted to do that. He said, "Come on down." I wrote that onto my calendar.

We returned to Canada again in 2017 for the Qatuwas Celebration (First Nation Canoe-In). This time it was held at Campbell River, BC, Canada with the Wei Wai Kum nation being the host. Many of our First Nation friends were there to greet us including Stewart Gonzales from Vancouver Island. Here our group rented a private home in upper Campbell River for our lodging. It always adds a twinge of Canoe-In authenticity when you can arrive at the Qatuwas Celebration by BC Ferry. The Big Canoe. It was so this year.

     DON McGEHE

CHAPTER 27

I'D HARDLY RETURNED TO KIRKLAND WHEN IT WAS TIME TO turn around and head south to Oregon for the total solar eclipse. I had arranged to meet Mel in the town of Mitchell, Oregon (population 130). This is the heart of the Painted Hills country along the John Day River. I arrived on Tuesday the 15th and found Mel with Rick and Laura Lee Gordley in colorful downtown Mitchell. I then followed them north about 13 miles to the Priest Hole Campground on the John Day River and their camp.

As the weekend neared folks began to arrive in greater numbers. Motor homes were pulling in. It soon appeared that rest room facilities would be at a premium. By Saturday afternoon there were easily 1,200 sun-worshiping eclipse seekers at Priest Hole. There was one restroom. We got in the habit of arising at 6 am to use the facilities and even at that early hour the wait was often 15 people deep already. BLM toilet paper ran out Friday noon. From then on, everyone in line had a roll of their own sanitary sheets under their arm. That line was an excellent place to socialize.

The big news of the week: there was no cell-phone reception or Internet connections at Priest Hole! People were using their cell phones to take photos. That was all. These were beginning to look like the good old days.

Campers in the next site over were Monica Lander and Jay Reeves from Bothell, WA. Down the river half a mile were Sean Walsh (Lake Stevens) and Bill Jones (Olympia). Bill Jones was an amateur astronomer who brought along a 10-inch reflector telescope with him. He offered nightly galaxy, star, and planet viewing sessions to anyone who was curious. It started to feel like "We Are Family."

One day Mel asked me how I was doing up in Kirkland. I told him I was being run out by traffic, population, and expense. He asked what I was looking for. I mentioned own-your-own (land and house) in a manufactured housing park where the owners formed their own condominium community by the Pacific Ocean. Mel had spent the past 20 years as a building and home inspector.

He knew Oregon Real Estate. He also said he knew just such a place. It was Florence, Oregon. "Follow me back down to my Lakeside, OR. home after the eclipse, and let's take a look around," was his response to the Kirkland problems which I had expressed. I told him that I had the time and would enjoy the visit to the coast.

The morning of the total solar eclipse, Monday August 21, 2017, was a warm 85 degrees. We set our deck chairs out in the open, donned our solar eclipse glasses, readied our cameras, and waited. Everyone's attention was focused on the northeastern Oregon sky. Soon the light began to fade slightly. As the moon came in toward the sun, at the "1:30" position on the sun-compass, it began to get darker. It was 9:06:43. When the moon first touched the sun's outer corona a huge cheer went up from the 1,200 viewers at Priest Hole Camp. Then the darkness began to set in on the entire campground.

A huge roar of cheers went up again at 10:19:36 when the moon reached its totality and blocked out the entire sun. Totality lasted until 10:21:38. Two minutes and two seconds. Bill Jones recorded his exposures through the camera attached to the 10-inch reflector telescope. These were our best images of the eclipse. By 11:41:06 it was all over. The heat began to build again and finally everyone relaxed. Many at Priest Hole checked off another box on their personal bucket lists. By noon, the exiting motor homes began to kick up the dust on the road to the south past the Painted Hills.

Mel and I waited until the next day to depart. It was a final and rather sad experience to strike camp and put everything back in the van for the trip to the coast. By Tuesday the roads were not crowded. Everyone who had to be back to work on Tuesday was gone. We made it to Lakeside, Oregon by 4:00 pm.

Mel had recommended realtor Melody Ann Beaudro to work with, saying that she knew the particular market I wanted to purchase in, and that she was honest. Melody knew that we were coming to Florence on Wednesday and she was ready with five homes in the Greentrees Village development to show us. Greentrees is a manufactured housing community, with an over-55 requirement to purchase, where you own your own home and land but have a condominium arrangement for running the community and also for services. There are 567 homes in Greentrees Village. Melody showed us four homes that first day, before we ran out of time.

One of these homes I really liked. I was nearly ready to make an offer. Knowing all the homes in the development, Mel took me aside and said that I really ought to sleep on it for a day. That night we discussed what we had seen. All the homes that were for sale that day had been in the "interior" of the complex. Of the 567 homes in Greentrees, only 36 were on the Siuslaw River and had river frontage, the remainder were "interior" placed homes.

The next morning Mel took me back into the community and showed me the river front homes. He knew what he was talking about. Over the past 20 years he had been the building inspector on many of those homes in Greentrees. There was a picturesque view of the Oregon Dunes National Monument off the decks, and across the river, of all those 36 river-front view homes. Compared to these, the "interior" homes had just a blah view of your neighbor's house, as you looked out through the windows.

That afternoon I went back to Melody's office and asked if any of the river-front homes were for sale. She said that none were, at that moment. I indicated that I wanted to work with her agency but that I wanted to wait until I could consider one of the river-front homes. She said that they do come up occasionally and that she would give me a call when she had one to show. I was happy with that agreement.

I wasn't really ready to buy at that moment anyway, if the truth be told. I knew I should wait until I had been in my current condo for two years to avoid any tax penalty with its sale. That two years would be up on March 15, 2018. I thanked Melody and Mel, got in my van and headed north. I'd seen Florence. I liked the city. I knew I could live there. It was now a matter of time and availability.

It took longer than I had imagined. That fall was busy with book-writer's weather. As soon as the Northwestern rains began again, I was busy researching and writing the memoir. My Holiday Card was written, printed, and mailed long before I heard from Melody again. One comment in the Holiday greeting on the card predicted, "Looking at possible relocation to the Oregon Coast next spring."

Melody e-mailed me on Christmas Eve day, with the word that two river-front homes had been listed that very day. I viewed them on the TR Hunter Real Estate web-site and e-mailed her back that I would be in Florence on December 26 to see them. Pay dirt. One of these two was just perfect. After the showing, we drove back to her office and wrote an earnest money offer on a 1,400 sq. ft., 2 bed, 2 bath unit on the Siuslaw River.

I remained with Mel in Lakeside that evening and drove back to Kirkland on December 27. Lots of driving: a seven-hour trip each way. I closed out the year with accomplishment, and a firm plan toward my next trip 'round the sun in 2018.

[Interjection. Somewhat out-of-time sequence. After 1990 See and I had virtually no communication for over 27 years. Finally on December 29, 2017, I got a letter in the mail from her. A brief section from this letter stated, "*From the address that I found, it looks like you might still be in the area. If that is the case, it sure would be fun to reconnect in person and catch up with each other. I actually have a fun/ironic story to share about our time together that would be more fun to share in person.*"

We did meet at a Starbucks in early January 2018. The "fun/ironic story" she shared with me over coffee was that she did not quit work as the office manager of the Seattle dental office. She was fired. She was so hurt, devastated, and ashamed by that firing that she had hidden that truth from me and everyone else in her life ever since. Had I known this at that time, it could have made a huge difference in our relationship in those last two years we were together. I'd been fired three or four times before. I knew what it felt like. It's a gut-wrenchingly ugly learning experience. That's why giving up corporate life for the weed business was so easy for me to do. I would have listened. I could have understood. But… hindsight is always 20-20. See showed true strength to admit that truth to me after 29 years.]

My first contact, after making the Florence offer, was to phone realtor Jeff Dilley to list my Kirkland condo for sale on January 5, 2018. By January 11 we had accepted an over listing-price offer on the condo. On January 15 all the paperwork for the Florence home was completed and signed off. The closing date for the Kirkland condo was March 15, 2018. Closing on the Florence home was March 16, 2018.

Before I left for Oregon, my associates in Kirkland threw a Sunday afternoon going-away party at the Springtree club house. Many of my friends came. It was a very touching experience to see them all, after years of caffeine and personal-experience-sharing at all the coffee shops we frequented. Renata painted up a large boulder with "Your Rococo Coffee Friends" inscribed on it and everyone signed it for me. It now rests beside my entry door on the south deck at my Florence home. I hope everyone comes down to see it so I can thank them with some Siuslaw River hospitality.

For the second time in two years, it was pack up everything and move. Even though it was exciting, this was beginning to be "been there, done that—again." From January through March, I was able to do some limited memoir writing, but most of the real work involved packing stuff up in brown cardboard again and stacking those boxes in the garage. Mel offered to bring two of his associates up from Oregon to load and move everything on March 15. This help was vital.

I rented a van from U-Haul and Mel's associates drove it down to Florence. Mel and I each followed, in our own vans (fully loaded), behind the U-Haul truck. The caravan arrived in Florence on March 16. All the cardboard was schlepped into the Siuslaw River House and garage by 6:00 pm. We then took a moment to sit down, in the late afternoon sunshine on the south deck, and relax in some classic teak deck chairs the previous owner, Bob Robertson, was kind enough to leave for us.

Following a hectic day, there are often small things that others do for you that you come to deeply appreciate. After Mel and the moving associates departed, I discovered that the seller had left the new queen bed in the master bedroom, fully made-up with new clean sheets, and ready to sleep in that very night. I grabbed my Dopp kit out of the car, brushed my teeth, and crashed in that pre-made bed. Thank you Bob Robertson. The move-in of the first cardboard box could wait until tomorrow.

Un-packing took two weeks. It was tough doing this all by myself. The benefit was, however, that I now know where everything was put. Provided, of course, that Alzheimer's doesn't make a sudden unexpected visit, and I can remember where I put it all tomorrow. I now realized the advantage of buying a home that is all on one floor. If I needed to go looking for something—and I would—there were no longer any stairs involved. Small favors.

When you move, you've got to get the layout of the new land you've moved into. First I found a supermarket, bank, library, credit union, post office, and gym. I then stopped by the Oregon DMV to obtain a driver's license. The DVM then sold me a new set of plates and re-registered the Mini-Van.

Over the next month I researched for a health care provider, ophthalmologist, dentist, and barber. Florence, Oregon is a small town. Its population is 8,700 souls. The City of Kirkland was populated with over 87,000 residents. The options here in Florence were far more limited. If you ask, neighbors can easily tell you which providers are good and which are not. I listened and learned.

One of my goals in moving to Oregon was to find a home where I could focus on, and finish writing, the memoir. After three weeks of move-in and orientation, I was able to achieve that focus and once again get serious about the writing. It seemed to flow well down here. It was quiet. I had a gorgeous river and sand dune vista just outside my computer room. The words accumulated easily.

On August 10, 2018, I quit shaving. My idea was to grow the beard in order to focus my mind on the writing of the memoir. It was my intention not to shave until I was finished with the writing. This backfired. Once I quit shaving, I discovered that that was one less thing that I had to do each morning. I liked that. I'm now in a quandary as to whether to shave when the writing is finished, or let it grow and be more in fashion with my fellow Oregonian males. Seems like 70% of the men here have facial hair. Stay tuned.

Another thing that has been postponed, in favor of the writing, is my exploration of the southern Oregon coast. There is outstanding photography here, which I am looking forward to, that is not particularly weather dependent. In winter, the coastal storms create scenic opportunities that are challenging and take-your-breath-away awesome. Fossil and rock hunting on southern Oregon beaches is often better in the winter when Pacific storms churn up the gravel to expose previously hidden treasures. There is also great history to be unearthed on this coast that only awaits time and low tide.

The weather in Florence is unique and ever-changing. I've found it seldom gets above 65 degrees F. There is less rain (so far) than I had been led to expect. I have only experienced six spring/summer months since moving, however, so I may yet be surprised by this climate. The wind is more persistent than I'd expected. I've just learned to live with that. My river home is snug against the gales and the wrap-around windows let me see what weather is coming at me, over the Oregon sand dunes, and out of the Pacific Ocean to the west.

As I conclude this writing I mark the Autumnal Equinox of 2018. I will close this memoir with several musings on subjects that I deem significant to life. The first is purely personal: diabetes. We each have a personal health concern. It is hoped that my reflections on diabetes will stimulate your thoughts on your own health issues. The remaining musings could apply to all of our lives.

Following the musings is an epilogue to wrap up some thoughts that I have mentioned above in the body of the memoir.

Closing Memoir Musings

Diabetes

Living with diabetes for 58 years, since 1960, has not been easy. It has just become part of my life and I have adapted to its regimen. The disciplines I've learned on this path came from many trials and considerable errors. Here is a brief history.

I have always had an addictive personality. When I was first hospitalized with diabetes in 1960, I got a visit from Arnie Sondergard. Arnie was a year ahead of me in high school and was also a type 1 diabetic. He had been diagnosed one year earlier. I asked Arnie if I could still drink with diabetes. Arnie assured me that he was able to consume alcohol and thought that I would be able to as well. I felt relieved.

Everything about diabetes was suddenly new to me and most of it sounded rather grim. In that first year with the disease, I decided that I would be able to live until I was at least 35 years old. That became my goal. I decided that I would just drink and have as good a time as I could, in the time I had left. Ironically I gave up alcohol in April of 1975 after 33 years of life.

When I reached 40, I decided that since I had made it this far I might as well start working out to continue in good health. I joined my first gym. I have been working out six or seven days a week ever since. It has paid off. After shooting insulin for 58 years (to date) I still have no end-organ damage (heart, kidneys, brain, eyes). Some would argue about the "brain," but that is more of a political and not a health discussion.

If I had developed type-1 diabetes before 1921, I would have been dead within three years max. We have now come a long way after the 1922 discovery of insulin. Every year since I was diagnosed, some well-meaning friend has sent me an article from a medical journal "forecasting" a "cure" within the next five years. So far, it has not come. I've just learned to live with the disease.

Diabetes has forced me to take care of my body. By "forcing" that discipline on me, it has become a total win-win situation. Without the needle, who knows where I would be now. I'm thankful for it.

Hobbies and Friends

I'VE HAD MANY HOBBIES AND FRIENDS. IF I EVER FELT THAT I was short of friends, especially after moving into a new community, I'd choose a hobby that I loved and find a club that I could join to pursue that hobby. It could be a photography club, a rock club, a book club, a cycling club—whatever hobby turned me on at the moment. By associating with folks who have similar interests I could quickly find new friends who shared those same common interests. When any group has shared interests, that interest acts as a bonding agent to strip away the discomfort normally associated with meeting new people. Your common love of the same hobby is the social icebreaker within the group.

Reading

TO ME, A LIBRARY HAS ALWAYS REPRESENTED AN OPPORTUNITY for geographic exploration and life expansion on a budget. Books have always been my passport, airline ticket and visa card expense to explore the world, and (with science fiction) the universe. I've always been a slow reader. With my slow speed, however, came near 100% comprehension. I did not begin serious reading until after I quit drinking. It was a late start. Suddenly my world became measurably bigger.

DON MCGEHE

Reading shares stories. Stories disclose character. People are nothing without their stories. To read is to expose yourself to those stories that make human beings unique and memorable. Understanding of, and empathy for, others is the end goal of storytelling. Verbal communication—storytelling—is what sets our species apart from the remainder of the animal kingdom. We are what we say—our stories.

Civil Disobedience

CIVIL DISOBEDIENCE HAS BEEN USED BY SOCIETIES SINCE THE 18th century to challenge and change unjust and inane laws. The Boston Tea Party, Montgomery Bus Boycott, Greensboro, NC Lunch Counter Sit-ins, and Mahatma Gandhi's efforts in India were all examples of civil disobedience. Throughout history, citizens have refused to accept unjust laws and to overturn them through the use of civil disobedience. United States Federal laws classifying cannabis as a Schedule 1 controlled substance is likewise unjust and inane. If anything, the "egos" of the federal officials who created this classification should be considered the "controlled substance."

I was involved in the civil disobedience to change these laws in the 1980s. My efforts were premature. I paid the penalty. As of this writing, the nation of Canada has legalized both the medical and recreational use of cannabis. Many of the states in the USA have done likewise. It is only a matter of time before the Federal Government, inside the Beltway, follows the lead of its citizens and changes the law.

Epilogue

THE SOCIETY IN THE UNITED STATES OF AMERICA WAS FOUNDED by colonies of emigrants purportedly escaping European religious intolerance. Once on these shores they proceeded to tolerate precious little deviation from the moral outlook and strict religious beliefs of their colony founders. Was this progress or just more prejudice? From the distillation of these moral codes of the founders we developed the laws of the nation. We are a nation of laws. If you don't like the laws you can either break them or change them. To break them has penalties; to change them takes time, education, and votes.

The term "society" is defined as "a community, nation, or broad grouping of people having common traditions, institutions, and collective activities and interests." If you believe in *all* those common traditions, institutions, and activities then you are following the "norms" of the society. If you disagree with them you are likely to call some of those ideas "societal B. S." I've often not bought the standard line. Not gone along with the norms. When my heart told me "no," I went with my heart.

The law that I fought to change was the Federal Schedule 1 classification on cannabis signifying "it is a drug of abuse with no accepted medical use." I do not now use cannabis. But I may, in the future, choose to use CBD products, derived from the cannabis plant, to help treat my diabetes. We now have discovered that there are many medical uses for cannabis. I want the law changed to allow everyone the privilege of choosing for themselves, in order to allow you and me to use the various cannabis derivatives to treat and improve our health.

You may not care about cannabis. You may have a totally different law you would like to see changed. You may want a change in the laws governing immigration, women's rights, gun control, abortion, LBGT rights, euthanasia, net neutrality, or political gerrymandering. Whatever you want to change, know this: Change is still the only constant in the Universe. If change is the only constant in the universe then *nothing is fixed and immutable.* Everything is within *your* power to *change.* In the 1980s "I fought the law. The law won." Now we are changing the law. Change happens.

To break the law is considered bad taste. I've always been more enticed by bad taste than good taste. Good taste is nothing more than a standardized way of looking at things. When you deviate from the norm you attract attention.

So…if you like change…if you want change…if you need change…follow your heart. Make yourself the change you are seeking in your world. If you follow your heart, you won't regret it.

To share this truth with another soul…is my story.

You've read my story.

Thank you.

Now go write yours.

Acknowledgements

I would like to thank all those who helped me write this memoir. It is an autobiography, but I prefer the term memoir. The differentiation is often unclear. I am telling you my story. Once you finish reading the last word of the last chapter, you may choose either term you wish.

To Charlotte Renata Simpson, my friend, who stimulated me to begin the writing. To poets Sheryl Sirotnik and Thomas Hubbard who read and critiqued the first three parts of the manuscript and offered moral support to continue the writing.

To my brother, John David McGehe, who flew to Seattle in the summer of 1989, after the bust, in a personal visit to listen, without judgement, to my story. He was able to keep his mouth shut so that my Mother would not have to know of the felony charges. He was also the initial beta reader of the first three parts of the manuscript and proof-read the final copy twice.

To Florence, Oregon author-journalist Catherine J. Rourke and Florence authors John Herbst and Tracy L. Markley who offered guidance into the mysterious world of self-publishing.

To my Oregon friend of 48 years duration, Marjorie Yokum, who was the first to read the entire manuscript and to Marjorie's daughter, Lee Erickson, who provided critical editorial guidance on the memoir and was an enthusiastic supporter of the writing effort.

To my good friends at Luminare Press in Eugene, Oregon. Owner Patricia Marshall and project manager Kim Harper-Kennedy coordinated the self-publishing efforts on the memoir and facilitated my discovering the magic of delivering a dream into a printed, published book.

To photography friend and graphic designer Rick Ferens who crafted a selling book cover.

And finally to my life-long friend William Frank "Bill" LaShell who offered continuing support and enthusiasm in the effort of writing the memoir. Bill knew that the stories from the old "hood" in Manhattan needed to be told and he did not wish to look as foolish as I was willing to look in telling them.